THE SUCCESSFUL SPEAKER'S HANDBOOK

Herbert V. Prochnow

PRENTICE-HALL, INC.
Englewood Cliffs, N. J.

By the same author:

The Toastmaster's Handbook
The Public Speaker's Treasure Chest
Meditations on the Ten Commandments
Editor of: Great Stories from Great Lives (*Anthology*)
With C. D. Murphy: The Next Century is America's
With Roy A. Foulke: Practical Bank Credit

The Successful Speaker's Handbook
by Herbert V. Prochnow

Prentice-Hall International, Inc., London
Prentice-Hall of Australia, Pty. Ltd., Sydney
Prentice-Hall of Canada, Ltd., Toronto
Prentice-Hall of India Private Ltd., New Delhi
Prentice-Hall of Japan, Inc., Tokyo
Prentice-Hall of Southeast Asia Pte. Ltd., Singapore
Whitehall Books Limited, Wellington, New Zealand

10 9 8 7 6 5 4 3 2 1

PRINTED IN THE UNITED STATES OF AMERICA
87253
0-13-872507-1 pbk.

PREFACE

THIS book aims specifically to help those who would like to learn how to speak well, and to assist those who have some experience in public speaking to speak even more effectively.

About the year 1800, David Everett, who apparently was young and inexperienced in public speaking, and who was about to make a speech, said:

> "If I chance to fall below Demosthenes or Cicero,
> Don't view me with a critic's eye,
> But pass my imperfections by.
> Large streams from little fountains flow,
> Tall oaks from little acorns grow."

Mr. Everett must have uttered these words with his tongue in his cheek. One's best efforts after years of experience at public speaking will quite likely fall below the speeches of the great Demosthenes and Cicero. One's first efforts certainly will. But if one follows the concise and simple instructions which are presented here, the fundamentals of good public speaking should be readily acquired and should give one confidence and reasonable competency in public speaking.

Few persons are called upon without experience or practice to give speeches on national coast-to-coast radio networks. However, millions of persons have occasions to speak for three, five, or ten minutes at conferences and meetings in their businesses, clubs, associations, churches, unions, neighborhood groups, and other organizations. These speeches may be quite informal, but they may play a very important part in one's advancement in business and in the professions, and in directing the affairs of clubs, associations, and all types of organizations.

The ability to speak effectively and to the point can be acquired, and it can become an instrument of power and usefulness. It can be invaluable in many ways in business, in the professions, and in one's social and personal life. Public speaking may not only be a practical and constructive tool in life, but there is a great deal of personal satisfaction in being able to present one's ideas clearly, concisely, and forcefully.

In this book there are presented the simple essentials which are so important in gaining the ability to speak to groups of persons. There is also explained, step by step, the course one follows to become more and more effective as a public speaker. The discussion contains many suggestions, exercises, and illustrations designed to help one present his ideas orderly, clearly, and fluently to audiences.

Public speaking should help one to organize his thoughts logically and to present them convincingly. It helps also to develop variety in delivery and in the manner of uttering thoughts.

Good public speaking ability is not something that is impossible or unattainable. While the extent to which one can develop and improve his speaking ability depends upon the amount of his study, improvement will certainly come with earnest effort. Intelligent and conscientious application should bring profitable and gratifying results and should promote the development of personal talents that may be of far-reaching value in life.

HERBERT V. PROCHNOW

TABLE OF CONTENTS

PART I

Fixing Your Aim and Getting Ready

Chapter 1

EFFECTIVE PUBLIC SPEAKING AND LEADERSHIP TRAINING

THIS book deals with effective public speaking and training for leadership—activities that can help you attain greater satisfaction and success in business or professional work and more complete enjoyment of the opportunities of social life.

In our complex and interrelated world with its streamline trains, jet airplanes, and television, the Biblical quotation, "No man liveth to himself," has acquired an even broader significance. A successful and happy life depends more than ever before upon one's relations with other people. No matter how intelligent you are, or how hard you work, you may at any time be blocked or hampered in achieving the purposes which you desire by misunderstanding or a lack of sympathetic cooperation on the part of other people. To secure the ready cooperation of others you often need a command of effective speech. You need skill in conveying your ideas and wishes to them accurately, quickly, and tactfully, so you will obtain from them the right reaction and response. It is not a question of whether you personally enjoy having the ability to present ideas effectively to others; if you do not have this ability, you are seriously handicapped.

A Powerful Instrument to Help You

This study aims at the heart of the problem of leadership with which so many are confronted. It considers primarily one very important phase of the subject which is often neglected, namely, how to acquire the ability to speak in public. Specifically, how can you train yourself to address a group of listeners of any size with assurance? If you work faithfully through the instructions and exercises given here, reading a few pages each day, you will find yourself possessed of a new and powerful instrument which you can employ profitably on a great many occasions whether speaking to one person or to thousands. In addition, the instructions in this book should be helpful in many other ways in your business, social, and personal life and in developing your leadership qualities.

Instructions You Can Apply at Once

We do not intend in this book to devote our attention merely to broad generalities. We propose to present as simply and clearly as possible practical principles and useful material that will help you. Full mastery of the art of public speaking will come gradually with experience. Men of great ability in public speaking give to it a lifetime of study, developing year by year added power and finesse. Here we discuss simply and briefly those fundamentals the intelligent man or woman should know in order to develop his own ability. Anyone who has intelligence, genuine interest in other people, and a general store of information can grasp these instructions easily and begin to put them to use almost immediately even though he has given no previous attention to public speaking. What you learn, moreover, you will not have to unlearn later on. The treatment is basic and comprehensive. It gives you the fundamental principles of the art of leadership through public speaking.

Motives for Study—Necessity, Enjoyment

There are two main reasons for systematic study of public speaking. The first is necessity. The need to speak clearly and forcefully is invaluable in achieving success in your business or professional work. The second reason is enjoyment. Intelligent study of public speaking for use in business, professional, and social life brings pleasures of various kinds which constantly increase as you become more expert.

Public Speaking in Business Life

If you are active in your business, your profession, or in your social circle, occasions frequently develop when you are called on to stand up and express your mind to a group of listeners. As you progress in business or professional work, you find yourself involved in an increasing number of meetings. There may be conferences, sales meetings, and conventions in your own business, when plans are presented and policies discussed, when committee reports are offered and considered, and instructions explained to subordinates. In many large organizations, participation in conferences and meetings constitutes a very important duty for almost everyone holding a position of responsibility.

For the business executive, whether he is president, sales manager, or personnel director, the ability to stand up and tell others what he means, clearly, concisely, logically and forcefully, is imperative. Anyone in business upon whom the responsibility of guiding others depends must be able to talk clearly and to the point if he wishes his management of a business to be productive. Only those who can express themselves effectively and tactfully can obtain the willing and intelligent cooperation of the individuals for whose guidance management is responsible.

There are also the meetings of business or professional associations and groups to which you belong (either from personal interest or as a representative of your business or your friends and associates) and in which every member is expected to share in the discussion. Participation in this discussion is often a helpful and speedy road to advancement. It makes you known to people of influence in your field and gives you opportunities of demonstrating your competence as a leader and executive. This in turn increases your value to your own business or to those with whom you are associated in a profession.

In Social Affairs

This is only one side of the picture. Outside of business hours much of the time of the active man or woman of today is occupied with meetings of community and civic organizations, fraternal or religious bodies, and social groups. Here also there is business to be transacted in which, as a member of the organization, he has an interest. Frequently some issue arises whose decision is of great importance to him. In social activities, the man who can express himself on his feet, as officer, member, or guest of an organization, will be sought after. He will stand out from the crowd. Furthermore, upon the person who is not afraid to voice his sentiments will depend in considerable measure the repute in which that organization is held by people in general and its members in particular.

The truth is that for anyone who means to be a leader in business, professional, or social life, a reasonable command of the technique of public speaking is almost as necessary as a command of effective conversation with individuals.

Neglected Responsibilities

There is a surprising difference in the attitude taken by most persons toward their responsibilities for conversation in contrast to public speaking. Almost everyone feels that he must hold up his end of a conversation. From childhood on, he takes part in conversation as a matter of course, and as a rule gives some thought to improving his ability to converse. Although one may at first be diffident or tongue-tied in conversations, he watches others and tries more or less consciously to imitate them, and through repeated practice to develop a degree of skill. But many persons never think of developing a similar skill in addressing groups of listeners. Perhaps we should say that many persons never think they can develop the ability to speak well. Public speaking, we should remember, is an activity of adult life, to which very few persons are "broken in" in youth. Too many men and women simply do not think of it as an accomplishment within their reach. They hold back, hesitant to try. Before long they come to believe that they have no ability in that direction.

Neglect Is a Handicap to Success

Such an attitude is most unwise. If you are unable to take your part in public discussion, you will almost certainly come short of meeting your business and social responsibilities. If you fail to get up and speak when a matter in which you are concerned is under discussion, you not only miss opportunities, but you may incur criticism. In fact, you may be considered either not interested or not informed.

As one result, you are almost certain to be passed over for many offices or functions, because you are presumed to be unable to meet the modest public speaking requirements of the position. You may resent it but at the same time have inward doubts of your ability. Everyone can think of instances in which men and women deeply interested in the work of an organization and well qualified for leadership have remained privates in the ranks merely because they so often insisted they could not "make a speech" that their associates finally took them at their word.

Rewards for Those Who Speak Well

On the other hand, if you come forward and take your part in the discussions of groups to which you belong, your rewards (if you do well) are immediate and very considerable. Many persons who speak on such occasions do it only passably. They escape criticism and put themselves on record, but no more. If you will give attention to the practical techniques of effective public speaking, you can learn with surprisingly little effort to do it very well. Then you may win attention and distinction.

In every field of work in every town, there are men and women who are looked to as leaders. Nine times out of ten these are the persons who have demonstrated the ability to express themselves well. They have taken an active part where matters of general interest were discussed. People have become accustomed to look to them for thoughtful opinions and suggestions. Thus they are able to make their abilities, information, and convictions count to a maximum degree. Every opportunity which such an occasion brings helps to develop their powers further and to broaden their knowledge of affairs and of people. Gradually, but surely, they come to handle still larger responsibilities. They capitalize on the opportunities before them for progress. In fact, they create such opportunities.

Development of a Leader—a Typical Case

In a small suburb of a large city, a few years ago, a young man we shall call John Harrison became interested in a plan to open the grounds of local school buildings for summer playgrounds. No provision had been made in that community of modest homes for places where the children could gather during the vacation season and work off their surplus energies. Harrison joined with others in organizing a committee to push the plan, but found that the effort got nowhere, because the members of the committee were unable to "speak up" in public and present the idea forcefully to their fellow townsmen. As for Harrison, he had never thought of making speeches. On two occasions he made an attempt to explain to an audience what the committee had in mind, but his presentation was so inexpert that it seemed almost comic.

Harrison was in earnest, however, about putting over the playground plan. The thought occurred to him that he ought to take a course in public speaking in order to learn what was needed to present his cause effectively. He was astonished to find how quickly he learned to speak well. He discovered that what was needed in addressing a group of listeners was merely a modification of methods which he used habitually in his sales interviews. In a few weeks he was able to stand up and present his cause in public. Every time he spoke he did better. Within a year the playground program was adopted by the town because of his speeches before the local service clubs and other organizations. But the results did not stop there. People had begun to think of Harrison as a person who had energy and good ideas. They got the habit of calling upon him in connection with other matters. As a consequence this man who had never expected to speak in public became one of the influential persons of his town, whose advice was sought and heeded on all kinds of matters. Incidentally, his personal development in confidence and assurance brought him advancement in his business. He possessed abilities which he had not been utilizing. His study of public speaking helped to bring these to the surface.

Advancement of this type is open to other persons of intelligence and energy. Skill in public speaking in business and social life can be acquired. It is a skill that is similar to the skill required in clear and effective conversation.

Self-Expression a Duty

There is another aspect of the matter. You have a responsibility for making known your ideas. As a member of your business or social circle you have convictions which ought to be placed at the service of your associates. If you are inexpert in public speaking, you are likely to fail in the full discharge of this duty. To illustrate, if you are in charge of a department in a business concern, at every department conference you will probably have to speak, whether you are an expert at public speaking or not. You will find it necessary to declare your views on matters under discussion, or perhaps to present information relating to subjects on which you are especially informed. If you are attending a meeting of an industry as one of the representatives of your organization, and if you sit still and say nothing, through fear of making a poor appearance, it may prove to be greatly to the disadvantage of yourself and your organization. There may also be some topic that has failed to receive intelligent discussion, and on which you have highly specialized knowledge which would enable you to make a real contribution. If you keep still, because you feel you are inexpert at public speaking, you are in a sense failing to meet your responsibilities.

Putting Your Powers to Use

The instructions presented in this book should help to show you how to make use of the ability you now possess but are not utilizing. Before you have completed the book, it is hoped you will find that when you are called upon to talk, when you feel it advisable to express yourself on some topic under discussion, and when you have some suggestion to make that will help you or your business, you will be able to do it satisfactorily. It is hoped that you will find you can express your thoughts as effectively to groups of listeners as you can to any one of your best friends.

A New Source of Pleasure

The ability to talk clearly and forcefully to groups is not only useful but also a source of personal satisfaction. It opens a new world of experience. You should enjoy the study of public speaking. There is pleasure in working with others for constructive and worthwhile purposes. There is satisfaction in knowing that one has the ability to present ideas to others effectively.

You are aware of the pleasure derived from a satisfactory conversation, in a business interview, for instance, when you present an idea you have thoughtfully developed and see it gradually find acceptance by the person with whom you are talking. It is gratifying to have a meritorious idea of yours gradually accepted by an associate until it becomes a part of his own thinking. You experience this sort of satisfaction in a much greater degree when you present your thoughts to an audience. You have an opportunity to develop your idea adequately without interruptions by the listeners' comments and replies. However, an opportunity of this character demands that one do his very best to present ideas of real value to listeners. It is a privilege which should never, never be abused by half-baked preparation and presentation.

For the same effort and time you can produce a much greater result by addressing a group than by conversing with the same number of persons one by one. The saving in time is obvious. The saving of effort is due in part to the fact that what you say makes a stronger impression upon each individual because of the silent influence of the group. When the audience as a whole is favorably impressed with your presentation, each individual is influenced that way. The judgment of the audience reinforces his own convictions.

Orderly Presentation of Ideas

Studying public speaking in the way that is outlined here brings an indirect benefit of great importance which at first may not be recognized. It improves your effectiveness in other relationships with your associates and friends. The training it gives you in organizing and uttering your ideas develops a readiness in adapting your conversation to listeners, which is useful many times. Good public speaking trains you to analyze beforehand the ideas you wish to present, to think them through clearly from the viewpoint of the person you are addressing, and to formulate them in a way that is logical and convincing. In conversation there is a constant temptation to utter ideas in a disconnected form and to assume that the listener will somehow piece them together. Practice in effective public speaking tends to safeguard you against that fault in conversation. Practice in public speaking also develops a fluency of language which is of use in conversation. Furthermore, the practice of public speaking develops greater variety in your delivery, in your manner of uttering your remarks. In the conversation of persons who have never developed the extra sensitiveness to their own manner of utterance which the right sort of public speaking brings, there may be a tendency toward monotony in the way the sentences are sounded.

A Power for Everyday Use

A thoughtful and conscientious study of public speaking and the possibilities it affords for developing leadership should help you to make greater use of opportunities for advancement in your business or professional work. It should enrich and enlarge your social life. It should assist you in the more orderly presentation of your thoughts and in their clear and effective utterance. It makes you more sensitive to human relationships and contacts, and better able to adapt yourself to them.

Chapter 2

THE SPEECHES OF BUSINESS AND SOCIAL LIFE

THE study of public speaking is not too difficult. It does not require you to undertake anything that is impossible or unattainable. You will find the exercises interesting and helpful from the beginning because they are closely linked with your regular activities. And you can be certain of profitable results. While the degree of improvement will depend upon the amount of attention you give to the study, improvement will certainly come. This is a game in which anyone who desires can win.

These statements may appear surprising. You may have thought of public speaking as something wholly foreign to your customary activities, and so difficult to master—even assuming you might be able to master it acceptably—that it would not be worth the effort and time involved.

Everyday Speaking vs. *Formal Oratory*

It is not unlikely that the source of this mistaken view is a misunderstanding as to the nature and implications of the public speaking which you are urged to undertake. Very possibly the term public speaking brings a mental picture of the orations of political leaders—Churchill's "Blood, Sweat and Tears," Bryan's "Cross of Gold," Patrick Henry's "Liberty or Death," Franklin D. Roosevelt's speech on "Fear,"—and you have an uneasy feeling that something like that is expected of you. It should be stated at once that you are not expected to compete with Churchill or Roosevelt, but with men of your own group, men in your own business or social circle, uttering ideas such as you are accustomed to express at a conference, in a letter, or in earnest conversation. A little reflection will show you that the public speaking which we are considering is of this fundamental character. Otherwise, men of your acquaintance would not engage in it, for they are not Churchills any more than you profess to be. However, we do hope to present helpful instruction and material so comprehensive in its character that there will be no practical limitations on your possible development as a public speaker.

Great Orations Exceptional

The truth is that great orations are not really representative of public speaking in general. They are the exceptions. They are high-water marks of the great masters of the art of speaking, like the championship golf of the leading professionals. Obviously they exhibit a finish, a massiveness or a compactness of substance, and an intensity of feeling that occur as a rule only in exceptional circumstances and in unusual situations. But their high standards do not apply to the everyday public speaking of business and social life. You need not think you must learn to talk in that way. To learn to talk in that way would probably be impossible. Those famous speeches were exceptional even for the men who uttered them. Their eminent authors were stimulated beyond their usual power by the importance and intensity of a momentous occasion. When the opportunity comes, if a man is at hand who senses the possibilities of the occasion, a speech of highly unusual significance is the result. But preparation solely to make such speeches, for which occasions seldom come in anyone's life, would be an unwise use of time.

Everyday Speaking Simple

The public speaking of business and social life is on an entirely different level because the demands made upon a speaker by the situation are much less exacting. The occasions, it is true, are of almost infinite variety and as varied as the purposes which bring people together, but the subject matter is generally less momentous than in the great efforts of the masters and the treatment is much less intense.

Here are a number of excerpts from speeches which illustrate the practical, everyday public speaking we are considering. They are taken from various phases of business, political, and professional life. While the actual range of such speeches is, of course, almost unlimited, this selection will suffice to give a perspective of how men in business, politics, and the professions succeed in making good speeches. These are the sort of speeches which men in all these fields may be asked to make.

Savings and Economic Security

From an address by Harold G. Moulton, president, The Brookings Institution, before The American Bankers Association.

Members of the Association: My address will have two merits. It won't be overly long and it won't be overly burdened with statistics. I shall, however, endeavor to cover a very wide range of history and economic development, with a view to bringing certain things which I regard of very great importance into a clear perspective. The significance of savings to individuals and to nations is one of the oldest themes in economic literature. From Biblical times until very recently the virtues of thrift have been incessantly extolled alike by bankers, economists, and ministers of the Gospel. The simple essence of the philosophy of savings is incorporated in such homilies as "a penny saved is a penny earned," or, in Franklin's language, "a penny saved is two pence clear; a pin a day's a groat a year"; and, also, in "take care of the pennies and the dimes will take care of themselves." By way of contrast, one cites the smile-producing illustration of the thrift-*un*conscious lad who wasn't interested in earning a quarter by mowing the lawn because he already had a quarter.

Individual Savings and Social Savings: In the literature of thrift and savings one finds that the emphasis is sometimes placed on the advantages to the individual and again on the advantages to society. The moralists, among whom I include Franklin, stressed chiefly the importance of savings from the individual's standpoint. The thriftless individual sooner or later goes over the hill to the poor house, while the thrifty may hope to live in mansions by the sea; the shiftless are buried in potter's field, the savers in the church yard, with a verse on a tombstone to perpetuate their memory. Those who save their money, especially if they put it in a savings bank, achieve economic independence and with it the self-confidence necessary to the exorcising of that inferiority complex with which most poor humans approach the age of manhood.

Who can say that these are not elementary facts of life? Can we, without the universal practice of thrift, develop that independent, self-reliant, fearless citizenry upon which the success of a democracy depends? Stating the matter the other way round, can perpetual dependence upon papa, or Uncle Sam, for present and future needs, fail to undermine the homely virtues and weaken the moral fiber of the people?

A Local World

From an address by Eric A. Johnston, when he was president of the United States Chamber of Commerce, before the British Chamber of Commerce, London.

I come from the extreme northwest of the United States, from the state of Washington, from the city of Spokane. Spokane is very remote from London. Or, to put it in a more American way, London is very remote from Spokane.

The first thing you have to remember in considering the United States in international affairs is the extraordinary localism on which the United States is built. We are a nation, yes; but we are a nation of ebullient localities and of regions which have a sort of patriotism of their own.

Some of my fellow citizens of Spokane are not content to call their region a region. They call it an Empire. Its immense wheat fields, its magnificent orchards, its colossal mountains, its stupendous waterfalls, its gigantic forest, call forth from them all the adjectives of Hollywood. To them the Northwest is something more than a geographical area. And, indeed, the states of Montana, Idaho, Washington and Oregon would make in many parts of the world a quite considerable country.

All these merits of the Northwest, however, are matters of good natured contempt and derision to the citizens of Fort Worth, Texas. Fort Worth is fifteen hundred air miles from New York. Its city motto is "Where the West Begins." Everything between New York and Fort Worth, according to Fort Worth, is mere East. Fort Worth, too, is an empire, the great empire of West Texas. Undoubtedly it was Fort Worth that produced the recent immortal Texan who before Pearl Harbor remarked:

"Well, if the United States goes into this war, Texas will go in, too."

This sentimental localism, which exists all over our country, is fortified by our economics and our policies. Many Americans, in addressing British audiences, stress the resemblances between the two countries. I think it wiser to begin by stressing the differences. Only through realizing those differences can we break through them and arrive at true terms of friendship.

Your financial system makes your country much more a unit than ours is. Your great banks have branches all over Britain. Our ideal, emphatically exemplified in practice, is strong independent banks in all localities.

You have London newspapers widely read all over your country. Few Americans outside Washington, D. C., ever regularly read a newspaper printed in our national capital. Even our great New York newspapers have mass circulation only in the New York metropolitan area.

All your radio stations are owned and operated by one public agency, the British Broadcasting Corporation. Our radio stations are all privately owned and operated under hundreds of different independent local ownerships.

Your national government is a truly completely sovereign government. It can do anything. Ours cannot. It has only such powers as the people may have given it. The most striking clause in our national constitution is that all other powers continue to reside in the states or in the people.

It is a great error to describe the United States as a sovereign union of sovereign states. In the United States it is the people alone who are sovereign. The people of each state give to their state government what powers they please. They retain the rest. The people of all the states together give to the national government such powers as they please. They retain the rest.

This practice and consciousness of popular sovereignty, of the power to *give* powers to government, of the power to *deny* powers to government, and of the power (above all) to *withdraw* powers from government, is the basic political psychological fact of America.

Add it to our sentimental localism and our localized diffusion of banking power and of the power of the radio and of the press, and what do you get?

You get an American who acutely questions all centralized dominance in any field and who is forever conducting crusades to break down private monopolies and public bureaucracies alike. He does not believe in irrevocably surrendered powers either in government or in business. He regards all powers, whether political or economic, as subject to daily revision—by himself.

SPIRITUAL SIDE

From an address by General Dwight D. Eisenhower at Columbia University, New York City.

. . . Man's spiritual side is still the dominant one. No human, whatever his position in the social hierarchy or his job in the working economy, merits more respect than any other animal of the woods or fields unless we accept without reservation the brotherhood of man under the Fatherhood of God. If men are not creatures of soul, as well as of body, they are not better than the field mule, harnessed to the plow, whipped and goaded to work, cared for in the measure of his cost and value. But too often, today, we incline to describe the ultimate in human welfare as a mule's sort of heaven—a tight roof overhead, plenty of food, a minimum of work and no worries or responsibilities. So far have we strayed in our sense of values. Unless we rekindle our own understanding, can we hope to make Marxist devotees see that things of the spirit—justice, freedom, equality—are the elements that make important the satisfaction of man's creative needs? If I doubted that man is something more than a mere educated animal, I should personally be little concerned in the question of war or peace.

Baseball Umpires

From an address by A. B. Chandler, former high commissioner of baseball.

Now, the job of an umpire is difficult. Some of you people, I know, think that we place the umpires at a disadvantage. You know, there has been a movement on foot for a great number of years—to take the umpires off the field and put them in the grandstand, on the theory that you can see the plays better from there. We never have become convinced that this is true, but I assure you that if we ever are, we'll make the switch, but until we do, you'll just have to put up with these umpires in the place of disadvantage where we place them on the field. . . .

I used to enjoy discussing baseball games with "Uncle Charlie" Moran. I'll never forget a lesson he taught me over in Philadelphia.

He was umpiring back of third base. About the fourth or fifth inning, the home team got a couple of men on, and some fellow hit a screeching line drive that went down the left field foul line. Well, I was sort of for the home team, as you are when you're some place—you like to see the home team do well. From where I sat in the stand, it looked to me as though the thing was close, or maybe all right. Both the runners scored, but they hadn't noticed that Uncle Charlie was waving—a foul ball. Pretty soon, after an argument (which he won—they always do, as you have observed), he sent the fellows back to their places. Well, the next fellow up popped out, the next one struck out, and the home team lost the game.

When the game was over, I said, "Ump, what about that ball that went down the foul line there?" (I had one of those preferred seats. I could see it better than he could.) I said to him, "What about that ball?"

He turned around and glared at me and said, "What about it?"

I said, "Wasn't it close?"

He said, "No."

I said, "Did you miss it?"

He said, "No." Then he grabbed me by the shoulders and started shaking me, and he said, "Boy, I want to give you a lesson. I'm going to tell you something, and don't you ever forget it. There are no close ones. They are either out or safe. And it ain't nothing until I've called it."

An umpire has to know something about the game, and if he's a diplomat, it doesn't hurt. Not long ago we had an unusual man umpiring a game down South, between two local teams. In the second inning one of the boys got on first base, and he undertook to steal second base with the pitch. Well, he went down in the dust, and the little local umpire went into the dust, and the second baseman was there, and they all went in together.

When they came out, the little umpire just stood there, and made no motions, so both sides went after him, asking him for his decision. Finally he confused the newspaper men and the radio men by putting the runner back on first. When the inning was over, they asked him to explain. He said, "Well, half of the gentlemen insisted that the fellow was out. The other half insisted with equal force that he was safe, but both sides agreed he was safe at first, so I sent him back to first and let the game go on."

A Commencement Address

Paul C. Packer, chancellor of the Oregon State System of Higher Education, spoke as follows at the commencement exercises of the University of Oregon Dental School:

I want to pay my respects to a few of the values . . . that are essential if we are to attain the superior living which ultimately will be our only insurance of maintaining any society worthy of human record. For the purpose of the moment I have chosen to comment on the following three values: integrity, tolerance, and security.

Noah Webster defines integrity as "Moral soundness; honesty; freedom from corrupting influence or practice; especially, strictness in the fulfillment of contracts, the discharge of agencies, trusts, and the like." For convenience and brevity I want to bundle all this into the quality of keeping obligations.

Fifty years ago the expression, "His word is as good as his bond," really represented a state that most individuals, no matter how far they fell short, wished to attain. Over the years this quality, though still prevalent in the public mind, has lost not a little of its sharpness. As a result, the highways of the world are strewn with broken obligations and promises, not only on an individual basis but on national levels. To illustrate specifically, we need only recall the bank failures of a few years ago which remind us that it came to be almost respectable to try to settle our obligations on fifteen or twenty-five cents on the dollar —even for those who, by sacrifice, could have paid in full.

Is it necessary to add that if we form the habit of dodging such obligations individually it would set the stage for the development of a society which would do exactlv the same thing on a national level?

You, your children, and your children's children have been handed a public debt of no mean proportions, plus an exceedingly heavy demand for ever-increasing public services. Both the debt and the public services necessary to effective living can be met only if the quality of individual integrity is maintained on a high level. Taking the long view, it is necessary to see that the youth of the nation are disciplined in the quality of keeping obligations. Unless we can achieve a generation that is intellectually and spiritually tough enough to meet this challenge on a high level, the type of life this country has enjoyed is in no little danger.

The second concept I want to discuss is tolerance. You remember that Voltaire said in effect that he would defend with his life the right of anyone to express his point of view but would, at the same time, reserve the right to battle to its death any idea with which he disagreed. Isn't it amazing how far away we have drifted from this concept? Daily we are being urged to be tolerant about this, that, and the other thing with few if any exceptions being made.

To counteract the misconception which is beginning to weaken the moral fabric of our society, I enter a plea for intolerance—intolerance, if you please, of poor work in any field of endeavor, intolerance of destructive gossip not only on an individual basis but upon a national and international level, intolerance of those who choose to make temporary popular decisions when they know them to be wrong, intolerance of such matters as poor sportsmanship and poor manners. This may sound like a play on words, but I assure you it is not so intended. It is but another way of giving emphasis to the necessity of recapturing the fine quality of tolerance in its true meaning. It means taking the flabbiness out of our approach to living so that we will not degenerate into a society that resembles a dish rag—and a pretty wet one, at that.

One other concept to which I wish to direct your attention momentarily is security. In the past, society has thought of security as something that is associated primarily with individuals nearing the sunset side of life. During this century, however, the idea of security seems to have grown so rapidly that the spirit of adventure, formerly the dominant tone of the youth of this country, has been a bit dulled. In a recent issue of *Fortune* magazine there appeared a report of a survey of the most sought-for objectives of this year's college and university graduates. The survey indicates that only in the states of Texas and Oklahoma does there seem to remain among the college graduates . . . any marked interest in gambling on the future. In all other sections of the country the majority of votes were cast for security.

Now I am quite aware that we have no comparable measure of the attitude that existed as respects the graduates of twenty-five or fifty years ago. However, the testimony of individuals who have experienced this period indicates that the present apparently overwhelming ambition of youth for security rather than adventure is something new. It may be that the defeating days of the thirties contributed greatly to developing the thought of security as a life goal of youth; or it may be that the recent war, in which so many of you and your millions of associates played so large a part, has temporarily reduced the zest for adventure. As someone has said, "Youth feels himself as a survivor in a long series of routs and massacres. Insecurity is his portion, and doom and death are to him familiar neighbors." All these and many other comments might be made respecting the issue of security versus adventure.

The important thing, however, about the whole matter is for us to recapture the age-old truth that security is an accompaniment of effort and sacrifice and not an end in itself. The days ahead will demand in even greater degree than in the past a sufficient quota of rugged, intelligent, generous, imaginative, gambling individuals who will once more give vitality to the spirit of adventure in our society. Unless these spark plugs arise in our midst—and I believe they will—we may well drift into a state none of us cares to contemplate. The heavy inheritance and the challenges that are the portions of the youth of today—and they were never greater—demand that adventure in living be made primary and security its accompaniment. . . .

In the long run these fundamental values of life will determine the degree of real achievement that is ours. Nothing short of superior living on the part of individuals has a chance in the days ahead.

Great Production and Wealth

From an address by Nathan W. Shefferman, executive director, Labor Relations Associates of Chicago, Inc., before the Union Delegates of the Western Conference of Teamsters.

Today I come with a message—also reliable facts and figures, not in apology but in reaffirmation of the comparative glories of our American way of life. . . .

For six thousand years of recorded history, all mankind has gone hungry and many have starved. Even among ancient civilizations with fertile lands people starved, babies were often killed—there was no food for them.

Rome fell apart in famine—one hundred and fifty years ago the French were dying of hunger—only one hundred years ago the Irish were starving. It's not more than a hundred years since Western Europeans have had food enough to keep them alive, bread in France, fish in Scandinavia, beef in England. On the rich farmlands of Russia thousands upon thousands starved as late as the 1930's. People right now are starving in parts of India, China, Africa. Famine has been the rule rather than the exception.

Then suddenly, in one spot in this world, hunger is forgotten, people have plenty to eat, America has never had a famine.

For six thousand years men carried goods and other men on their backs, then, suddenly, in one small part of the earth's surface, nature's forces are harnessed to do the bidding of the humblest citizens.

For six thousand years, families lived in caves, floorless hovels, not even a chimney; then within a few generations we in America take for granted floors, rugs, chairs, tables, windows, chimneys, electric lights, refrigerators, running water, bathtubs, toilets.

For six thousand years men and children worked desperately from dawn to dark barefooted, half-naked, unwashed, unshaved, uncombed, with lousy hair, mangy skins and rotting teeth. Then, suddenly, on a spot of this earth there are all kinds of food, rayon underwear, nylon hose, shower baths, razors, ice cream sodas, lipsticks, permanent waves.

In less than a hundred years, we in America have conquered darkness—from pine knots and candles, to kerosene lamps, gas jets, electric bulbs, neon lights, fluorescent tubes.

We have set up new defenses against weather, from fire to fireplaces, to stoves, furnaces, automatic burners, insulation, air-conditioning.

Disease and pain are being conquered, life is being prolonged with anesthesia, surgery, sanitation, hygiene, dietetics.

Space has been annihilated from ox-cart to rafts, canoes, to railroads, steamboats, streetcars, subways, automobiles, trucks, buses, seaplanes.

Time is being saved by telephone, telegraph, radio. Drudgery is no more, steam, electricity, gasoline, all substituting for the brawn of man. No telling what may come from atomic energy.

Coal, copper, alumnium, zinc, lead and other materials can be found all over the world. Our natural resources are no greater than any other nation's. We started with virgin forests, untouched mines, unharnessed water power, fine farming land, but not yet tilled.

We had no monopoly on creative and inventive talent. They were discovering and inventing in the Old World long before the white man came to America, but new ideas, like natural resources, are as useless as a ribbon on a frog until something is done about them.

In the early days, we had no production goods, no raw materials, no livestock, no tools, no machines, no equipment.

We had no good roads, most everybody was poor—but by thrift, setting aside some savings, capital grew and through far-sighted leadership, individual initiative and imagination, tools were developed to make tools that could produce things that could not be produced without tools. We became the greatest producers and the wealthiest nation in the world.

Remarks at a Boy Scout Convention

Still another type of informal speech may be illustrated by the following delivered by Mr. Dan Beard, father of the Boy Scouts of America, at an annual meeting of the National Council of the Boy Scouts. Frequently, on an occasion of the kind, some prominent member of the organization, one whom all know and honor, will be called upon for remarks. The listeners are not expecting a connected speech, but merely a frank, informal presentation of whatever thoughts may occur to the speaker on the spur of the moment. This also is the sort of demand with which one who has been prominent in an organization is at any time likely to meet.

What we have to inculcate in boys, and they will believe in it because it appeals to them, is rugged manhood. We do not have to be prudes to be decent. A man can be decent and be rugged and strong; a man can be decent and be manly. He can be much more manly than the indecent man. And you can appeal to the boys, because the boys have that urge, they have that—well, we Quakers call it the inner light. That is the reason we have a vigorous program; that is the reason for the outdoor program, and all of those things which Scouting has inaugurated, which interest the boys, and their interest is necessary.

I attended a boy's club the other day, down in a tenement house district in New York City. And up on the roof of a house there, with dingy back windows, with clothes hanging out on the line, there was a campfire and a tent, and a canvas drawn, and some of the dirtiest youngsters you ever saw in your life were camping out and enjoying it. It might make you laugh, but it had the contrary effect on me; it almost made me cry.

As long as there are any underprivileged boys in this country, we are unsafe. It is up to you men, the men of this land, to see that there is no such thing as an underprivileged boy. Every boy has a right to life, liberty and the pursuit of happiness if he is down in the slums or hasn't the proper school facilities, or if he hasn't the opportunity to become a Scout. While I was visiting the Museum of Natural History, a group of dirty youngsters came up to me and said, "Uncle Dan, how can we become Scouts?" That is the question that is up to you, individually, and us as a body, to answer, "How can they become Scouts?"

There is nothing in the world bigger than this. There is nothing in the world that has happened since the beginning of Christianity that has as great a possibility as the Scout Movement, and consequently there is no body of men in the world that has greater responsibilities for our country and the salvation of the world.

Simplicity of Such Speeches

If you will examine these speeches, you will see that most of the material in them is not too difficult to prepare. The speeches vary in quality, it is true, just as the conversation of various individuals will vary, but it is possible for an earnest student of public speaking to prepare equally effective speeches. Undoubtedly you have at times expressed yourself with similar clearness and detail upon topics not essentially different, in animated conversation with friends, or perhaps in a letter or memorandum. There is no reason why you cannot express your ideas of this kind before an audience. It is simply a matter of acquiring the technique which is involved. From this book you can learn the technique and be aided in your effort to become an efficient public speaker.

Opportunities for Effectiveness

The examples shown here indicate that public speaking offers great opportunities for skill and art. If it is done clumsily, it may produce, as is true of a clumsy letter or a blundering sales interview, only passable results or none at all. It may, however, be done very skillfully, and produce results that are far-reaching. Many of the speeches delivered at conferences within a business organization, at dinners or luncheons of trade bodies, at meetings of local lodges or clubs, display examples of admirable skill in presenting ideas to suit the occasion.

The standards, however, are always those of common life. When you participate in the speaking on such an occasion, you are measuring yourself, not with Churchill, Eisenhower, or Daniel Webster, but with men of your own grade in your own circle or elsewhere.

Chapter 3

EVERYDAY SPEAKING IS NOT DIFFICULT TO LEARN

FROM the examples in Chapter 2 it is apparent that the speeches required in professional, political, and business life are not too difficult to prepare. They are entirely within the capacity of an intelligent person's thought upon matters in which he is interested.

No Special "Gift" Required

You may, however, be harboring another misunderstanding with regard to the procedure itself, the act of making and delivering the speech. Very often a person who has never faced an audience looks upon the act of addressing a group of listeners as something requiring special powers or "gifts," powers which most persons do not possess. This notion is as erroneous as the one about subject matter. You can learn to make a speech as surely as you can learn to write a letter, drive a car, or handle a sales interview. You will be surprised, indeed, at the ease with which you can pick up the necessary technique if you go about it in the right way.

Expert versus Beginner

At first, it is true, you may be dismayed by the expertness in public speaking of some of the people in your own circle of acquaintances. As you listen to the representative of a rival concern in your trade association or to a fellow member of a civic organization, or even to a ready talker among your own subordinates at a conference within your own company, you may be tempted to think that these persons have some special endowment which you lack. Their thoughts, it may seem to you, run on so smoothly; their delivery is so easy and impressive; they seem never to hesitate for words, so that you wonder how they do it.

You say to yourself, "I could never talk like that!" Naturally, you shrink from getting up and inviting comparison with them.

This feeling may be even stronger if you realize that they have no actual advantage over you in understanding of the matters under discussion, or in general mental ability. Someone gets up —someone who really knows less of the situation than you and whom you could easily equal in effective conversation. He carries the group successfully with him to a decision that you feel is wrong. You are inclined to attribute his success to some mysterious personal "gift" which makes you feel impotent beside him.

Then some other acquaintance, perhaps much more capable and experienced than the first person, but without that strange "gift" of speech—as you suppose it to be—will get up and try to answer him and do a very poor job. His looks and manner reveal intense nervousness; he hesitates for words; perhaps he even gets his ideas twisted; and he sits down in obvious discomfiture. Watching such a performance may prompt you to a determination not to cut such a sorry figure yourself, to keep still even though it means remaining in the background, rather than attempt something you feel you cannot do successfully.

Expertness a Matter of Practice

But you would be in danger of making a serious mistake. You have no reason whatever to be dismayed by the performance of these persons in your own circle of friends and acquaintances. Actually, what produces the impression upon you and the others who listen to them is not, in most cases, any exceptional or unusual power. It is merely the expertness that comes from practice. These persons have given intelligent practice to an activity which the others, who make a poor impression by comparison, have never studied. The right kind of practice will enable you to develop similar skill for yourself. The chances are that the first attempts of these men whom you admire, when they began earnestly to practice public speaking, were just about as faltering and ineffective as those of the beginners for whom you feel sorry and with whom you may now classify yourself.

You Can Learn

When you watch a good amateur tennis or golf player, you are likely, if you have never played tennis or golf, to have the same feeling of amazement at the skill which they display with a tennis racket or golf club. But in that case you realize at once that the skill is the result of constant practice and study of the game; that if you were to set about it, you could develop considerable skill yourself. On every hand we see the results of practice—in swimming, bridge, knitting, painting, playing the piano, cooking, and writing.

Now this applies to public speaking. Skill in public speaking is pre-eminently something that comes from intelligent practice. Some people acquire it more rapidly than others, just as some learn more quickly to play a good game of tennis or bridge, or to swim; but anyone of intelligence, energy, and patience can learn. You can learn.

You Have the Ability

You have as much ability as those persons whose ease and readiness before the group so impresses you. They are not geniuses. They are merely competent persons with normal ability. Indeed, it is *that* fact which wins them a hearing. They are putting into words ideas which seem to their listeners sensible and sound, which come as the opinions and suggestions of people like the listeners, whom the listeners can trust. You simply need good common sense and normal ability. Therefore, you also can make yourself an impressive and influential speaker if you will take the trouble to learn the simple techniques of addressing a group. In fact, it is entirely possible that when you in turn have had the advantages of practice, you will be even more effective in the public speaking of daily life than some of these persons whose performance now appears so remarkable to you.

No Mysterious Procedure Involved

In the first place, there is nothing essentially strange or mysterious in the procedure involved when you stand up to address a group of persons. You do not need to learn to do something different from anything you have done before. It is merely a matter of employing in a somewhat modified way the techniques you have acquired in conversation, and you have been practicing conversation your entire life.

Let us suppose you are conversing with a few friends in the front of an auditorium. You are telling them about an experience you had on a recent trip to another city. Your story is very interesting. Some other friends of yours come along and stop to listen. Gradually the group becomes larger and as it does, those on the edge of the group are unable to hear you. They suggest that everyone in the group sit down so they can all hear you as you stand and continue telling of your experience.

Now at what point did your conversation change to a speech? Was it when the group grew larger? Was it when everyone else sat down? You were telling the same story after your listeners were seated and you were standing alone. If, when you stood alone, you suddenly realized you were about to make a speech, you might have lost your nerve and the story would not have been finished. But you just kept on conversing and, therefore, held your listeners. It is that simple.

Public Speaking Is Enlarged Conversation

There is no major difference between conversation with a few friends and conversation with an audience, except of course that we must use our voices to a little better advantage; we must speak a little louder and more distinctly when talking to an audience. We get some of the same help from an audience that we get from our friends in a conversation. Of course, John, Henry, and Mary do not break into our speech by asking a question or by objecting to this or that statement. They do not give voice to their thoughts, but we find that they do take part in our speech by their general attitude, their facial expressions, a shake of the head or a nod, the attention they give. All these take the place of the verbal agreement, disagreement, or question which is given in conversation with a small group. Therefore, the public speaking that we wish to use in meetings and before public groups, is *merely enlarged conversation.*

No Special Vocabulary Required

Perhaps you think that your command of language is not adequate for public speaking. Men and women may say that they cannot address an audience because they do not have sufficient education. Those very same persons have no hesitancy in expressing their ideas to their friends and associates and they can often be exceptionally interesting in conversation. They imagine that their language is not good enough for making a speech to these same friends and associates.

What words do we need in order to express our ideas to others? There are many persons who go through life, express their ideas, make known their wants, get the results they desire, and have only rather limited vocabularies. Your vocabularly is probably much larger than the meager stock of these individuals. You have no hesitancy in taking part in conversation. You should not hesitate to get up on your feet for the "enlarged conversation" with an audience.

Listen carefully to the speeches and sermons you hear. You will be surprised how few words you hear in them that are not in your own everyday vocabulary. In many speeches you may hear no words at all which would not come to your own lips in careful conversation.

Simple Words in Formal Speeches

We may go further. Let us look at excerpts from the addresses of a number of speakers, some of them orators of world fame, with respect to the *words* they used.

Problems for Thought

From an address by Herbert Hoover, former President of the United States, at Stanford University, August 10, 1949.

We must wish to maintain a dynamic progressive people. No nation can remain static and survive. But dynamic progress is not made with dynamite. And that dynamite today is the geometrical increase of spending by our governments—federal, state and local.

Perhaps I can visualize what this growth has been. Twenty years ago, all varieties of government, omitting federal debt service, cost the average family less than $200 annually. Today, also omitting debt service, it costs an average family about $1,300 annually.

This is bad enough. But beyond this is the alarming fact that at this moment executives and legislatures are seriously proposing projects which if enacted would add one-third more annually to our spending. Add to these the debt service and the average family may be paying $2,900 yearly taxes. They may get a little back if they live to over 65 years of age.

No doubt life was simpler about 147 years ago, when our government got well under way. At that time there was less than one government employee, federal, state and local, including the paid military, to each 120 of the population. Twenty years ago, there was one government employee to about 40 of the population. Today, there is one government employee to about every 22 of the population. Worse than this, there is today one government employee to about 8 of the working population.

Twenty years ago, persons directly or indirectly receiving regular monies from the government—that is, officials, soldiers, sailors, pensioners, subsidized persons and employees of contractors working exclusively for the government—represented about one person in every 40 of the population.

Today about one person out of every 7 in the population is a regular recipient of government monies. If those of age are all married, they comprise about one-half the voters of the last presidential election.

Think it over.

In the long run it is the Average Working Citizen who pays by hidden and other taxes. I have made up a little table showing the number of days which this kind of citizen must work on average to pay the taxes.

	Days' work
Obligations from former wars	11
Defense and Cold War	24
Other federal expenditures	12
State and local expenditures	14
Total thus far	61

But beyond this the seriously proposed further spending now in process will take another 20 days work from Mr. and Mrs. Average W. Citizen.

Taking out holidays, Sundays, and average vacations, there are about 235 working days in the year. Therefore, this total of 81 days work a year for taxes is about one week out of every month.

You might want to work for your family instead of paying for a gigantic bureaucracy.

Think it over.

To examine what we are doing, we must get away from such sunshine figures as the gross national income. We must reduce our problem to the possible savings of the people after a desirable standard of living. If we adopt the federal government's estimate of such a desirable standard, then the actual, and the seriously proposed, national and local governmental spending will absorb between 75 per cent to 85 per cent of all the savings of the people. In practice it does not work evenly. The few will have some savings, but the many must reduce their standard of living to pay the tax collector.

And it is out of savings that the people must provide their individual and family security. From savings they must buy their homes, their farms, and their insurance. It is from their savings finding their way into investment that we sustain and stimulate progress in our productive system.

One end result of the actual and proposed spendings and taxes to meet them is that the government becomes the major source of credit and capital to the economic system. At best the small business man is starved in the capital he can find. Venture capital to develop new ideas tends to become confined to the large corporations and they grow bigger. Governments do not develop gadgets of improved living.

Another end result is to expose all our independent colleges and other privately supported institutions to the risk of becoming dependent upon the state. Then through politics we will undermine their independence which gives stimulus to government-supported institutions.

No nation grows stronger by subtraction.

Think it over.

It is proposed that we can avoid these disasters by more government borrowing. That is a device to load our extravagance and waste on to the next generation. But increasing government debts can carry immediate punishment for that is the road to inflation. There is far more courage in reducing our debts than in increasing them. And that is a duty to our children.

And there is no room for this spending and taxes except to cut the standard of living of most of our people. It is easy to say increase corporation taxes. That is an illusion. The bulk of corporation taxes is passed on to the consumer—that is, to every family. It is easy to say increase taxes on the higher personal income brackets. But if all incomes over $5,000 a year were confiscated, it would cover less than 10 per cent of these actual and proposed spendings.

The main road is to reduce spending and waste and defer some desirable things for a while.

Change Is the Order of the Day

From an address by Virgil M. Hancher, president, University of Iowa.

The state of Iowa was admitted to the Union in 1846. It has 99 counties. Most of them are at least 90 years old. Each county is approximately 24 miles by 24 miles. The size of the counties was fixed in the horse-and-buggy days, and their size was fixed so that a trip to the county seat by horse and buggy or team and wagon from any part of the county would not be too laborious. But the world has changed, and the counties have not. The horse-and-buggy days are gone, and the 99 horse-and-buggy counties remain. Political scientists may agree that with present means of transportation and communication 10 counties would be more realistic for present needs than 99 were for the needs of

1858. Nevertheless, 99 counties have become so much a part of the thinking of our people, interests in political and official positions have become so vested, relationships between counties have become so firmly established, and the lag between physical fact and social thinking is so great, that something more radical than the teachings of the professors would be required to effect a rapid change in the status quo.

It may be regrettable, but it is nonetheless true, that rapid and fundamental changes in the structure of our modern American society have not been achieved in this fashion. The changes which threaten to alter fundamentally the long-established structure of our society have come from sources outside the colleges and universities.

From whence have these changes come? They have come primarily from business and industry and finance, the very areas that fondly fancy themselves as the staunch defenders of the status quo. And first and foremost, I would say that they have come from rapid means of transportation. When the Mormon settlers of Utah left Nauvoo they traveled overland by ox teams and wagons. The trip took months to accomplish. Yesterday I accomplished substantially the same journey in seven and a half hours! What theory or what dogma of any living social scientist is one-half so significant as that simple fact? Or is one-half so cataclysmic in its effect upon the habits, the customs, and the traditions of our people?

Let me repeat an illustration which I have used on other occasions. Iowa City, the seat of the State University of Iowa, is 120 miles from our state capital in Des Moines. By ox team and wagon the 120 miles was traversed in 12 to 20 days. By stage-coach, it was traversed in 2 to 3 days. By horse and buggy it was an overnight trip of at least a day and a half. Today by slow train it can be traveled in five hours, by streamliner in two hours, by commercial airplane in less than one hour, and by the fastest plane now known—from point to point without starting time or landing time—the distance can be covered in something under twelve minutes!

Most of these changes have taken place in the lives of men now living. What social scientist during the same period has produced anything so revolutionary as this in its effect upon the social order? Or, have all the social scientists in all the colleges and universities of the country produced anything so revolutionary? If the capital invested in railroads is in jeopardy today, is it because of the teachings of social scientists or because of the competition of automobile, bus, truck and airplane?

What academic person ever revolutionized the life of America in the way that it was revolutionized when Henry Ford hitched the internal combustion engine to a four-wheeled conveyance and introduced the low-priced automobile to America and to the world? The barriers of provincialism were broken down. Mud roads gave way to paved highways. The one-room country school gave way to the consolidated high school. Horses gave way to tractors and trucks. Farm life ceased to be an endless round of toil. American farmers and American laborers were no longer bound to the soil, and the American people became the greatest nomads since Tamerlane. The family car became more important than house or apartment. The closely knit family life of pioneer days came to an end. It disappeared and has never returned. The church and the school ceased to be the center of social life. Old habits, old customs, and old moralities broke down. The age of ceaseless motion was ushered in.

What the rapid means of transportation began, the rapid means of communication have augmented and stimulated. The telegraph and transatlantic cable first broke the monopoly of the written and printed word. The telephone came, and voice answered voice across the continent. Then radio came and sent its messages around the world in the length of a heart beat—the wit and wisdom and folly of mankind are heard in every tongue and in every capital. Crises flourish, and the breathless newscaster races from sentence to sentence while nerves grow taut and arteries harden. Finally, television has come to add its bit, so that we may be spectators as well as auditors of both great and trivial events.

Not one of these has come without uprooting the customs and habits of the people. If the fabric of our common life is threatened, if the status quo has been jeopardized, if the dear dead days of long ago are now beyond recall, if the American Way of Life, as envisioned by the Founding Fathers, has been shaken to its deepest foundations, neither credit nor blame can be laid at the door of the historian, the political scientist, the sociologist, or the economist. Nor can it be laid to colleges and universities. For this, education can be neither scapegoat nor whipping boy.

Although institutions of higher learning cannot be held responsible for the uprooting of our people, for the disintegration of family and community life, for the destruction of old habits, old customs, and old traditions, they would be derelict to their duty if they failed to note the essential characteristic of the age and to prepare young men and women for the conditions and the environment in which they will live.

The essential characteristic of our age is change. The one certainty upon which we can agree is the certainty of change. Moreover, this change appears to progress at an ever-accelerating tempo. It has been pointed out that the life of George Washington as a Virginia gentleman was not unlike that of a Roman noble in the first century B.C. More fundamental changes in the living conditions of men have occurred in the last 150 years than in the preceding two thousand.

If the current universal tendency toward change is to be effectively arrested, industry and business and finance must close their laboratories and research departments; they must agree that no new inventions will be made and that no new models, designs, or styles will be created; they must agree that change is hostile to the social order and that hereafter there shall be no new thing under the sun. One need only make such a proposal to see its utter impossibility. It would mean the end of free enterprise and of individual initiative. It would mean the substitution of private monopoly and state controls for the free and indomitable spirit which has done so much to liberate the American from the slavery and serfdom of the toiling masses throughout the rest of the world. It would mean the substitution of the safety and stagnation of the status quo for the glories and hazards of the never-ending creativeness and ingenuity of the mind of man.

America is not finished. It has not exhausted its strength. It will not be content with things as they are. Change is the order of the day. It has been our heritage. It will be our future.

Essentials of Popular Government

From the Farewell Address of George Washington.

Of all the dispositions and habits which lead to political prosperity, religion and morality are indispensable supports. In vain would that man claim the tribute of patriotism who should labor to subvert these great pillars of human happiness, these firmest props of the duties of men and citizens. The mere politician, equally with the pious man, ought to respect and to cherish them. A volume could not trace all their connections with private and public felicity. Let it simply be asked, Where is the security for property, for reputation, for life, if the sense of religious obligation desert the oaths, which are the instruments of investigation in courts of justice? And let us with caution indulge the supposition that morality can be maintained without religion. Whatever be conceded to the influence of refined education on minds of peculiar structure, reason and experience both forbid us to expect that national morality can prevail in exclusion of religious principle.

It is substantially true that virtue or morality is a necessary spring of popular government. The rule, indeed, extends with more or less force to every species of free government. Who that is a sincere friend to it can look with indifference upon attempts to shake the foundation of the fabric?

Self-Government

From the First Inaugural Address of Thomas Jefferson.

If there be any among us who would wish to dissolve this Union, or to change its republican form, let them stand undisturbed as monuments of the safety with which error or opinion may be tolerated, where reason is left free to combat it. I know, indeed, that some honest men fear that a republican government can not be strong; that this government is not strong enough. But would the honest patriot, in the full tide of successful experiment, abandon a government which has so far kept us free and firm, on the theoretic and visionary fear that this government, the world's best hope, may, by possibility, want energy to preserve itself? I trust not. I believe this, on the contrary, the strongest government on earth. I believe it the only one where every man, at the call of the law, would fly to the standard of the law, and would meet invasions of the public order as his own personal concern. Sometimes it is said that man can not be trusted with the government of himself. Can he, then, be trusted with the government of others? Or have we found angels in the form of kings to govern him? Let history answer this question.

Eulogy of a President

Here is a part of the impassioned conclusion of the eulogy of President Garfield by James G. Blaine, delivered at the memorial service in Congress.

Surely if happiness can ever come from the honors or triumphs of this world, on that quiet July morning James A. Garfield may well have been a happy man. No foreboding of evil haunted him; no slightest premonition of danger clouded his sky. His terrible fate was upon him in an instant. One moment he stood erect, strong, confident in the years stretching peacefully out before him. The next he lay wounded, bleeding, helpless, doomed to weary weeks of torture, to silence, and the grave.

Great in life, he was surpassingly great in death. For no cause, in the very frenzy of wantonness and wickedness, by the red hand of murder, he was thrust from the full tide of this world's interest, from its hopes, its aspirations, its victories, into the visible presence of death—and he did not quail. Not alone for the one short moment in which, stunned and dazed, he could give up life, hardly aware of its relinquishment, but through days of deadly languor, through weeks of agony, that was not less agony because silently borne, with clear sight and calm courage, he looked into his open grave.

Cardinal Newman

Here, finally, is a passage from a lecture by one of the most highly cultivated men who have ever spoken our language, John Henry Newman, a Cardinal of the Roman Catholic Church in England.

If, then, the power of speech is a gift as great as any that can be named—if the origin of language is by many philosophers even considered to be nothing short of divine—if by means of words the secrets of the heart are brought to light, pain of soul is relieved, hidden grief is carried off, sympathy conveyed, counsel imparted, experience recorded, and wisdom perpetuated, if by great authors the many are drawn up into unity, national character is fixed, a people speaks, the past and the future, the East and the West, are brought into communication with each other—if such men are, in a word, the spokesmen and prophets of the human family—it will not answer to make light of literature or to neglect its study; rather we may be sure that, in proportion as we master it in whatever language, and imbibe its spirit, we shall ourselves become in our own measure the ministers of like benefits to others, be they many or few, be they in the obscure or the more distinguished walks of life—who are united to us by social ties, and are within the sphere of our personal influence.

Your Own Vocabulary Adequate

In these examples, also, are not most of the words simple and familiar, words that you might employ in earnest conversation? There are a few uncommon words, but is it not quite likely that if you were speaking on a subject that stirred you to the depths of your nature, you would find yourself employing, instinctively, words not essentially different in quality from the few unusual words in these passages?

It is true that a number of these extracts from addresses by able speakers have a smoothness, dignity, and vividness that are far out of the ordinary. But these qualities come from the way the words are combined. That is primarily a matter of practice. It is at this point that the expertness that grows out of intelligent study of the art of speaking manifests itself.

The words that will express your ideas in conversation are the same words that you should use on your feet. Simplicity of expression makes for ease in understanding. The simpler you can make the talk—that is, in the words you use—the more assurance you have that everyone in your audience will be able to follow you. You will know that the least educated will understand what you are saying; and you cannot offend the most educated, because he, too, will know what you mean and will have your idea vividly impressed upon his mind.

What Those, like Yourself, Have Done

The best proof that you can master this simple and useful art of everyday public speaking is the fact that so many other people like yourself have done so, by means of intelligent effort.

A Store Executive

Some years ago a man who had never made a speech was promoted to the position of general manager of a retail store in a large city. It was somewhat unusual, it may be noted in passing, that a man who seemingly did not have the ability to express himself should be selected for the position—or rather, that he should have gone as far as he had without acquiring that ability. When he became general manager, he felt that he had to learn to speak. He was over fifty years old at the time. He took some private lessons covering substantially the material in this book, and began experimenting.

He discovered a power whose existence he had never suspected, which has aided him immensely in his work as a general executive. He was a man of exceptionally clear and straightforward mentality. The little talks that he delivered to employee groups, and later to outsiders, had a definiteness and directness that won and retained attention and respect. Among executives of his organization, there were several men who were much more fluent as speakers than he was. But no one compared with him for effectiveness.

An Advertising Man

Another similar illustration is that of a young man in a large advertising agency—a college graduate, thirty-six years old, quick-witted, personally rather thin-skinned and sensitive, a ready and skillful writer. He felt he was utterly unable to face an audience. He had an actual aversion to speaking before a group. Throughout his high school and college years he had managed to dodge all the instruction in public speaking that was offered to students.

Unexpectedly, another man in the agency, who was closely associated with the young man, came down with appendicitis just as he was starting on a trip to address groups of salesmen on behalf of one of the agency's leading clients. The speaking tour could not be canceled. There was no way of arranging for one of the other men in the agency to take the assignment. This young man, who had never made a speech, but who knew the account intimately, had to go.

There was no time to prepare, no time even to hunt up a public speaking instructor for a few lessons. One of the men in the agency had on his desk a volume of text material which he was using in a course in effective speaking. The young man took it on his way to the train, much as a drowning man grasps at a straw. In the Pullman that night he opened the little volume and read it through. He was not reading for entertainment, he was actively seeking help. To his amazement, what he read seemed to have been written for his own case. In the words of the old saying, he put his prejudices in his pocket and determined to try the suggestions offered.

His first attempt was only partially successful, but before the week's series of five talks was completed, he was entirely converted from his former attitude. He had discovered that he was able to speak effectively to one audience of strangers after another, and that he actually enjoyed the experience. He became one of the outstanding public speakers among advertising men. His mental alertness, his responsiveness to other people, and his rich background of information made his progress rapid, once he had permitted himself to try the thing which he had supposed was both impossible and unpleasant.

A Woman Active in Community Work

Still another typical instance is that of a woman in a small city, a leader in church and club activities, capable, an excellent organizer with an unusual power of getting other people to work with her. But she could not stand up and talk to even a small group of the women with whom she was continually working. She "just knew she couldn't." So she would never consent to be president of any of the organizations which she directed, or even chairman of any committee which had to make a formal report. She would be vice-president and do all the work, but someone else had to do the speaking.

Then one day the inevitable happened. There was to be a large public meeting for the community chest drive. The hall filled with people. A telephone call came advising that the president's car had broken down on the way from another town and she could not get there for the meeting.

There was nothing for the vice-president to do but take the chair and carry through the program which she had planned for the other woman. Her trial was more severe than that of the two men just described, for she had no warning and no preparation whatever. She said afterward that she thought she would die when she got up before that crowd and first heard her own voice in public.

But she found she could speak. She knew what had to be said, and after the first moment, she forgot all about herself in her eager desire to have the program go through without failure.

Thereafter, like the store manager and the advertising man, she also was able to utilize the power which she had always possessed, without realizing the fact.

Sure Rewards from Careful Effort

After all, the question of whether or not you develop skill in public speaking depends on whether you have anything to say. That thought bears repetition—it depends on whether you have anything to say. If you have, you can learn to say it effectively. That is only a matter of following certain simple directions that have been developed by ages of experience. You can make speeches—when the occasion calls for them—that are as good in their way as those cited earlier, if you will invest in your own future to the extent of careful and systematic practice. You can progress, if you continue your experimental study of this practical art, until you are able to meet with ease the responsibilities of any occasion that may come to you.

Learning to make full use of your power will of course require care and attention on your part. It will require acquisition of habits of steady self-control with respect to some things which in the past you have done on impulse, or even automatically. But the benefits you will receive for such effort and care should be rewarding to you. The work itself will be interesting from the start because at every moment you are studying people and their reactions, which is one of the most interesting of all human activities. And you will be able to put your efforts to practical and worthwhile use.

Chapter 4

TAKING THE FIRST STEPS

MERELY thinking about the matter will not achieve what you are seeking—the ability to think on your feet and express your thoughts. Action is necessary. Prove to yourself that you *can* do it in the only way possible—that is, by actually making the attempt.

Therefore, make an opportunity to stand up and talk. Get up at a conference of your business associates. Say something at the lodge or club. Do not try to make a speech at first, merely stand up and say something. Make a motion, object to something with which you do not fully agree, or ask a question. Make it as short as you like, but say something. You will have started. Putting off the trial until some other occasion will not help you.

A Good Way to Begin—Asking Questions

Probably the best of all ways of making the first plunge is by asking a question. Or rather, to begin by asking a question enables you to slip into the speaker's attitude by easy stages, and without ever having to make a sudden plunge.

Accordingly, at the next meeting of your club, civic or church group, in a business conference or trade gathering, watch the discussion and when something is said that is not entirely clear to you stand up and ask a question. Do not break into a speech by someone else, but wait until the speaker has finished. Interrupting a speaker is permissible in conversation, but not, as a rule, in a group discussion.

Address the Chairman

There are two points of technique to bear in mind. The first has to do with observance of the rules of group discussion, or what is called parliamentary practice. In group discussion all questions and remarks are supposed to be addressed to the presiding officer.

Therefore, remember to "address the chair" and direct your question to him and not to the person who has been speaking. The correct form to employ is, "Mr. Chairman, may I ask the last speaker a question?" or, "Mr. Chairman, I should like to ask a question." The chairman will answer, "State your question," and then you may proceed.

Expand Your Question

The second point of technique concerns only yourself. In order to obtain full benefit from your first practice step in public speaking, do not compress your inquiry merely into three or four words, as you would do in conversation. Instead, expand it a little, into three steps, as follows:

1. State your question briefly.
2. State briefly the reason for the question. Indicate the point which you find obscure or inconsistent.
3. Repeat the question.

AN EXAMPLE

Suppose, for example, that your club is considering a report from the entertainment committee, and certain figures seem to you indefinite. You might say something like this, "Mr. Chairman, I should like to ask a question on an item in this report."

The chairman will say, "State your question," and you will proceed, "Does the figure given by the committee for the price of the hall represent the total cost? The reason I ask is that on such occasions we have found previously that there are usually a number of service items, such as janitor's fees, that have to be covered. Sometimes these are included in the charge for the hall and sometimes they are not. I should like to know whether the figure we have been given includes all expense items connected with the use of the hall."

Do the same thing at the following meeting, and so on for a while. It will break the ice for you. Many persons who are now expert speakers began by thus asking questions, in that way becoming accustomed to standing up and hearing their own voices.

Offering a Brief "Remark"

Another way of getting started is to get up, in the course of a discussion, to utter a brief remark, just two or three sentences. In a courteous manner, challenge some statement made by one of the speakers, or add a brief expression of your own view. Some of those present have given their ideas in regard to the subject. You have some feeling on the matter. You have some thoughts relative to this topic. Because of what the others have said, you will have no difficulty in expressing yourself regarding it. You may elaborate on what they have said, or you may disagree with them and give your own ideas.

As a matter of fact, you may already be saying to yourself what you feel should be said, even if you do not get up; you are making a *mental* speech. The trouble with that kind of speech is that no one will hear it and have the benefit of your constructive ideas. Make yourself heard; get up and tell the others what you are thinking.

Do not elaborate your statements, but merely utter two or three sentences, as you would in conversation, taking care to speak somewhat louder, so that you may be heard. After resuming your seat, watch the effect of your remarks. Listen closely to any replies or comments made by other speakers. That will show you whether you made your point clear, and whether you expressed it effectively.

Only you can help yourself. The first time you rise in this way, you may feel like the man who said, "I do my hardest work before breakfast." "What is that?" asked his friend. "Getting up," he said. Getting up may seem, the first time, a severe task, but make the attempt and you will find that it was easier than you thought.

Acquiring the "Speaker's Attitude"

Repeat these exercises—asking questions or injecting brief remarks—in every meeting in which you take part, for several weeks. Every time you get an opportunity to join in a discussion, seize it. It is good practice, and practice is what is necessary. Practice to give yourself self-confidence. Practice to prove to yourself that you can talk standing up.

Gradually you will get used to hearing your own voice in public. This will gradually beget a freedom of expression. You will come to feel as easy and composed when expressing your thoughts to a group of listeners as you do in conversation. Then, on some occasion, you will undoubtedly have the impulse to extend your remarks on a subject that interests you particularly, and you will find yourself making your first little speech.

The Question of Stage Fright

If you set about the study of public speaking in the systematic way just described, you are likely to escape altogether those queer panicky sensations which come to most persons when they first face an audience, and to which the name "stage fright" has been given. It may be, however, that you will find yourself called upon for a regular "speech," a connected talk of several minutes, without having put yourself through the preliminary breaking-in process of questions and remarks. In that case, when for the first time you rise to speak, you may be assailed by a sudden feeling of extreme nervousness.

You see all those pairs of eyes fixed upon you; you start to speak and your voice sounds strange in your ears. You are struck with a sudden thrill of fear, fear lest you may say or do something inappropriate or ridiculous, or may forget entirely what you want to say.

Its Cause

Consider the nature and cause of this feeling. Then we shall find that the cure is not difficult. It is a combination of two main elements. Although you may have no fear in speaking to individuals separately, there is, first, a natural excitement, a heightened sensitiveness, which is involved for you in the act of standing up before a group. It is entirely natural. A person who has this extra nervous energy will probably make a better speech because he is "keyed up." If you did not have it at all, you would be abnormal. In substance, it is not different from the feeling you experience when you are introduced to some distinguished individual. In an inexperienced speaker there is, secondly, a feeling of self-distrust, lest he may not be able to meet the demand—whatever it may be—that will be laid on him as he talks. With some persons this distrust amounts almost to panic. In some cases the unhappy speaker pictures himself making some stupid blunder. In other cases everything seems to go blank for him. Sometimes the panic-stricken individual halts, hesitates, mumbles some inane remark, and sits down in confusion. This is a wretched experience, like seasickness. People who have had a serious case of it often have a permanently timid attitude toward any effort to address an audience.

A Natural Result of Excitement

Now we should understand that this particular feeling is prac tically universal. Almost everyone who rises to address a group of people experiences it at first. Many expert public speakers continue to experience these sensations, to a degree, all their lives. William Jennings Bryan, a few months before his death, told a friend that he had never ceased to experience it whenever he faced an audience. The fact that you do experience it is some evidence that you possess the responsiveness which is essential for effective transmission of your message to other people. Do not worry over the fact that you have these sensations. Just consider what to do to tone them down so that they do not hinder the effectiveness of your talk. That can be done.

A Simple Remedy

In the first place, the purely physical sensations, the pumping of the heart and the trembling of limbs, can be at least partially overcome by merely remembering to stop and take a few deep breaths before beginning to talk. That will temper your excitement and will help you to restore your ordinary self-control. Do not rush in to your remarks. Just stand still, look steadily at your audience, and take two or three good deep inhalations of breath. You will find that the deep breathing will help to allay the feeling of oppression. Your nervousness will in some degree disappear as soon as you hear your own voice at the beginning of your talk.

Incidentally, the fact that you stand there a moment, quietly looking at the audience, will help to make them think of you as composed, self-possessed, probably an experienced speaker—which will tend to make them listen respectfully.

Useful Mental Treatment

The procedure which has just been described should assist in overcoming any stage fright. You will start on your talk, and then your interest in making your point will help you forget about your own nervousness. With some individuals, it is true, the sensations of nervousness are so strong as to persist in spite of the practical first-aid remedy just mentioned. The reason is, almost always, that these people cannot get over the feeling of strangeness, unusualness, in the situation. If you are one of these extra-sensitive people, give yourself some mental treatment.

Conversing with the Audience

As already noted, you have no fear of the individuals in that audience. It is the act of standing up and addressing them as a group, which you feel to be unusual. But is talking before a group really unusual? After luncheon the other day, you and a number of friends and acquaintances stood in a group and discussed some subject in which you were mutually interested. There may have been ten in the group. There was nothing unusual about talking with them. Suppose the ten had been casually seated around and you had been standing in the room? Could you not have discussed the same subject without feeling that you were doing something out of the ordinary? Convince yourself that talking before any group is merely an enlarged conversation.

Do not talk *to* them, *at* them, or over their heads. Talk *with* them and they will, in effect, take part in the conversation. Though they will not speak, they will manifest their interest on their faces and in their appearance.

If you "converse" with your audience in this way, the unusual aspect of public address will be eliminated. The chief difference between everyday conversation with one or more individuals and conversation with an audience is a mental one. You have been led to believe that public speaking is entirely different from what you ordinarily do when you talk. It is not. Once you realize that your relation with your audience is a normal and natural one, fear, doubt, and worry can more easily be dissipated. When you stand up to present your thoughts to a group, do so with courage, confidence and faith in yourself.

Above All, Trust Yourself

Above all, do not let yourself be troubled by doubt of yourself, of your own competence, or of your ability to express your ideas to any individual or any group. Trust yourself. The things that you have to talk over with your hearers are things with which you are thoroughly conversant. You know what you wish to say. Your audience will be interested in proportion to your own interest. You cannot be sufficiently interested in the things you are saying if while uttering them you do not trust yourself.

Do not be unnecessarily timid. The timid individual always suffers from the illusion that everyone is seeking to criticize his faults. The worrisome, nervous, timid man, because of his pessimism, distorts every expression into one of criticism. He imagines every whispered remark must be aimed at him. Even the look of interest directed toward him must, he feels, have back of it some sinister meaning. In every smile, he imagines, ridicule lurks. Timidity makes him self-conscious and makes him awkward—awkward in carriage, awkward in speech, awkward in expression. The sure cure for timidity is for the individual to face squarely and bravely that which overwhelms him. If you fear ridicule, know that the strongest armor against it is the lack of fear. The man who does not mind being laughed at will not be laughed at. Force yourself to do that which timidity would ordinarily prohibit you from attempting. Ability to speak in public, as well as leadership in life, depends on overcoming extreme timidity.

Challenge Boldly Your Timidity

Challenge boldly the feeling of being the target of the unspoken critical thoughts of your listeners. Not everyone who hears you will agree with all that you say. It is not necessary that they do so. The disagreement they may manifest may come from misunderstanding, and in that case you can remove it. It may come from a conviction which you cannot overcome. But it does not come from an attitude of attempting to embarrass you. On the contrary, all of us like to hear men express themselves. Not only do we like to hear them, but we applaud those who do it fearlessly.

Therefore, if you express your thoughts boldly, even those who disagree will respect you and admire you. Train yourself to look directly at your listeners. Looking squarely into their eyes will give you confidence. You will perceive and interpret rightly the response they are silently making to your remarks.

And remember, finally, that normal listeners are not seeking things to criticize. They want to be interested in what you say. They are not expecting you to say anything out of the ordinary. If you have made careful preparation of your comments, you may be able to contribute some worthwhile ideas to your listeners. They will appreciate them and will value your remarks.

Stage fright, like seasickness, is annoying but not fatal. It is in large measure an imaginary malady, a sort of hysteria. The malady is real, but the cause lies in the imagination. If you recognize clearly that the difficulty is not with the audience or the situation, but with yourself, with your own mental attitude, you will be well on the road to relief.

Questions and Remarks Ward Off Fear

But if you follow the plan suggested in the first part of this chapter, of asking questions and making brief remarks, before you attempt formal talks, you will avoid serious difficulty. Then the sensation you experience when you rise for your first real "speech" will be merely a mild and rather stimulating excitement.

Chapter 5

WHAT TO TALK ABOUT

SUCCESS in addressing an audience depends first of all upon having something to say, having a message. We talk for the purpose of conveying ideas. Unless we have worthwhile ideas to present to listeners, we cannot expect to retain their attention and support, for we have no right to take up their time. There is no excuse for making a public speech unless one has conscientiously prepared worthwhile ideas to give his audience.

Always Have a Message

You should apply this principle also as a matter of course in conversation. Sensible men and women do not just chatter. What you say in conversation bears upon the subject under consideration, or opens another subject which you believe your companion will be interested in when he hears of it. Everyone feels embarrassed, awkward, and ill-at-ease when he has to "make conversation" or talk just to fill time, for example, with a stranger at dinner. If you will remember always to make a worthwhile contribution when you address an audience, your progress in public speaking will be rapid. You will have accomplished the most important objective in public speaking: presenting something of value to an audience. The fact that you have something worthwhile to give will affect both your audience and yourself. It will show in your own manner, giving it an impressive, composed, businesslike character. This in turn will impress your listeners and dispose them to pay respectful attention to what you have to say.

This, therefore, is the first rule for success in public speaking: Always have something to say that you feel certain is worth saying. That involves thorough and conscientious preparation.

What the Rule Means

This rule may not at first seem very helpful to one who has

shied away from opportunities to speak in public and who has been told that he must now take every opportunity for *practice*. For you say, "I don't often have a real message for an audience. It is rare, indeed, that I have anything in mind which I feel might be a worthwhile contribution to a group of listeners. If I speak only when I have something which I very much desire to convey to the group in which I find myself, my speeches will be few and far between."

Well, let us see. Is this really the situation? Perhaps you have misconstrued the expressions, "messages," and "worthwhile." Perhaps you are making the error noted in Chapter 2 with respect to the *nature* of the speaking in business, professional, and social life and assume that you must champion some great cause or attempt the explanation of some intricate idea. It is not necessary that your message be mighty or momentous. It need not sway nations! If you have some contribution to make to subjects under discussion among your business or professional friends and associates, the members of your Rotary, Kiwanis, Lions, or Optimists club, the social groups of your church or your chamber of commerce, you can make a worthwhile speech.

The Impulse to Speak

Perhaps the desire to present an idea to an audience, with definiteness although not in a life-or-death attitude, comes to you more often than you realize. However, because public speaking is now an unfamiliar activity, you do not try to carry out the desire. You are by no means mentally passive, uninterested in other people and their affairs and ideas, and in their reaction to your opinions and purposes. If you were thus lacking in responsiveness to what goes on around you, you would not be reading about public speaking. In conversation, certainly, you do not sit mute and tongue-tied until one of the great dominating interests of your life comes up; instead you take an interest in whatever topic is under discussion and participate to the best of your ability. Do the same thing when participating in group discussions.

The probability is that if you were accustomed to addressing groups of listeners you would often find yourself prompted to "make a little speech," in order to express opinions about some topic brought up by another speaker or to introduce a topic that had been developing in your own mind. That is to say, you would find that you really have a much larger store of worthwhile contributions to offer to an audience than you now realize.

What Can You Talk About?

This book is designed to help people who desire to learn how to "make speeches," to help them in the first place to utilize that power when its employment is necessary or desirable; and in the second place, to obtain the indirect improvement in business interviews and ordinary conversations which the study of public speaking brings—as shown in Chapter 1. Therefore, it is very important to learn, at the start, how to discover the topics which you really desire to employ for speaking to groups.

We come then to the question: What are the matters regarding which you desire to convey your thoughts to others? The natural answer will be: Matters which you think are important for the other people to know—useful, instructive, profitable, beneficial, or entertaining to them. The question becomes finally: What material of this character is there in your own mind, either impressed on it by your daily experience or developed through your private observation and reflection? With the answer to that question we shall begin to get somewhere.

Talk of What You Know

This is the answer: You will talk about matters with which you are intimately acquainted, those which pertain to your business, your occupation, or your personal life. If you want to get helpful practice in public speaking, utilize subjects related to your business, your profession, your work.

Do you think there is little about such topics that would interest others? Let us see. You are so close to your work that everything about it is familiar to you. It is not familiar, however, to other people. Some aspects of it are not familiar even to fellow members within your organization. It does not matter what your business is, whether it is operating a railroad or raising oranges, inventing electrical devices or selling shoes, plumbing or trucking. The story can be made interesting. There are all around you men and women who do not know how your business is run; what is necessary to carry it on; the future which might be in store for anyone entering your field of endeavor.

When you build a talk on your business, start at the bottom of the ladder. That is what you tell young men to do who are entering business: start at the bottom of the ladder and climb. Describe the business all the way to the top. A talk on the manufacture of clothing or toothpicks could be made intensely interesting. These subjects are not complicated. Can you think of anything better known than clothing or a toothpick? And yet relatively few persons would know much about these subjects.

Never forget that public speaking is merely conversation—enlarged conversation, carried on with more than one individual, but still conversation. You can interest your friend in a conversation on almost any subject if you are really interested in it yourself. You can interest also the composite individual constituting your audience.

Opening Up the Subject

But remember to *open up* the subject. Otherwise you will merely scratch the surface of your topic and fail to tell the things about the subject that are really significant and worthwhile. For instance, suppose that your subject was matches and that you were "merely talking." You might simply state what a match is, and where it can be purchased, and then conclude with "I think that's all that can be said on the subject." Why would that be all? Because you had not really thought about the subject from the standpoint of attempting to pass on to listeners really significant facts or comments with reference to it. You did not develop your ideas.

That is not the way to make an interesting *speech* on the subject. If your business was matches, and you were to try really to make a speech about matches, you would very likely take an encyclopedia and read something regarding matches. You would familiarize yourself with the whole history of matches and perhaps the part fire played in the development of modern civilization. A little reading would enable you to give a very interesting talk.

The Question of Clearness

Someone may object that the subject of matches would not be a worthwhile topic. "A talk about matches could not be clever." This comment, which might be made by one who has not given much thought to the question, needs to be considered. Let us see what truth there is in it, and how far it is justified. It may be conceded at once that almost everyone likes to be considered "clever."

At the last banquet you attended, one of the speakers may have been applauded because of his clever address. Everyone commented upon it. Many of those present, perhaps you among them, thought, "I wish I could talk like that." Cleverness, we feel, always receives the approbation and acclaim of others.

When we call a speaker clever, we may mean one of two different things. We may mean that he expresses his thoughts in a surprising form. When a person deliberately sets himself to make his talk "clever" in this sense, there is great danger that his talk will be amusing momentarily, but will leave no worthwhile ideas.

The Essential—Knowing Your Subject

The other meaning of clever is that the speaker gave an able talk; he proved himself a talented speaker. Now who is the able speaker? The man who knows his subject, who handles it in such a way that he interests and convinces us. The word "talented" should not lead you to believe that public speaking is an *unusual* talent. Any average person can be an able talented speaker. There are certain subjects on which you are an able conversationalist—subjects concerning which you would be called talented—subjects which you know thoroughly—subjects about which you are thoroughly informed and enthusiastic.

A Golfer

To illustrate, there is a quiet individual who belongs to your organization. It is hard to draw him out. His only sociability seems to be that he plays golf. He is not an expert, just a fair golf player. The other day he made a hole in one. Did you hear him telling about it? If he can buttonhole you, he will tell you the next time you meet. He has something that he is interested in; he is enthusiastic; he is overjoyed. He wants the world to share in his excitement, in his enthusiasm, in his joy. He becomes on that one subject, an able, talented conversationalist.

A New Car

Another man in your organization has recently bought a new automobile. He will tell you the fine points of his car, the number of miles he can make on a gallon, and its wonderful pick-up. He can take any hill easily; he is bubbling over with enthusiasm. He is an able speaker on the subject of that car.

All Have the Power

We are all talented with the power of speech and expression. We should use that gift and obtain the most from it. The talented man makes an able speech, because he knows what he is talking about, has put thought on it and developed it. Because he is convinced of the value of his subject, it necessarily follows that he will paint mental pictures with power, force, interest. He must and does dominate. Unless you are extremely timid, unless you fear, unless you are worrying about the outcome, unless you lack self-confidence, you can do the same with a subject in which you are interested. You can get a reputation for being a talented speaker.

A Speech about Packing Cases

A very interesting speech was delivered in a debating club, by a young man who worked in the receiving department of a big retail store. A member of the club who was a golf enthusiast had given a vivid and instructive description of the way to make certain golf strokes, using a golf club to illustrate the proper stance and swing. Later in the evening the man in the delivery department, who was a quiet chap weighing perhaps 130 pounds, borrowed the golfer's club and described the way to handle big packing cases weighing up to 350 pounds. He held the club like a box-hook and illustrated the stance and movements by which a slender man is able to handle boxes more than twice his own weight.

No one would have supposed that an interesting speech could be made on that subject. But when he finished he had given his listeners some unusual ideas. He brought out points of human dynamics which his audience had never considered.

Therefore, talk about ordinary things, but think them through. Talk about the things you know, but develop your knowledge so it is unusually complete. Make yourself the master of your subject.

Subjects Familiar to Others

Do not be afraid to talk about subjects regarding which your hearers also are informed, even if they know more about the subject than you do. No man knows everything on any one topic. The learned man will tell you that the longer he lives the more he realizes how little he knows. We can all learn from the college professor, from the professional writer, and from the laborer. The man digging the ditch that you passed this morning knows more than you do on some topic, if you could get him to discuss it.

There may be, therefore, people in your audience who know more about the subject than you do. Still there may be just one phase of the subject, one point about it that they have not observed as you have. There may be just one side of it on which you can give them a new viewpoint. We all have ideas, which, if communicated, would help others.

Your Thoughts Are Different

"Oh, but my thoughts on that subject are obvious. Everybody must know them." That is just the point! *They do not.* You are so well acquainted with your business, are so close to it, that there does not seem to be anything out of the ordinary in it. Your ideas, your thoughts, being yours, seem obvious to you. You assume that everybody must have the same thoughts and you think that there is no use discussing what everybody knows. You want to be able to say something new, something that is startling.

Remember, however, that people are not always interested in things about which they know nothing at all. In your conversation with friends, you discuss matters that are of mutual interest. You do not talk about things your friend does not understand.

A traveler in Africa discovered a lake on an oasis. He asked an Arab chieftain whether there were any fish in it. The chieftain had never seen a fish and, in attempting to make him understand, the visitor drew the picture of a fish for him. The chieftain merely looked at the drawing and shrugged his shoulders; he knew nothing about fish, had never seen one and therefore was not interested. He was not even curious about it.

Since, in conversation, we talk about things concerning which our friends have some knowledge and find of interest, we should realize that the same kind of talk will interest the members of any group when we stand up to address them. Therefore, talk about ordinary topics. Talk about things that you know and about which you realize your listeners also have some knowledge. Pass on to them the special ideas which *you* have thought out about these common subjects.

SELF-RELIANCE

Consider the following quotation from Emerson's essay on Self-Reliance:

To believe your own thoughts, to believe that what is true for you in your own private heart is true for all men—that is genius. Speak your latent conviction and it shall be the universal sense; for the inmost in due time becomes the outmost, and our first thought is rendered back to us by the trumpets of the Last Judgment. Familiar as the voice of the mind is to each, the highest merit we ascribe to Moses, Plato and Milton, is that they set at naught books and tradition, and spoke not what men, but what they, thought. A man should learn to detect and watch that gleam of light which flashes across his mind from within, more than the luster of the firmament of bards and sages. Yet he dismisses without notice his thought, because it is his. In every work of genius we recognize our own rejected thoughts; they come back to us with a certain alienated majesty. . . . Tomorrow a stranger will say with masterly good sense precisely what we have thought and felt all the time, and we shall be forced to take with shame our own opinion from another.

A Man Who Spoke Out

The truth of what Emerson says is clearly shown in an experience related by an advertising executive who said:

"A certain chemical company started a national advertising campaign for marketing a baking powder. The product was good. Those who used it were strong in their praise of it. The testimonials were extraordinarily good, but despite all of the commendation, despite the great amount of money spent for advertising, the baking powder did not sell. The reason seemed so obvious to me that I feared to express it. The president of the company was talking to a number of department heads about the failure of the baking powder to appeal to the housewife.

"One of those present said, 'We made a mistake in the marketing. We advertised, on the package and in the newspapers, that the baking powder was made by a chemical company. The public always views with suspicion food that is made chemically. We should have marketed our powder under the name of some subsidiary.'

" 'You're right,' said the president, 'that's the answer. Why didn't we think of that?'

"I thought of that too, but I had only *thought* of it. I sat back and said nothing about it. It seemed too obvious. That incident taught me to have faith in my thoughts."

Courage to Utter the Obvious

Have the courage to express what you think. Express it even if you think it is obvious. If others have the same idea, they will agree with you. We all like to be able to sit back and hear a speaker give opinions or enunciate thoughts which agree with ours. When his ideas agree with ours, we feel he is right. For that reason we tend to agree with his subsequent statements. So what seems obvious to you may be the means of winning your audience.

Have the courage, therefore, to give voice to your opinions. Think them through carefully, and if, in your good judgment, they are correct, then have the courage to express them.

Common Topics Earnestly Treated

What topic should you pick? The topic that seems an ordinary, everyday topic to you. That will be the subject with which you are conversant. You will talk about the things you understand thoroughly. You will express what you believe. There is a speech in almost any subject. When you express effectively what you think others already know, you will interest your listeners. They will agree with you and will be gratified. If some speaker with a splendid reputation delivers a speech and so handles his subject that we are forced, because of our own knowledge of it or our own thoughts on it, to say, "That's right," we are flattered. We have thought the same things that this well-known or famous individual expressed.

Great men are not always great because they have thoughts differing entirely from the ideas of others. They are great because they have the courage to express those thoughts publicly, because they can express them with conviction, because they express them with interest and enthusiasm.

Some years ago Louis D. Brandeis, then Justice of the United States Supreme Court, delivered an oration on "True Americanism." Justice Brandeis' judicial opinions have been widely quoted by the legal profession. He did not in this oration give to his listeners any thoughts that were startlingly new. His oration is made up of your and my ordinary thoughts.

He begins his talk with the motto adopted by the founders of our republic:

> *E Pluribus Unum*—out of many, one. Many states—peoples from many lands—one nation. We welcome and make citizens of the immigrants to our shore. All citizens, both native and foreign-born, are Americans. All show reverence to our flag. The immigrant becomes a loyal citizen. This Fourth of July has been termed Americanization Day.

What is Americanization? It manifests itself superficially in dress, manners and language. It is founded upon deeply rooted interests and affections which bring us all into complete harmony with American ideals.

American ideals compel the development of the individual man. He must observe the American standard of living. We in America have become our brothers' keepers. The American standard of living implies the guarantees of our Constitution—life, liberty and the pursuit of happiness. These necessitate the means to live well; to be politically and industrially free; to be enabled to fully develop and utilize our faculties.

For this purpose we need an education that is broad and continuous. We need adequate food, proper working and living conditions and leisure.

The American must be capable of ruling. He needs industrial liberty and financial independence.

The child being the father of the man, must be brought up in surroundings that are in accord with the American standard of living.

The difference between the American standard and the standard of other nations is brotherhood.

Other nations limit their citizenship. America declares for equality of nationalities and individuals.

American democracy is opposed to the theory of aristocratic government. The eighteenth and nineteenth centuries were devoted to establishing the equal rights of every person.

America dedicates liberty to the brotherhood of man. It rejects the principles of the superman. America believes that in differentiation—not in uniformity—lies the path of progress. Europe generally believes in the aristocratic theory.

It assumes that the stronger must dominate others to advance civilization.

Nations have individuality no less than single persons. America proclaims that both have the right and duty to develop.

The United States is called upon to point the way. America says, "Go the way of Liberty and Justice—led by Democracy and a new nationalism."

There are the thoughts developed in the talk by Mr. Justice Brandeis. Are there any but ordinary thoughts expressed therein? In your own words you could express the thoughts that are given in this oration. You could have done it before you read the oration. There are no particularly startling ideas. One finds just an expression of thoughts which many Americans might express. They are simple, forceful, easily understood. The language convinces you of what you already know. Yet this is an oration. Stirring, patriotic, moving. An oration that swayed others and vivified thoughts which were perhaps dormant in the minds of his hearers. You could give a speech like that if you had the courage.

Believe in Your Own Mind

Believe in your own thoughts. Express what you think without fearing that it is commonplace. Think—then say what you have to say with courage, conviction, and enthusiasm. Subjects on which you can speak effectively to audiences should not be hard to find. They may or may not be connected directly with the subjects that are being discussed at the time by others. *Pick your subject and stick to it.* Think it out. Make your decision and then hold to that decision.

Chapter 6

DETERMINING WHAT YOU WANT TO SAY

WHEN asked the secret of success, Chauncey M. Depew once replied, "There is no secret about it. Just dig, dig, dig."

What is the secret of effective speaking? There is no secret about it. It is just *practice, practice, practice.*

A Gift to be Developed

Public speaking is a gift, but it is a gift that is yours and mine. We do not call walking—the power to walk—a gift. Yet it is just as much of a gift as effective speaking. You had to learn to walk. So also you learned to talk. If you can talk in conversation, you can just as easily talk standing up before a group. You probably could not win a walking or running race without training, but training and practice at accelerated walking or running would help make you an athlete. Training and practice in accelerated thinking and speaking will help make you effective when you stand up to talk. While age may hinder one from becoming an athlete, age will help one to be effective as a speaker. The older the person, the longer has experience been his tutor. Because of your experience you have the foundation for talking interestingly. What you need is to add sufficient preparation to the knowledge gained by experience.

Preparation—Various Meanings

There are various methods of preparation for effective public speaking. Some instructors lay special stress upon the importance of detailed and elaborate preparation before making a speech. "Know your subject," they repeat again and again. This sort of preparation is necesssary for many types of speeches. You cannot talk on anything about which you have no knowledge, but sometimes you have no opportunity to prepare a speech before you are asked to talk briefly on a subject.

To speak extemporaneously does not mean speaking without preparation. You may not prepare a written speech for a talk, but you will still be prepared. You are prepared by your knowledge of the subject, by your life's experience. While you may not write the words for a particular talk that you will give, back of every talk is the experience of years.

What, then, do we mean by talking in this instance without preparation? We mean that you do not prepare the words. The subject will be related to matters with which you are already familiar, and therefore you will be ready to speak. The subject which may be given you will be in the field in which you are prepared to talk from your experience and knowledge. In this sense, your "extemporaneous" talks, as well as the "extemporaneous" talks of every worthwhile speaker, have taken a long time to prepare. The preparation has been going on for years.

Subjects on Which You Are Prepared

Whether or not you are aware of the fact, you have made preparation for effective public speaking of this character. There are topics on which you are able right now to talk convincingly even without further study. In fact, the type of subject that you, as a business man or officer of a fraternal or service organization, will be called upon to discuss is almost certain to be one of which you have definite knowledge. You obtained that knowledge from observation, from experience, from conversation, from reading.

It should be emphasized that with respect to these subjects your preparation has been going on for a long time. Your experience, which is your preparation, is so close to you that it may not seem to you an adequate foundation for presenting trustworthy material, but in reality it is a very good foundation. It will take practice, of course, to attain the readiness and fluency for which well-known speakers are notable, but practice will bring this also in sufficient degree.

Subjects That Call for Study

You may be asked, however, to talk on some subject for which experience has not thoroughly prepared you, or on an occasion when a more formal address is imperative. In that case it is necessary to make definite preparation by means of reflection, reading, and conversation. You may make a detailed outline and write the complete speech. You may speak from written notes or from mental notes. Public officials sometimes feel it necessary to read a speech because of the danger on an important public issue of not expressing exactly the thoughts they have in mind. They wish to be quoted in the press just as they have carefully set down the words in writing. Ordinarily it is not as effective to read a speech as it is to speak from mental or written notes one has made in advance of a speech. Sometimes one may also have a speech fully written, keeping it before him as he speaks merely to remind him of major thoughts and of the sequence of his ideas. The written manuscript is also available for publicity releases.

Your Idea versus Its Presentation

The specific preparation required before you can work up an effective speech includes two different lines of activity. There is your own *mental* preparation, which is requisite before you can determine what you want to say. There is also the preparation required for determining how to present your ideas to the listeners you are to address. In the case of an experienced speaker both processes may be carried on very rapidly—almost instantaneously. For the inexperienced speaker, on the other hand, both aspects require careful attention.

Preparation in its second aspect—that is, determining how you will present your ideas to your listeners—will be taken up later. Here we must consider your mental preparation, the preparation required in determining what you desire to say.

Reflect, Read, Consult

With regard to your personal preparation, which is certainly necessary when you have to talk on a subject not wholly familiar to you, or when you are given time to prepare a more formal address for some special occasion, the formula to follow may be summed up in three words: *Reflect, Read, Consult.* That is to say: Turn the subject over carefully in your mind, to make sure of just what you actually think about it at present. Then read books, magazines, and other written matter, to see what others have said about it. Finally, make opportunities of conversing upon the subject with other persons, as often as time permits, to discover how it appears to people who are probably somewhat like those you are to address.

Senator Beveridge's Advice

Albert J. Beveridge, at one time United States Senator from Indiana, was not only the author of two outstanding books on American politics, the life of John Marshall and the life of Lincoln; he was also one of the most eloquent and skillful orators our country has known. In an article on "Public Speaking" he speaks of two important steps in one's mental preparation for making a speech—thinking and reading. He does not believe you should read at all until you have first reflected on the subject, until you have examined the present contents of your own mind.

These are his words:

The method commonly employed in preparing speeches is incorrect. That method is to read all the books one can get on the subject, take all the opinions that can be procured, make exhaustive notes, and then write a speech. Such a speech is nothing but a compilation. It is merely an arrangement of second-hand thought and observation, and of other people's ideas. It never has the power of living and original thinking.

The true way is to take the elements of the problem in hand, and, without consulting a book or an opinion, reason out from the very elements of the problem itself your solution of it, and then prepare your speech.

After this, read, read, read, comprehensively, omnivorously, in order to see whether your original solution was not exploded a hundred years ago—aye, or a thousand; and also, to fortify and make accurate your own thoughts. Read Matthew Arnold on "Literature and Dogma," and you will discover why it is necessary for you to read exhaustively on any subject about which you would think or write or speak. But, as you value your independence of mind—yes, even your vigor of mind—do not read other men's opinions upon the subject *before* you have clearly thought out your own conclusions from the premises of the elemental facts.

If you follow this method, you begin by thinking about the subject. Have a pencil and paper handy. Jot down your ideas. Do not write the speech; merely put down the ideas. Concentrate on them. Then, after thoroughly weighing them, read as widely as you can.

This method may be helpful to many persons, but there is no rigid method of preparation which must be followed. Many of the most able and effective public speakers may first read widely on any subject on which they expect to speak. They read conflicting viewpoints to get all sides of a question. They do not try to form a final opinion until they have read exhaustively on the matter. Follow whichever method you find is particularly helpful to you. But —and this is exceedingly important—be sure you have thoroughly informed yourself regarding the subject by reading, thinking, and conversing with others. Then prepare your notes or written draft of the speech or organize it mentally into a logical presentation.

Using the Thoughts of Others

Do not fear to use ideas that have been expressed by others, but put those thoughts, unless you are quoting, in your own words. Elaborate them as you see fit. Draw your own conclusions from them. Make them your own. Your ideas will then be augmented and clarified by the ideas of others.

This use of other men's ideas as a basis for your own is a perfectly legitimate practice. It has been followed in all ages. With respect to ideas, thoughts, and reflections which grow out of observing life, there may be only a little that is new. Many of the ideas that we call new and modern are merely a restatement of ideas that were first conceived ages ago. Many of your own thoughts which you regard as completely original have undoubtedly been expressed before. You have a right to utilize any idea, provided that you do not merely "parrot" it, but give it an original application.

Shakespeare

The great master writer of all time, Shakespeare, did not hesitate to take the ideas, the plays, of others. He used their plots, and some of their scenes, and from them developed his great dramatic masterpieces. But remember he made the thoughts, the plots, his own.

Lincoln's Gettysburg Address

Lincoln's Gettysburg speech will live while the English language exists. His great conclusion is quoted in patriotic speeches on many occasions. Was the wording, "government of the people, by the people, for the people" original? No. Lincoln had a copy of Theodore Parker's speeches. Parker had used the words, "A Government of all the people, by all the people, for all the people," in a speech at Boston in 1850. In 1795, Thomas Cooper had said, "Government of the people and for the people." Years before Lincoln's address John Marshall had stated, "Government over all, by all, and for the sake of all." Webster had used almost the same sentiment in his reply to Hayne in 1830, when he said, "The people's government made for the people, made by the people, and answerable to the people."

Some of your thought combinations may never have been expressed until now. Those that have been voiced differed in the manner of expression from the form and language you will use. While there is little new under the sun, by taking the old, dressing it in a new garb of language, you can interest others. Because it seems new it will have a freshness of appeal.

Make the Ideas Your Own

It is imperative that you make the ideas you express really your own, for as William Jennings Bryan said: "One cannot communicate information unless he possesses it. There is quite a difference in people in this respect; we say of one that he knows more than he can tell and, of another, that he can tell all he knows." It is impossible for one to tell more than he knows.

On the other hand, it is not a compliment to say of any individual that "he knows more than he can tell." What you *know* you can talk about. If you cannot tell us about a thing, you have no clear knowledge on the subject. Make your knowledge clear. Think it out and you will be able to talk about it.

The Value of Consultation

In addition to reflecting upon the subject, and reading widely and attentively, discuss it with other persons of your acquaintance, or with strangers when you have an opportunity. Ask questions. Find out what others know about the subject. Conversation with others is a most valuable element in preparing your own thought.

Almost anyone can learn from books. Many learn a great deal also by observation. Few learn all they could from other people. Yet almost everyone you meet can teach you, can tell you or show you something worthwhile if you know how to ask intelligent questions, and if you are really interested in learning. The person who wishes to grow must be a human interrogation point.

Alertness Finds Material

Suppose, then, that you have selected your topic. It is being held before your mind, and you are actively examining it, thinking through it. You will be amazed to find how material will collect.

To your surprise, when reading your morning newspaper, you will find a paragraph or comment that bears on your subject. In casual conversation a remark will be made that will help you in developing it. A lecture, a sermon, a book, will give you a suggestion that will aid you. Why? Because your mind is awake, alert. It is receptive on the subject. It is eager to grasp whatever will help in making the topic clear. Bryan defined "eloquence" as: "The speech of one who knows what he is talking about and means what he says." An unknown author once said, "Eloquence is logic on fire."

Above All, Think It Through

Knowing your subject may involve reading; it may involve conversation. It will certainly involve thought. On the walls of a certain university are inscribed these words of Owen D. Young:

> Facts can be applied in any field. Our course is ignorance. Facts are our scarcest raw material. This is shown by the economy with which we use them. One has to dig deep for them because they are as difficult to get as they are precious to have.

Do not confuse thinking with a mere readjustment of your prejudices. Prejudice means arriving at an opinion without getting the facts. If you think conscientiously after you have the complete facts, you cannot harbor prejudice.

It has been said that only a few people think. But the thinkers are the leaders. Get the facts and think the subject through to a logical conclusion. Then you will be mentally prepared and your preparation will make it possible for you to secure the results you seek.

Whether you employ the method of preparing your thought which was once suggested by Beveridge—beginning by thinking the subject through for yourself—or whether you seek first to obtain the opinions of others through reading and conversation, you must thoroughly digest the matter which you are going to discuss. You will begin to have faith in your power to talk on the subject. You will make your hearers remember what you have said. You will have made them think.

PART II

Methods of Delivery

Chapter 7

READING, RECITING, OR TALKING EXTEMPORANEOUSLY

YOUR work of preparing a speech really begins after you have chosen your subject and have determined what you wish to say. Up to that point you have merely been clarifying your ideas, for yourself. But a speech is an effort to convey ideas to other people. In a speech you are not just revealing your thought, talking to yourself, soliloquizing, as the characters do sometimes in Shakespeare's plays. When Hamlet says:

> To be or not to be, that is the question, whether
> 'tis nobler in the mind to suffer the slings and
> arrows of outrageous fortune, or to take arms
> against a sea of trouble and by opposing, end them,

he is thinking aloud. The listeners are merely overhearing him. They get a glimpse into his mind and watch him thinking. He makes no effort to convey his ideas to them. Hamlet is not making a speech.

But when Patrick Henry said: "If we were base enough to desire it, it is now too late to retire from the contest. There is no retreat but in submission and slavery," he was manifestly addressing other people. He already knew what he thought and was now presenting his ideas to the members of the Virginia legislature, to win them to his view. A speech is an effort to reach the minds of other people.

Planning the Presentation Essential

To succeed in this step involves arranging, explaining, and wording your ideas in a way that the audience you are addressing will find easy to understand, interesting, and convincing. In preparing a speech it is necessary to plan it to fit the needs of the particular audience you have in mind.

Even when speaking on a subject with which you are thoroughly familiar, you have the same need of considering the requirements of the audience. You may, for example, find yourself in a situation like that of a business man who was invited to address the Rotary Club in a Wisconsin city on current problems of business. The principal of the high school also asked him to address the students at a morning assembly. Two speeches on the same subject were to be given within three hours. Obviously, a different presentation was necessary for each occasion. Some time in advance, the business man sat down and worked out carefully the ways he would present the same subject to the two audiences. Both speeches treated the same subject, but they were different in their method of presentation.

The Main Steps in Planning

You face the need of working out carefully your manner of presentation with every speech, whether the subject matter is familiar to you or whether it is one that you must look up. We shall consider now the main aspects of such preparation for the audience, what things you need to consider, and how you go about it. Since these matters must be considered in all speeches, determining what to do about them forms a large part of your work. We shall break down the general subject of preparing speeches for an audience into a few main subdivisions; these are:

The general idea you wish to present
Planning the main steps or sections in developing this idea
Shaping up each step or section to give it an effective form
Shaping and polishing the statements or sentences
Choosing the right words

Two Matters to Consider Beforehand

We shall take up these topics in successive chapters. There are two points, however, which should be considered here.

One of them is the general method you will use in presenting or delivering your speech; the other relates to your memory. As your decisions on these points will affect all aspects of your presentation, you will find it helpful to consider them before going further.

Methods of Delivery

First, in regard to the method of delivery which you will employ, there are many methods of presenting a speech, of which some of the principal ones follow:

1. You may write out your address and read it from a manuscript.

2. Having written out your remarks you may commit them to memory.

3. You may memorize your opening words, your closing sentences, and such other passages as you wish to make sure of, and extemporize the rest.

4. You may extemporize the whole address, appearing before your audience with no visible manuscript. You will seem to be giving your audience the thoughts of the moment, but actually you will have prepared your remarks well in advance.

5. You may write your address and have it before you on the speaker's stand, but you will only read from it occasionally. A substantial portion of your remarks will be extemporaneous, especially any illustrations and stories. This procedure is effective, but it requires thorough familiarity with your manuscript.

6. You may write an address in full but only have with you a small card or two of notes containing an outline of the essential points.

7. You may write an address in full in order to have thought through the subject carefully. But you will make only a mental, not written, outline of the major points, and you will talk extemporaneously.

Writing and Reading

The method of reading is used by many successful speakers. It has the advantage of definiteness. You can set down exactly what you want to say and be sure of giving it without change. Men and women in important positions in government may wish to follow this procedure when announcing important policies. They must state a policy precisely and accurately. Business and professional men and women also may make public statements of such significance that they cannot rely on extemporaneous speech. There is always the danger that poor memory may result in forgetting a very important point. Moreover, it is not always possible for busy men and women to take the time to memorize a speech.

The reading method has some disadvantages. It makes it difficult to adjust one's remarks to the situation. In rare instances what you write beforehand may not fit closely with the situation or with the mood of the audience. The listeners may then admire what you have written but they may not feel that you are talking directly to them.

Reading a talk may mean monotony. Your voice may become singsong. If you have not read the talk often enough so you can occasionally look at your audience, you lose the powerful effect of the eye in holding their attention. You may not so easily interest them. You may not gain the intimacy which makes a speech effective.

As we have already indicated, one major reason for reading a talk is to guard against being misquoted.

The President of the United States, when talking on some subject which might have important public reactions, very often reads what he has to say. The scientist who is developing a formula for the guidance of other scientists may read. The head of a great corporation, talking on a matter that may affect stock or commodity markets, may prefer to have his speech in written form, so that he may not inadvertently make wrong implications. But for the usual talk of a business or professional man or woman, reading an address in its entirety may cause lack of interest on the part of the audience.

Methods number five, six, and seven given above are variations of method number one. Speakers may use any one of these methods which they find most helpful with their speeches.

Memorizing

Some good speakers commit their speeches to memory. This has been the practice of many famous preachers with their sermons, of many eminent lawyers with their pleas to the jury, and of many public men in speeches on political issues. Some of these men seem to possess a photographic memory. They can write a speech that will take a half hour to deliver, read it over to themselves, and repeat it practically word for word from memory. It should be said, though, that those who employ this method are not infrequently professional speakers, in the sense that they make many speeches. For the man or woman who makes a speech only occasionally, the method may be too laborious. It is not necessary to memorize your talk word for word, and depending upon memory may be hazardous. If in the course of your delivery your memory fails, you may be left helpless. There are too many instances of speakers who had to stop and sit down in discomfiture because they could not remember.

With this method also there is the problem of delivery. Very few persons can give a talk from memory and get the best results. It requires acting ability of the highest order. The experienced speaker may accomplish wonders by this method. The speaker with little experience may be less successful. Like the talk that is read, the memorized talk may sound written. There is a difference between written and spoken language. Few persons write as they speak. The freedom of offhand speech is lacking.

The most serious objection to both of the methods already described is that they may handicap you when you are caught in an emergency, without time to write out a speech in advance.

Memorizing Important Passages

The third method, writing out and memorizing certain passages, is used to good effect by many prominent speakers. It has obvious advantages, when you need to cite statistics or definitely worded opinions. It enables you to frame your opening, or your conclusion, or important transitions, so as to be sure of saying what you have planned.

With this method one must be careful that there is no difference between the spoken and written language. If you can write in the same style that you use when you talk, well and good. If not, your memorized passages may be rhetorical while the extemporized part of your talk may be colloquial. The difference will be noticed. It may be a distracting element, calling attention to your language rather than your idea. The audience should be attentive to the thought, not to the vehicle of the thought.

Speaking Extemporaneously

The fourth method, speaking extemporaneously, has a number of good points. It gives you the power to look at your hearers. You will be natural. You will be actively thinking. Your hearers will appreciate it. You will make them think. You will therefore get results much more easily. Said Dr. Lyman Abbott, a great preacher and successor of Henry Ward Beecher in the pulpit of Plymouth Church, Brooklyn, "The best manuscript address is the most admired; the best extemporaneous address is the most effective."

You want to be effective. If you read your address you may not be so effective. Your hearers will be annoyed. You can and should know your subject, and if you do know it, you are able to talk ex temporaneously. Make the attempt. You will astonish yourself. Calvin Coolidge said, "Most people have failed because they did not really try."

To succeed you must *do*. Doing is necessary to build mansions, reputation, or ability. To acquire the ability to make speeches demands that you make speeches. Do not become discouraged. As the late George Bernard Shaw said, "Success covers a multitude of blunders." At the first attempt the speech may not be good. Your next attempt at this method of presenting your ideas will be better. But the tenth speech made on this plan will in all probability be very good.

The extemporaneous wording which you give to your prepared talk will be spontaneous. Your talk will not seem artificial. You will be thinking before your audience and for them especially. They will sense it and appreciate it, and their interested response will help you.

Preparing for Extemporizing

Speaking extemporaneously, however, does not mean speaking without planning what to say. Far from it. If you are wise you will go over the speech beforehand, perhaps several times. Only, do not try to memorize it.

Here is a method which you will find helpful. Write the talk out in advance, just as you think you would deliver it. Write it quickly, with a "running pen" as the old saying goes, not pausing to correct or recast any more than when actually talking. Write it all out and then take it up and read it over several times to yourself aloud—*as if delivering it to the audience*. That will show you how it sounds. It will also reveal to you places where recasting will improve the speech.

Familiarizing Yourself with Your Idea

You have expressed your thought on the subject in writing the speech, and in reading it aloud. You should now be able to express it again when you get up to face your audience; you are prepared to talk extemporaneously. The words you utter to the audience will be the words of the moment. They will clothe the thought as they do in conversation. The thought, however, will not be extemporaneous in the sense of being hasty or accidental. The thought is the result of preparation, through your study, and through your experience in business and social life—the experience that you gained back in your school days—the experience that your mind has been storing up over the years. When you thus present to your hearers in concentrated form the result of your experience, study, judgment, imagination, and enthusiasm, you will interest them.

Trying Out the Speech

When time permits, carry this preparation one step further. In addition to writing the speech in rough form and reading it aloud to yourself, make opportunities of trying it out by actually delivering portions of it to listeners, in conversation, or in a definite rehearsal.

The late Alfred E. Smith was once lunching with a group which included Bourke Cockran, an eloquent New York congressman. After the others had gone Cockran repeated to Smith a speech an hour and a half long, which he later delivered to Congress with hardly a change in wording.

The head of a large business organization who is in demand as a speaker lately revealed to a friend the secret of the orderly and smooth presentation of his material. He makes it a practice, he says, when getting ready for an important speaking date, to give himself two or three rehearsals by delivering the speech in advance before little groups of his intimate friends. In that way, when he stands before his real audience, he knows his way through the subject. He can talk as easily as if conversing. You may, perhaps, be able to do the same when preparing for some of your own speaking dates.

Rehearsing to Yourself

But if this is not practicable, you can secure virtually the same effect by rehearsing the speech to yourself.

After definitely organizing a speech, planning it, writing it out, and reading it over, stand up in your room alone, and *talk through the speech to an imaginary audience.*

Do not try to recall all the words. Just begin and let your mind plow ahead through the subject. Talk for the length of time you have set for the speech—five minutes, ten minutes, half an hour, as the case may be—and then stop. Whether or not you have finished, when the set time is up, stop. Sit down and think it over. See how near you have come to saying what you intended.

The next day do the same. You need not try to recall your first scheme of treatment. It may be better to try a different beginning, and follow a somewhat different path. But try to get to the same conclusion in the same number of minutes.

Do this day after day, each day varying the approach and the detail of treatment.

A "Sure-fire" Method

Then when you face your actual audience, you will be prepared. You will "know the country." You will have been over the subject by this path and that path, and you will be able to move easily from one point to another.

The drill you thus obtain is somewhat like that which is received by the politician in a campaign who speaks several times a night to audience after audience. He has a few points which he wants to present to every group. But according to the make-up of his audience he emphasizes one of these points on one occasion and another point on another occasion. He changes his introduction, his illustrations, and his words, for different situations. Thomas Marshall tells in his autobiography about his campaign for governor, in Indiana. The way he expresses it is somewhat like this. "I made three hundred and twenty-six speeches in the campaign, or rather I made *one* speech three hundred and twenty-six times. It was the same material altered to suit the audience."

This method of talking extemporaneously, but rehearsing as often as time permits without memorizing words or sentences, is a flexible and effective method. Anyone can learn to employ it. It will take more time in the first stages of your self-training in public speaking, but it will help to insure results. As time goes on, you will find that the time required for adequate preparation of the ordinary speech will be greatly reduced. Finally, you will be able to make an effective talk with a minimum of time to get ready.

Using Notes

The question is sometimes asked, "May I have any notes at all, when I rise to speak? Will it not be a safeguard if I have a little outline, on a paper or card? If I *should* forget, I could look at this and recover myself."

Many good speakers use cards on which they have written the outline of the talk. You will see them occasionally refer to the outline to recall the points which they are to discuss. You may use such a guide to give you the topics. Some speakers fear that when you have an outline you will not use your full mental faculties. You may make too much use of the outline. But other speakers have found an outline helpful because it assured them that they would not wander far from the subject. One of the great dangers of extemporaneous speaking is that the speaker will merely "run off at the mouth" without knowing when to stop. "Extemporaneous" speaking requires thorough preparation.

Memory–Fixing the Points in Mind

To use the method of extemporaneous speaking with full effectiveness you need to train your memory. This statement may appear surprising in view of what has just been said about memorizing a speech, but there is a distinction. To memorize the language, or a particular form of presenting an idea is ordinarily unwise. But, of course, you need to remember your outline of points, your plan for developing the subject. You need to train yourself so that you can be sure of remembering the outline, however the situation may develop as you speak.

The psychologists tell us that there are two necessary factors in remembering. The first is *vividness of impression.* The second is careful *association of impressions.*

You remember easily things in which you are deeply interested, things to which you have given close attention. Therefore, when trying to fix in mind the main points of your speech, or particular items that are of importance, concentrate attention upon them beforehand. Make yourself *study* them, as you used to study for an examination in school.

Further, to reinforce your recollection of the different steps or passages, try to fix in mind some kind of frame or sequence. For example, you may fix in your mind just how your speech outline, your plan, looks on paper.

Or, you can make up short word-headings for the successive points, all beginning with the same letter. If you were advocating the establishment of a new adjustment system in a business house, you might summarize your main points under the four headings: complaints, causes, cure, cost. For a short speech such a scheme is hardly necessary, but when your speech is to run to twenty minutes or more, it may be very helpful.

Sometimes you can give this little frame a humorous twist and announce it to the audience. An oldtime clergyman, it is related, announced to his congregation that he was to preach on the text: "The devil goeth about like a roaring lion, seeking whom he may devour." He would discuss the subject, he said, under these headings: what the devil was; where the devil was going; and what the devil was roaring about.

Enriching Your Mental Store

In addition, and this is the more important point, it is eminently wise to have in your mind, to be drawn upon at a moment's notice, an ample supply of material for your speech. This supply of material will include a stock of words, a stock of sentence patterns, a stock of methods of developing an idea in a paragraph or a group of paragraphs, and of course a stock of stories and specific subject matter to illustrate the points you may make. You wish to give the impression of having at your complete command every mental resource. This requires having a good memory.

We see how this applies in conversation. The best conversationalist is the one who can talk on a variety of subjects. Good conversation depends on the speaker's retention of facts or ideas. It is obvious that the more ideas you possess—the more able you are to recall them when you desire—the more interesting you will be as a conversationalist.

Now what is true for conversation is even more true when you are making a speech to a group. If you cannot recall names, dates, and other items of fact that come up in your talk, the audience gets an impression that you are either unfamiliar with your subject or lacking in mental grip. If, on the other hand, you have a well stored and well disciplined memory, that hands you item after item as your talk requires it, the audience gets an impression of adequate knowledge and full mental control.

Alertness, Attention at All Times

It is, therefore, important for anyone who wishes to be an effective speaker, able to meet any emergency that may arise, to train his memory. Practically all men or women who have been successful as public speakers have recognized this fact. If their memory was not naturally strong at the beginning of their speaking career, you will find that they gave systematic attention to strengthening it. With many of them, as in the case of William Jennings Bryan, their trained memory was a very large element in their success. It supplied them instantly with just the illustration, the fact, the word which they needed for the occasion, and thereby enabled them before an audience to apply their greatest energy to the speech.

You will see that training your memory means much more than merely fixing in mind certain ideas, patterns, illustrations, or words for use in a particular speech. It is much more important to develop your memory in general, as Bryan and the others did. Then it will pick up and retain, almost automatically, the specific items needed for the single speech. A football player must learn and keep in mind the particular plays that are to be used in tomorrow's game. But he needs even more to have his mind full of football tactics and expedients, so that he can be ready to take advantage instantly of the unexpected developments in the play.

In connection with the work of preparing subject matter for audiences you need to store your memory with the following types of material:

Methods of developing an idea
Illustrations and stories
Patterns of sentence structure
Words

The best way to do this is through developing the habit of alert attention. Whenever you listen or read, note and fix in mind items which may come in handy in your own speech.

Chapter 8

THE CENTRAL IDEA

THE first step in preparing your speech for the audience consists in determining carefully your central idea, your main thought, just what it is you wish to say. This is the most important step in preparation. It is one which the beginner almost always neglects but to which the experienced speaker has learned to give close attention.

Always an Idea, When You Talk

In earlier chapters we spoke of choosing the subject to talk about. Now when we talk about a subject either to another person or to a group, it is always for the purpose of making some statement, expressing some comment, view, or opinion. For example, the subject which you talk about in conversation with a friend may be a topic like one of the following:

Reducing city taxes
The dinner you attended last Thursday
Your company's new promotion campaign
The coming Red Cross drive
The new gas furnace you are selling
Your fishing trip in Canada

But what you say is:

Our city taxes could come down a great deal with efficient management.

The dinner last Thursday was a dead affair. I wish I hadn't gone.

The new promotion campaign is going to make things a lot easier for salesmen in this territory.

The Red Cross drive will need to raise more money this season, because of the bad storms we have had, not to speak of the drought and several large disasters.

This new gas furnace will actually save you money in operation, besides being far more convenient than your former method of heating.

In Canada last week, I had the best fishing I have known.

Determine the Idea Beforehand

In conversation you do not stop and explicitly consider what this central idea of our remarks is to be. You "just know" what you wish to say; your thought comes to you in a flash—automatically, subconsciously. You utter it with almost as little conscious reflection as moving your legs when you walk. But when you make a speech, it is different. When you have to go into a matter in detail before a group of people, it is wise to consider definitely beforehand just what it is that you intend to say; in other words, to determine the central idea of your speech.

If you are urged to go to the Town Improvement Association meeting and give them the views which you have expressed to your friends on reducing the local budget, you will have to think over your case and make up your mind as to what you will recommend. For you will be challenged, you will have to support your statements. Or, if you are asked to tell about your fishing trip in Canada at the monthly meeting of your club, you will also find it wise to determine carefully the central idea of your remarks. Otherwise, you may run on indefinitely and weary your listeners.

The Danger of Rambling

The fact is that everyone tends to ramble when making a speech. Unless you know clearly just where you are going, you may start with one idea and then unknowingly detour to another which is somehow related to the first but on a somewhat different subject, then to another, until you wind up far from the point where you started. Failure to keep on the subject is a common experience with after-dinner speakers. Dr. DeWitt Talmage, an eloquent preacher and popular orator, once characterized the subject of an after-dinner speech as merely a point from which to depart. The dinner speaker, he believed, started with the subject assigned him and then merely rambled ahead as this or that thought occurred to him. Such a talk is uncoordinated. It is not focused. It is only a series of remarks.

The Rare Exception

Once in a while, it is true, this is what is desired by the audience.

Professor Brander Matthews of Columbia University, after his retirement from teaching, was invited to address a group of friends at dinner and just reminisce. Professor Matthews in his long life had been in touch with many phases of literature, drama, and life. For fifty years, he had known practically every person of importance who had come to New York. On this occasion, he held his listeners spellbound for two hours, while he rambled on from one topic to another. The reason was that his experiences had been so significant and so close to the field of his listeners that merely to wander with him held them in rapt attention. They had the background which enabled them to understand each item and place it in its proper setting. Listening to such a talk is like strolling through an art gallery or museum, stopping here and there to look at whatever catches your fancy. If you are familiar with the field of art or science represented in the museum, you comprehend the significance of each object on which your eyes fall and you are not confused.

As a Rule, Chart Your Course

But for one who lacked this background, the confusion would be hopeless. An outsider listening to Professor Matthews on that memorable occasion would have been held to attention, if at all, merely by the entertaining treatment of single items, the picturesqueness of the illustrations, the neatly turned sentences, or the expressiveness of the words. For the outsider it would have been merely a long vaudeville show. For most of us on most subjects, and even for Brander Matthews on most occasions, such rambling would be a very poor way to make a speech. It would be almost certain to confuse and tire the listeners. Professor Matthews himself once said:

> Even a man who has no gift for oratory, no enthusiasm, no fervor, no magnetism, as it is called, can make a presentable figure on the platform if he rises knowing exactly what he wants to say, if he says that and no more, and if he sits down as soon as he has said it. . . .

Take time in determining your central idea. It will save you time at every later step. It will enable you to make an adequate and creditable presentation of your view. It will make your speech easier for your audience to grasp and enjoy, and that is one of the most important factors in speaking effectively.

Determining the Results You Desire

Determining the central idea involves in the first place, deciding just what effect you want to produce on the minds of your listeners, what result you want to secure by your speech. We might classify the possible results or effects of a speech under four headings. Actually, of course, the four groups shade into one another and overlap. For convenience of analysis, however, the grouping will be helpful.

Winning a Vote or Decision

First, the object may be to make the listeners decide to grant a request. For example, you may desire a committee to award you a contract. Or you may desire a body of citizens to go to the polls and vote for a candidate whom you favor. Here, for example, is a speech made by a man running for alderman in a municipal campaign:

Ladies and Gentlemen: May I take this opportunity to thank you for having honored me by selecting me your candidate for alderman. I am appreciative of the hard work you have done and will do to insure my election.

With registration behind us and the election but two weeks away it is fitting that we consider the issue in this year's municipal election.

I do not pretend to be a brilliant orator or speaker. I am merely a plain-spoken man sincerely interested in the people of this aldermanic district. I shall refrain from excursions into the fields of state and national politics and confine my attention to the needs of this neighborhood.

This year's municipal election raises but one issue and that issue is: Do you approve the present administration of this city or do you wish to hamstring that administration by the election of its boss-controlled opponents?

To answer the question fairly we should briefly review past events. From 1934 until July 1, 1946, the people of this city entrusted the management of their affairs to the bosses. It was a picturesque period, but what direct benefits did the people get from their city? Did the schools, hospitals and parks increase in step with the needs of the people? Did the conduct of the police department, fire department, sanitation department and municipal courts raise the standard of public service? Were the rapid-transit facilities improved? Was the local tax burden lightened? Were housing conditions brought up to date?

In other words, was the management of the city such as to improve living conditions for all the people?

If we are honest, there is but one answer and that is, "No." The bosses had the opportunity and failed to produce. They have made their record and must be judged on that record of failure.

Henry Jones was sworn in as mayor by our good neighbor, Judge John Harrison, on January 1, 1947. What has been his record in the months that he has held office? Let me briefly summarize it:

1. He saved the credit of the city.
2. He drove out of office the grafters and racketeers who masqueraded as public servants.
3. He raised the standard of public service in the various city departments.
4. He improved the schools, the hospitals, the parks.

In other words, he has run the city for the benefit of the people and not the political bosses. For a change the people got a break.

Ladies and gentlemen, I hold that Henry Jones has done more in 42 months to make this city the finest place to live in than was done by the political bosses in the twelve years they controlled the city.

Mayor Jones deserves a board of aldermen that will cooperate with him in serving the people, and to this end I ask that I be elected.

As your alderman I shall wholeheartedly support the mayor, so that the people of this district may benefit by a continuation of the honest, humane, efficient and progressive city administration they are now enjoying under the able leadership of Mayor Jones.

The central idea of this speech is: "Elect me alderman as evidence of your support for Mayor Jones's administration."

Winning Attention from an Idea

Second, the purpose of your speech may be to discuss an important business, political, economic, or other type of problem and give your views of what needs to be done about it. The following excerpts from an address by Elvis J. Stahr, Jr., dean of the University of Kentucky College of Law illustrate an address with this objective. Dean Stahr is explaining that this century is a critical one in the life of America and faithful citizenship and faithful stewardship are required of all Americans.

There have been critical centuries before, to be sure. The first century after the crucifixion of Christ was critical. Would Christianity survive? We now know the answer—it did survive—but only through the courage and the vision and the leadership of a relatively small group of early Christians.

The century before the fall of Rome was critical. What was to be the future of Western civilization? We now know the answer—the loss of courage and of vision and of leadership plunged the western world into a thousand years of darkness.

The century from 1775 to 1875 was critical. Could a nation, a great nation, be founded on untried political foundations—be "conceived in liberty and dedicated to the proposition that all men are created equal," be launched on the thin edge of a new continent, with an ocean at its back and a wilderness at its front—could it be thus born, and flourish? We now know the answers—it was thus born—but only through the courage, the vision, and the leadership of a relatively small group of American Revolutionaries. It did flourish—but only through the courage of a relatively small group of pioneers—and the vision and leadership of farseeing ones among our forefathers.

Yes, there have been other critical centuries—yet I repeat that never in the history of civilization has there been a century so critical as the twentieth will prove to be. With this solemn statement surely no thinking man on earth has disagreed since August, 1945. Why? Because this time *everything* is at stake—*all* we know and cherish—our progress, our culture, our freedom, our civilization, our ability to make a living, our sacred rights, indeed our very survival as rational beings and children of God. Do we now know the answer?

Let's put this critical century in such perspective as we briefly can. By 1900, the people of America had realized that their physical frontier was gone, that the industrial revolution was indeed a revolution, and that their nation was a power on the earth. In 1917, it was seen by all the world that war could not be localized. In 1918, a new concept of the state hit the world with dramatic impact and there arose a powerful ideological rival to the still-young western ideal of individual liberty through representative government. Call it black fascism or red fascism—totalitarianism was rapidly to split the world asunder.

In 1930, the American people began to realize that their economic system was not impregnable, that their resources were not unlimited, that adjustments must be made, that wilderness trail-blazing and urban mass production were not so closely akin that individualism could be applied in exactly the same way to the two situations. In 1940, the American people began to realize that their problems were no longer isolated—and could never be again.

Then, in 1945, the machine age, and the age of electricity, moved suddenly into the atomic age—before we were ready for it.

And now—we must recognize that we stand on the threshold of disaster—that the answers to the greatest problems of all history must now be found—and quickly—or it will forever be too late. That is the challenge of this critical century!

What are the odds?

They are heavily against us, in my judgment, unless there shall emerge again in this country a group of men with the courage and the vision and the leadership that are always imperatively needed in critical times. And this time it must be a relatively large group—indeed it must include all our best citizenry—all across the land. . . .

That old phrase, "good citizenship," must now be made to mean even more than it has in our finest hours of the past. It is something we must work at—constantly. We must face the necessity that we must all rise above ourselves. For it is my conviction that unless the local citizens throughout this country, the men and women who understand and cherish the blessings and opportunities which we enjoy, almost alone of the peoples of the earth, the men and women of standing in our American communities—become aroused to the awful gravity of our times; unless we cast off inertia and prejudices; unless we squarely meet the challenge of this critical century—the blessings of liberty will not be secured to our posterity; the land of opportunity will not be known to our posterity—for there will be no liberty, no opportunity, and possibly no posterity.

Therefore, now, at the fulltide of this dramatic century, let us rededicate ourselves to the great business of making democracy work; let us resolve to meet this mighty challenge by faithful citizenship and faithful stewardship—by being alert to change what is bad, by being determined to hold fast to what is good—so that the kind of government of which Lincoln spoke shall *not* perish from the Earth.

Inspirational and Informative Addresses

In the third place, the purpose of your speech may be to give your listeners an inspirational, philosophical, educational, or informative address. This type of address may be very similar to that we have just discussed and may also include an analysis of some problem. However, it is generally characterized by an analysis of some situation, a moral to be gained from some observation, a study of some interesting life or experience, or some other type of informative discussion. The two addresses which follow illustrate speeches of this character.

Lincoln and Edison

An Address by George F. Sokolsky, journalist.

Two birthdays are being celebrated this week end. Yesterday was the birthday of Abraham Lincoln; on Friday was the one hundred and second anniversary of the birth of Thomas A. Edison.

In these days of universal fear and government control of the individual, these two figures stand as peaks of human liberty.

I speak of liberty not in general terms but specifically as the right of the individual to think, to plan, to dream, to experiment, to create, to build, according to his own judgment, assuming his own responsibilities and obligations without fear of any man, any government, any majority or minority, anyone upon this earth. That is liberty.

We all know the personality and character of Abraham Lincoln, but few realize how lonely he was; how he walked alone in this sad world where man so often hates man, where man's inhumanity to man brings in its wake wars, destruction, chaos.

I once visited the little village of Salem in Illinois. It still stands, much as it used to be, in a state park. Every American should make a pilgrimage to that village to see the lowly origin, the humble beginnings of one of the greatest figures in our history.

Lincoln read by candlelight in the attic of an inn. There all alone, without the aid of teachers, of high school, of college, he mastered the English language until he could speak with a beauty of words altogether unknown in our day of slang, of double talk, of cheap vulgarities. Here, in the log building, in a village remote from big cities and great centers of learning, among farmers, lumbermen, and small storekeepers, he made of himself a competent scholar, a lawyer, a great thinker and debater, eventually President of the United States.

We always think of Lincoln as the emancipator of the Negro slaves, as the author of the Emancipation Proclamation and the Gettysburg Address. But there is one thing that Lincoln wrote that I love for the grandeur of its thought and language. It was only a presidential proclamation announcing a day of thanksgiving. Every President writes several of those and nobody bothers to read them. But each year, on Lincoln's birthday, I like to read out loud parts of that proclamation. I like to read it because it belongs to these days as it did to his day. It belongs to all time.

Let me read you some of it:

"Whereas it is the duty of nations as well as of men to own their dependence upon the overruling power of God, to confess their sins and transgressions in humble sorrow, yet with assured hope that genuine repentance will lead to mercy and pardon, and to recognize the sublime truth, announced in the Holy Scriptures and proven by all history, that those nations only are blessed whose God is the Lord:

"And, insomuch as we know that by His divine law nations, like individuals, are subjected to punishments and chastisements in this world, may we not justly fear that the awful calamity of civil war which now desolates the land may be but a punishment inflicted upon us for our presumptuous sins, to the needful end of our national reformation as a whole people? We have been the recipients of the choicest bounties of heaven; we have been preserved these many years in peace and prosperity; we have grown in numbers, wealth, and power as no other nation has ever grown. But we have forgotten God. We have forgotten the gracious hand which preserved us in peace and multiplied and enriched and strengthened us, and we have vainly imagined, in the deceitfulness of our hearts, that all these blessings were produced by some superior wisdom and virtue of our own. Intoxicated with unbroken success, we have become too self-sufficient to feel the necessity of redeeming and preserving grace, too proud to pray to the God that made us.

"It behooves us, then, to humble ourselves before the offended power, to confess our national sins, and to pray for clemency and forgiveness."

Let us pause a moment to look at this tall, homely man, walking the world alone and sadly, foreseeing the future with great uncertainty.

Abraham Lincoln never forgot humility; never hated any man; always dreamed of a world of justice, of the brotherhood of man in the fatherhood of God.

Thomas A. Edison also walked alone. He also was unable to have much schooling. No professor in a college taught him physics. No university gave him a Ph. D. or a Phi Beta Kappa key. He wrote no learned thesis nor did anyone laud him for his brilliance.

Whatever he achieved was his own doing—the product of one man—of the genius, the perseverance, the diligence of one man. The disappointments were his; the achievements were his.

No government subsidized him. No bureau or commission directed him. No RFC made loans to him. He passed no civil-service examinations, nor did he ask the consent of any presidential commission to pursue his experiments. Thomas Edison was a free man. Untutored, unschooled, the master of his personality, he went his way, and before he died he had 1,097 United States patents issued to him—more than to any other individual.

I stand here tonight and talk to all of you through a microphone and over electric wires. You are far away, but, were I on television, you would see me in all my fullness. You are sitting in your well-lighted homes, comfortable perhaps with a cold drink out of an electric refrigerator. You take all this in your stride. Many of you have never known when such wonders were not possible. You press a button and a dark room is illuminated. You are bored and go to a movie to spend an amusing evening or you sit at home and see a performance on your television set. The room can be light or dark at your wish and convenience.

I remember when I was a small boy on the East Side of New York. The only light we had was an open gaslight. Then came the Welsbach mantle and we were all excited by the great improvement. Then, one day, we saw electric lights all about us. We were amazed at this wonder. But soon we took that in our stride. We even complained that the streets were still lighted by gaslight. We demanded streets lighted by electricity.

In the many years I lived in China I saw literally millions of men and women who had never seen an electric light. The only artificial lighting they had—as a matter of fact, still have—was an oil lamp or a candle; most of them go to bed with the dark and rise at dawn. They are limited in their reading, their learning, their leisure by the darkness, and what I say of peasant and village life in China was equally true of Siberia in very recent years. It is true of much of this world. They live in darkness.

Thomas Edison's lamp, which we, in our generation, take in our stride, is the product of the unending labor of a free man—financially poor, uneducated, insecure—who dared to dream. He often failed, and after each failure he had to borrow the money to take another risk.

He had to find a container for his light. The sealed glass bulb that would not collapse when it warmed up was no small matter to work out. Then the problem of finding a filament that would produce light but not burn itself out or overheat the container—that problem faced the inventor with many failures. He tried every known fiber. He even tried hair out of a beard. Everything went wrong, except his great soul, which shouted, "There shall be light."

And finally, he found the exact carbonized cardboard which was suitable. But he still faced problems. He had to generate the electricity and to carry it from the generator to the light. This he had in 1879, but it was not until September 1882 that a service for the public was started in New York City.

Altogether, Thomas Edison had to obtain 356 patents, involving original inventions in an altogether untried field, before he could call his work in power generation and distribution a success.

Had he only done this, he would have been one of the greatest minds of all time. But Thomas Edison invented the phonograph, the motion-picture camera, and he laid the foundation for electronics which makes possible radio and television.

No government, no committee, no majority, no minority could ever produce the genius of Abraham Lincoln or Thomas Edison. No group ever wrote a poem or painted a picture. Nor need a man be rich in money or have the advantages of formal education or the assurance of security from the cradle to the grave to achieve greatness. What were the advantages of Beethoven or what the security of Mozart? Were they greater than those of Lincoln in the log house in Salem or Edison when he peddled newspapers on a railroad train?

The gods among men walk alone. They dream and create and nothing can hold them back. They do not fear failure any more than they fear insecurity. They are driven by their personalities to high accomplishment and when they have completed their work, the world is a better place to live in because they have been of it.

And this happens in every age, in every country, among all peoples, great and small. Perhaps someone who is listening to these words has in his soul some task to do. He may fear the consequences of his dream and courage.

Go forth, as Lincoln and Edison did, for your start today could not be more lowly than theirs; your disadvantages today could not be as great as theirs. They hurdled every handicap, alone, unaided. They reached their goals alone—by will and choice and daring.

And America remembers them everlastingly and celebrates their births.

Thank you.

The Art of Contemplation

An address by Virgil M. Hancher, president, State University of Iowa.

The staccato tempo of modern life has made difficult the art of contemplation. The days pass, they gather into weeks and months, arteries grow old and reactions slow down without the acquisition of that wisdom which comes only from the distillation of experience. Cynicism may also be the distillation of experience; but it is a bitter brew. The wise man, no less than the cynic, will not be taken in by life; but neither will he let the weaknesses and frailties of men blind him to their aspirations. Wisdom knows that men's eyes can be, and are, sometimes turned toward the stars, even though at other times they may be turned toward the gutter.

"Instinct, Intelligence, Wisdom" are the categories named by Whitehead, and they arrange themselves in an order of progression. If life is to have meaning, if the things we do are not illusion, if there is reality in our efforts and our undertakings, the freedom of choice and of action, which we appear to possess, is more than appearance. It is a real freedom, and the choices which we make are real choices.

To come to such a decision is in itself an act of faith. It assumes that the universe is not driven by blind, mechanistic forces which we can neither resist nor understand—and, indeed, of which we are a part without our knowledge. Our ultimate view of the universe is always an act of faith, rather than of reason, because our ultimate view of the universe rests upon a first postulate which cannot be proved.

The ancients said that there could be no dispute in matters of taste. "*De gustibus non disputandum.*" Men differ in matters of taste, but there are no absolutes. Perhaps the same might be said of postulates, although this will be disputed and disputed vigorously. For with one postulate you will become a religious orthodox and with another you will become a dialectical materialist.

I do not mean to imply that it is a matter of indifference that you become one or the other, or that you arrive at any one of the infinite number of destinations between the two. Neither do I mean to imply that all postulates are equally valid. What I do mean to imply is that with the infinite variety of men, there will be diversity of outlook, and now, and for a long time to come, one man's meat will be another man's poison.

What I would desire for you is an apprehension of the postulate upon which your faith is founded. Because you do have a faith, or at least a working hypothesis of your relation to the entire scheme of things, on which your life is founded. Whether this hypothesis is formulated or unformulated in your consciousness, it still exists—and your actions, if not your declarations of faith, are witness to it. Indeed your actions may be the true witness.

Your hypothesis may range all the way from a belief that life has purpose to a belief that it is utterly without purpose—that nothing can be done to give it sense or meaning. But your hypothesis exists. Do you know what it is?

The staccato tempo of modern life makes difficult the contemplation necessary for self-knowledge. I make no plea for the good old days. Most of us would not be here if the good old days had not been changed for the better. Disease or famine would have cut off us or our ancestors, and of those who survived only a fortunate few would have achieved the luxury of an education. The triumphs of science and of scientific method are not to be overlooked. Nevertheless the balance sheet has its debit side.

Somewhere along the pathway of progress, the art of contemplation has been lost. The Society of Friends, certain Roman Catholics, an occasional mystic or band of mystics have preserved the art. They retain an anchorage in a sea of ceaseless motion, of disquiet, of drifting. They possess an integrity, a calm and assurance, a wholeness of mind and body that is a kind of holiness. This wholeness, this holiness, I crave for you.

It will be difficult to achieve. All the forces of modern life conspire against it. The Church which once exercised such great dominion over the bodies and souls of men now competes with a thousand secular rivals. Competition, activity for its own sake, the lust for success and power make difficult the art of self-mastery. We are slaves and not masters. "Things are in the saddle and they ride mankind." The newspaper, the radio, and now television, interrupt our days and disturb our nights. Everyone is a little tired, a little distraught, a little below par, a bit inaccurate in judgment.

Yet this need not be so. It is so, because others have willed that it be so, and we have let them have their way. Mark Twain has been quoted as saying that he once stopped reading the newspapers for seven years and they were the seven happiest years of his life! This remedy for our modern distemper seems a bit drastic, but perhaps nothing less than a radical remedy will now halt the disease. Until the radio and the newspapers have learned that men cannot survive in perpetual crisis, they are in danger of reprisal. A populace made schizophrenic by perpetual crisis and inaccuracy may well construe "the freedom of the press" and the radio to mean freedom to publish the truth—and nothing less.

But nothing compels you to give up your sanity, even though the world conspire to drive you mad. You can make it a rule of your life to withdraw each day into quiet and contemplation—religious quiet and contemplation, if you will, but quiet and contemplation, in any event—so that you may put aside the pressing and temporal things, and look upon those which come out of the deep places of human experience. "The heavens declare the glory of God," said the psalmist, "and the firmament showeth his handiwork." Modern man cannot afford to lose the sense of wonder. Perhaps it has been recaptured by some in the fission of the atom; but, for most of us, this must remain as great a mystery as the origin of life or the nature and destiny of man. Yet against this mystery we pit our intellect and our wills, however feeble they may be, confident that the unexamined life is not for us, but that out of our struggle we shall apprehend the postulates of our faith, and achieve that distillation of experience which is wisdom.

History records the ebb and flow of civilizations, the aspirations and failures of men and nations. Whether it possesses a rhythm or pattern is still a matter for dispute—yet, as one surveys the record, the trend has been upward. There is little evidence that modern man has a better brain than the prophets of Israel or the sages of Greece or Rome, but modern man is the inheritor of ideas and instrumentalities without which our modern civilization could not exist.

These ideas and instrumentalities have come to us because men have believed that they were free to make choices, and that the choices were real. They have believed that what they did, as individuals and collectively, made a difference in the long history of mankind, even in human destiny itself. They counted it the better part of wisdom to be on the side of the angels.

You, too, have a choice, and the choice is real. It should be made, not in response to the staccato drum-beat of temporality but in the quiet and contemplation of eternity. You have but one life, and a short one, at your disposal. There is not time to squander it hastily. Only in leisure can you savor it to the full. "Be still and know that I am God," said the voice to the psalmist long ago. "Be still and know the good" is as modern as tomorrow's television set.

Wise choices are the distinguishing mark of an educated man. You, too, can be on the side of the angels. Can you afford to be anywhere else? With what greater wisdom can you be wise?

Entertaining the Listeners

In the fourth place, your purpose may be principally to entertain the listeners and to give them a good time. However, even in speeches of this type, a speaker may often leave a message of real value. In fact, to provide entertainment or humor alone for fifteen to thirty minutes is a very difficult assignment. Most speakers will find it advisable to include a message along with the humor or entertaining remarks. As an example of this, we may take a toast on "The Legal Profession" which was at one time delivered by John S. Wise at the annual dinner of the New York State Bar Association.

The chairman, in introducing him, said: "I call upon a gentleman to respond to this toast who, I venture to say, has practiced law in more states of the Union than any other gentleman present. I allude to the orator of the day, the Honorable John S. Wise, formerly of Virginia, but now a member of the Bar Association of the State of New York." Mr. Wise replied:

Mr. Chairman and Gentlemen of the Bar: It may not be true that I have practiced law in more states of this Union than any one present, but it is certainly true that I never did as much speaking in the same length of time, without charging a fee for it, as I have done within the last twenty-four hours. At two o'clock this morning I was in attendance, in the city of New York, upon a ghost dance of the Confederate Veterans; at two o'clock this evening I resolved myself into a deep, careful and circumspect lawyer, and now I am with the boys, and propose to have a good time. Now, you know, this scene strikes me as ridiculous —our getting here together and glorifying ourselves and nobody to pay for it. My opinion is, that the part of wisdom is to bottle this oratory and keep it on tap at five dollars a minute. The legal profession—why, of course, we are the best fellows in the world. Who is here to deny it? It reminds me of an anecdote told by an old politician in Virginia, who said that one day, with an employee, he was riding to Chesterfield court, and they were discussing the merits of a neighbor, Mr. Beasley, and he said, "Isaac, what do you think of Mr. Beasley?" "Well," he said, "Marse Frank, I reckon he is a pretty good man." "But," the employer replied, "there is one thing about Mr. Beasley, he is always humbling himself." Isaac answered, "Marse Frank, you are right; I don't know how you is, but I always mistrusts a man that runs hisself down." Isaac continued, "I don't know how you is, Marse Frank, but I tell you how it is with me: I scarcely ever says no harm against myself." So I say it of the legal profession—it don't never scarcely say no harm against itself.

Of course, we are the best profession in the world, but if any of our clients are standing at that door and listening to this oratory, I know what their reflection is. They are laughing in their sleeves and saying: "Watch him, watch him; did you ever hear lawyers talk as much for nothing? Watch them; it is the funniest scene I ever saw. There are a lot of lawyers with their hands in their own pockets."

Mr. Chairman and gentlemen, another thing. We are not fooling with any judges now. I know who I am talking to and how long I have been doing it. Sometimes you can fool a judge into letting you have more time than the rule allows; but with lawyers, enough is enough. We know exactly when to put on the brakes with each other. We are not now earning fees by the yard or charging by the minute, and when a man is through with what he has to say, it is time to sit down, and all I have to say in conclusion is, that the more I watch the legal profession and observe it, the more I am convinced that with the great responsibility, with the great trusts confided to it, with the great issues committed to its keeping, with the great power it has to direct public feeling and public sentiment, with the great responsibilities resulting, take it as a mass—and there are plenty of rascals in it—but take it as a mass, and measure it up, and God never made a nobler body in these United States.

The following excerpts from an address on "Successful Worry" by Tom Collins, humorist and philosopher, illustrate how Mr. Collins could insert thoughtful observations on life in his humorous remarks.

I am here, frankly, ladies and gentlemen, to listen to my own favorite speaker on your time. . . . Today, I don't want to talk about my business. I can't talk about yours. I've got to have something to talk about. . . . I have my troubles; you have yours—I don't know the answers to yours; you don't give a hoot about mine, except to be glad I've got them, maybe. And I am not here today to solve anybody's problems at all. I am here in the hope that maybe we can relax a little; maybe you can take a minute or two off from your jobs and maybe it won't hurt you. I get a little sick of work occasionally. I think it is kind of an overrated sport once in awhile.

I one time met a gentleman who was sitting on an empty wagon and he was bogged down to the hubs in the mud. There he sat, moaning, "Here I am, hub deep in the mud and nothing to unload!"

I believe that, as hard as you work, you've got to have a little moment occasionally to relax, have a little strength saved for the hills that come in your business, I guess, the same as they do in mine. I met a fellow once, driving a mule along a level road. He wasn't doing very well with it. I don't know anything about mules, but I am anxious to give anybody advice. I went over to tell him what I don't know about mules, and said, "Brother, did you ever try twisting his tail?" He said, "Man, I'm saving that for the next hill." . . .

My theme today is to talk to you in terms of successful worry. Now, I would be the last fellow in the world to urge you not to worry. I can think of no worse world than a smug one in which people said, "It's all going to be all right. I haven't a thing to worry about," and who lived like the lady in the back seat of a taxicab who beat on the glass and said to the driver, "You are scaring the living daylights out of me every time you go around a corner." The driver said, "Why don't you do like I do when we go around a corner—why don't you shut your eyes?" . . .

Every day is different, until I am a little bewildered. I don't think I know as much as I did a few years ago, and so I go around like the young fellow who didn't know the answer when his teacher asked him a question. So he pitched it right back at the teacher, and he said, "Professor, what do you think?" The professor said, swelling up, "I don't think. I know." The young man said, "Well, I don't think I know either." . . .

We've got a million worries, all of us. Some of them come because we want more than we have any right to want. Some of us have said, "I want it this way because I am me and I ought to have it that way." And then we found out that sometimes you don't get your choice.

There was a gentleman came in a restaurant one night, and the waiter said, "Will you have veal for supper?" The fellow said, "No," and the waiter said, "In that case, supper's over."

A lot of times you didn't get what you wanted. Sometimes maybe it turned out to be a little better if you couldn't get your way all the time. I have a friend who is engaged to one of twin blond girls. They are mighty pretty; they look so much alike that I can't tell them apart. I wondered how he did. I said to him, "When you want to kiss the girl to whom you are engaged, how do you tell her from her sister?" He said, "I don't even try." Sometimes you get unexpected rewards.

Many of the things we worry about are foolish. Do you remember the old story of the man sitting in the restaurant eating and another fellow comes running in and says, "McGuire, your house is on fire!" So the fellow goes tearing out and running down the street. He raced on for about six blocks and then suddenly he stopped and said, "What in the world am I running for? My name ain't McGuire!"

A lady in a hotel one time had one of those phobias, a fear of fire. She wouldn't go to bed nights until she knew just where the fire escape was. She went up and down the halls, looking for a fire escape, and she opened the door on a gentleman taking a shower. She said, "Mister, I'm sorry. I didn't mean to disturb you. I am just hunting for the fire escape." And she went on down the hall. In a minute, the fellow came running after her, with a towel wrapped around him, and said, "Where's the fire, lady?"

Sometimes you waste energy on somebody else's worry.

I think a good many of your worries and mine are pretty selfish, based on the fact that you like to have it your way, thinking about yourself. A woman called up the fire department one night and said, "I've got a new rock garden. I put a lot of time on it, and a lot of money." They said, "Madam, we have no interest in your rock garden. This is the fire department." She said, "I know it. My neighbor's house is burning down, and, when you all come over to put out the fire, I don't want you to trample on my rock garden." . . .

My wife used to get me out of bed past midnight, when she would hear a burglar downstairs, with the ridiculous suggestion that I go down and catch him. Well, I reasoned with her, and said, "Now, look here, my good woman"—which was what I was calling her at the time. I said, "If there were a burglar downstairs, he would be a professional. He would be no amateur. He wouldn't be crawling on his face. You wouldn't hear him." Now she worries because she doesn't hear any noise. You see how unbeatable it can become. It can be an attitude.

There is an old story of a gentleman who left his home, and said to his wife, "I am going to John Jones and borrow his ax." She said, "Do you think he'll lend it to you?" He replied, "Why not? He's the best friend I've got. We've been borrowing for fifteen years." Then he began to worry—what does my wife know that I don't know? Has John been complaining to her? He got himself in such a mental state that, when he got to John's door, the first thing he said to him was, "Keep your old axe. I don't need it." That is what a worry in advance does sometimes. It stops you before you begin. . . .

There was a heavy freight train pulling up a hill one time, and it pretty nearly didn't make it, but with a kind of grunt and a snort, it got over the hill. The conductor came over to the brakeman and said, "Brother, we almost got stuck." The brakeman said, "That's right. We never would have made that hill if it hadn't been for me. I'm the fellow that kept the brake on to keep us from slipping back."

There is a lot of worrying over the fact that maybe something won't be right because we don't know enough about it, and we've got the brake on a little. Maybe it is holding the whole works back. I think the old train has got all the steam it ever had if we would just light in with a kind of optimistic view and say, "If I can't help it, I can't do anything about it and I will be flexible minded. Every day is a new adventure. I'll take it that way. Too many yesterdays weren't too bad; too many tomorrows can be what we want."

Relation of Purpose to Idea

It is evident, of course, that the purpose of your speech will affect your choice of what to say and the way you will say it; it will affect the method of arranging your ideas, the illustrations which you insert, the way you build each section or paragraph and the way you word the individual statements.

You have a definite idea to express. You must not compromise or alter it. But if you are to present it successfully you must consider how to adjust it to your listeners and to the conditions of the occasion.

Character of Audience

In the first place, you will find that the character and mood of the audience has a great deal to do with the determination of the central idea. It is one thing to address the Executives Club of Chicago. It is another matter to address the Boy Scouts of the same city. Always be certain that you know the composition of your audience so you can appeal directly to their interests.

Condition of the Occasion

Equally important with the need of adjusting the speech to the character of the audience is the need of adjusting it to the time and conditions of the situation. With any subject of real interest, it is impossible to give an entire treatment in the time allotted for a speech. If you undertook to do so you would outwear your welcome, and when you got through your listeners would be critical. The deluge would be too much for them. Consequently, you must select from the many aspects of your subject which deserve treatment the one or more aspects which can best be treated in the time available. To put the matter in very homely terms, do not try to serve your guests the whole animal, but cut them a steak.

Expressing the Central Idea

Another point that needs to be considered is the manner of expressing your central idea. Generally, you will express it rather plainly at the beginning of your speech; sometimes you may express it at the beginning and repeat it again and again through the talk; on some occasions you may find it best to hold it back until near the end. Somewhere, however, it should be definitely stated. A maxim in salesmanship is, "Ask for the order." In the same way, if you want your central idea to get over, you should state it somewhere in so many words. You may divide your subject into two, three or four subdivisions. Generally it is better not to have more than four, or the listener will become confused and will fail to remember them.

Notice how M. R. Franks, director of the National Labor-Management Foundation, states in the opening paragraph of an address exactly what he proposes to discuss.

I am genuinely pleased to be with you on this occasion because it offers me an excellent opportunity to discuss with you a subject very close to my heart—namely, industrial harmony and the means at our command to bring it about in the final interest of the worker, his employer, the general public—and the happy and prosperous future of this great nation of ours.

Note also how James A. Farley, business man and statesman, shortly after he began an address on the subject, "The Nation Faces a Serious Dilemma," stated clearly the subject he was going to discuss.

Can we set aside an increasing part of our incomes, profits and in some cases our capital for taxes? Can we afford all we want in public service?

We may have differences of opinion among ourselves as to the forms and amounts of such service. We may believe that government should help the farmer and at the same time not believe that it should socialize medicine. We may believe that foreign commerce ought to be stimulated by government while domestic commerce should be left to natural economic laws. But in general this country has long since given up the notion that all that can be expected of government is the maintenance of an army and navy, a post office department and a diplomatic service.

Undoubtedly there are many of you, and I think I share your views on this subject, who fear that in the multiplication of services we shall load down our government and taxpayers with financial obligations that will ultimately destroy our way of life. There is a place, economists tell us, where taxation not only yields a diminishing return but also stifles the productive activities that in the long run support the government. I do not know exactly where that point may be in this economy. I do not even know whether we have approached it at the present time. But I do know that there must be ever-increasing caution lest we do reach that point without anticipating it. Therefore, we face, as a nation, the serious dilemma of a demand for increasing governmental services on the one hand and the danger of excessive taxation on the other. As a business man I am keenly aware of the second of these circumstances and as a former member of the government I am keenly aware of what the public expects. It is about this dilemma that I want to talk with you today.

In perhaps most speeches the principal idea to be discussed is presented at the beginning of the speakers' remarks.

Central Idea at the End

Occasionally, the speaker prefers to withhold the statement of the central idea until the end of the speech. Because of some feature in the situation he feels it important to get the audience ready before giving them his message in definite terms. A speech given by Walter Alexander Groves, president of Centre College of Kentucky, on the subject, "The Christian College Today," contains its central idea (Christian People Must Support Christian Institutions) at the end of the address as follows:

But, and here is the point, can we continue to lament the misunderstanding of the meaning of freedom in our land and undercut and neglect the institution that has been its bulwark, can we complain that more and more of our people expect society to provide for them and then fail to support the one institution that has been and is educating our young men and young women for creative activity in the service of mankind, can we go on orating about the necessity of free enterprise and yet fail to exercise our freedom in the support of the institution that is helping to make our system of free enterprise intelligent and Christian, and finally, dare we continue in the Church to put every cause first from the building of a church to the installation of one more stained-glass window and leave at the end of the list, if it gets on the list at all, the institution from which we expect our trained leaders, both ministers and lay people?

Let me close with this little Negro story. A farmer was driving to town one day with a load of garden manure, and on the way he picked up a Negro named "Jim." On the way he passed a neighbor who called to inquire what he had on his wagon. "Oh," he replied, "just a load of manure and old Jim here." This happened a second time, and again the jovial farmer replied in the same way. After it had happened a third time, the old Negro tugged the farmer's sleeve lightly and said, "Boss, if they asks yuh again, do yuh mind mentioning me fust?" I want to ask that more of you think of Centre College first these days.

In an address on "The Plight of the Conservative in Public Discussion," before the Speech Association of America, James H. McBurney, dean of the School of Speech of Northwestern University, summarized at the close of his address four major suggestions as follows:

Several suggestions for developing effective spokesmen in deliberative councils are implicit in what I have already said. I should like to spell these out in greater detail.

In the first place, men in executive positions in business and industry must be willing to participate in public discussion. As the president of the United States Rubber Company put it last June:

"The eleventh hour is here for business to speak for itself. Now, and from now on, the men who run American business must devote as much—if not more—time and effort to the public relations of their business as they spend on finance, production, and distribution. Unless they do, they will not need to worry about the latter problems. Government will be glad to handle them all."

In the second place, the paid spokesmen of the conservatives, the public relations officers of business and industry, must be selected with careful attention to their qualifications for serious intellectual discussion and vigorous public debate. The main job of such officers is developing relations with the public rather than with their brothers in the bond. This requires social, political, and economic literacy of a high order and topnotch dialectical ability.

Thirdly, the conservatives urgently need to develop greater sensitivity to the changing pattern of communication in America. This pattern is characterized by a growing emphasis on logical values in place of high pressure mumbo-jumbo; by simple, direct statement rather than verbal obfuscation; and by a sense of relativity in language usage in place of arbitrary, dogmatic assertion. These changes are inevitable in a democratic society which is becoming more conscious of the processes of communication and more sophisticated in their use. Any speaker ignores them at his own peril.

Fourthly, the conservatives must rid themselves of some unfortunate stereotypes. In this so-called era of the common man, the conservative is depicted as the foe of the common man. Unfortunately, this role can easily be given specious plausibility because the conservative does have vested interests in the status quo. In a society in which men are living longer and specialized economic functions tend to draw class lines, it is easy to think of the conservative as an old man who has lost the common touch. Actually, the interests of the common man on any given issue at any given time and place may be just as completely identified with the conservatives as with the liberals. Most certainly it begs the question to assume otherwise. The lines between conservatives and liberals in America need not, and should not, be drawn on the basis of age or class. They should be determined in free and widespread discussion, and the conservatives must learn how to conduct themselves in such discussions in ways which will enlist the sympathy and understanding of common men.

The conservatives have also succeeded in alienating many of the intellectuals in America. Witch hunts in the colleges and universities, journalistic caricatures of the mortar board, and frantic name calling are hardly designed to win the understanding of men who place a high premium on objectivity in discourse. Moreover, there are echelons in the intellectual hierarchy in which there are fashions in ideas just as there are in goods. In some of these quarters, I fear, the conservative position has lost caste for reasons which have very little or nothing to do with its merit. . . .

In conclusion, I wish again to make clear that I do not present this analysis to plead the cause of the conservative, nor do I mean to question the ability and integrity of the conservative. It is my purpose rather to point out that conservatives generally are not doing their cause justice in public discussion and debate, explain why this is the case, and suggest some of the ways in which this weakness can be corrected. I believe this is to be a problem of more than ordinary importance in American public life, and certainly one of great significance to students and teachers of speech.

As Aristotle put it, over two thousand years ago, "Truth and justice are by nature more powerful than their opposites; when decisions are not made as they should be, the speakers with the right on their side have only themselves to thank for the outcome."

An Unusual Speech

One of the most interesting examples of a speech which holds back the central idea until the end is the following address delivered by George William Curtis, editor, orator and litterateur, at the annual dinner of the New England Society of the City of New York, December 22, 1876. It was an anxious time throughout the country. The presidential election had resulted, seemingly, in a tie vote, and no one could think of a method to determine whether the Republican or Democratic candidate had been elected. Men's passions ran high. Strange as it may seem to us to-day, there was open talk of Civil War. Mr. Curtis, one of the best-known writers and orators of his day, determined to discuss this subject, a subject charged with dynamite, in his speech at the New England dinner.

The difficulties were so great that his friends strongly advised him not to make the attempt. He felt it to be the duty of some one to speak up, however, and he set himself to build his speech very carefully. There were two main difficulties. In the first place, the subject was one on which all his listeners had strong feelings. At every moment he ran the risk of angering one faction or both factions of his listeners and making the situation even worse than it had been. In the second place, the audience he had to address was composed of the most cultivated and sophisticated men in the United States, who would be quick and critical to catch any slip either of thought or expression. If his speech was clumsy or dull, even though the ideas might be good, the ultimate effect of it might be unfavorable for his great purpose. The speech follows:

Liberty under the Law

Mr. President and Gentlemen of the New England Society: It was Isaac Walton, in his *Angler,* who said that Dr. Dotelier was accustomed to remark "that doubtless God might have made a better berry than the strawberry, but doubtless he never did." And I suppose I speak the secret feeling of this festive company when I say that doubtless there might have been a better place to be born in than New England, but doubtless no such place exists. [applause and laughter] And if any skeptic should reply that our very presence here would seem to indicate that doubtless, also, New England is as good a place to leave as to stay in [laughter], I should reply to him that, on the contrary, our presence is but an added glory of our mother. It is an illustration of the devout missionary spirit, of the willingness in which she has trained us to share with others the blessings that we have received, and to circle the continent, to girdle the globe, with the strength of New England character and the purity of New England principles. [applause] Even the Knickerbockers, Mr. President—in whose stately and splendid city we are at this moment assembled, and assembled of right because it is our home—even they would doubtless concede that much of the state and splendor of this city is due to the enterprise, the industry, and the genius of those whom their first historian describes as "losel Yankees." [laughter] Sir, they grace our feast with their presence; they will enliven it, I am sure, with their eloquence and wit. Our tables are rich with the flowers grown in their soil; but there is one flower that we do not see, one flower whose perfume fills a continent, which has blossomed for more than two centuries and a half with ever-increasing and deepening beauty—a flower which blooms at this moment, on this wintry night, in never-fading freshness in a million true hearts, from the snow-clad Katahdin to the warm Golden Gate of the South Sea, and over its waters to the isles of the East and the land of Prester John—the flower of flowers, the Pilgrim's Mayflower. [applause]

Well, sir, holding that flower in my hand at this moment, I say that the day we celebrate commemorates the introduction upon this continent of the master principle of its civilization. I do not forget that we are a nation of many nationalities. I do not forget that there are gentlemen at this board who wear the flower of other nations close upon their hearts. I remember the forget-me-nots of Germany, and I know that the race which keeps "watch upon the Rhine" keeps watch also upon the Mississippi and the Lakes. I recall—how could I forget?—the delicate shamrock; for

"There came to this beach a poor exile of Erin," and on this beach, with his native modesty
"He still sings his bold anthem of
Erin-go-Bragh."

[applause] I remember surely, sir, the lily—too often the tiger-lily—of France [laughter and applause] and the thistle of Scotland; I recall the daisy and the rose of England; and, sir, in Switzerland, high upon the Alps, on the very edge of the glacier, the highest flower that grows in Europe, is the rare edelweiss. It is in Europe; we are in America. And here in America, higher than shamrock or thistle, higher than rose, lily, or daisy, higher than the highest, blooms the perennial Mayflower. [applause] For, sir, and gentlemen, it is the English-speaking race that has molded the destiny of this continent; and the Puritan influence is the strongest influence that has acted upon it. [applause]

I am surely not here to assert that the men who have represented that influence have always been men whose spirit was blended of sweetness and light. I confess truly their hardness, their prejudice, their narrowness. All this I know: Charles Stuart could bow more blandly, could dance more gracefully than John Milton; and the Cavalier king looks out from the canvas of Van Dyck with a more romantic beauty of flowing love-locks than hung upon the brows of Edward Winslow, the only Pilgrim Father whose portrait comes down to us. [applause] But, sir, we estimate the cause beyond the man. Not even is the gracious spirit of Christianity itself measured by its confessors. If we would see the actual force, the creative power of the Pilgrim principle, we are not to look at the company who came over in the cabin of the *Mayflower;* we are to look upon the forty millions who fill this continent from sea to sea. [applause] The *Mayflower,* sir, brought seed and not a harvest. In a century and a half the religious restriction of the Puritans has grown into absolute religious liberty, and in two centuries it had burst beyond the limits of New England, and John Carver of the *Mayflower* had ripened into Abraham Lincoln of the Illinois prairie. [great and prolonged applause] Why, gentlemen, if you would see the most conclusive proof of the power of this principle, you have but to observe that the local distinctive title of New Englanders has now become that of every man in the country. Every man who hears me, from whatever state in the Union, is, to Europe, a Yankee, and today the United States are but the "universal Yankee nation." [applause]

Do you ask me, then, what is this Puritan principle? Do you ask me whether it is as good for today as for yesterday; whether it is good for every national emergency; whether it is good for the situation of this hour? I think we need neither doubt nor fear. The Puritan principle in its essence is simply individual freedom. From that spring religious liberty and political equality. The free State, the free Church, the free School—these are the triple armor of American nationality, of American security. [applause] But the Pilgrims, while they have stood above all men for their idea of liberty, have always asserted liberty *under law* and never separated it from law. . . . Those men stood for liberty *under the law.* They had tossed long upon a wintry sea; their minds were full of images derived from their voyage; they knew that the will of the people alone is but a gale smiting a rudderless and sailless ship, and hurling it, a mass of wreck, upon the rocks. But the will of the people, subject to law, is the same gale filling the trim canvas of a ship that minds the helm, bearing it over yawning and awful abysses of ocean safely to port. [loud applause]

Now, gentlemen, in this country the Puritan principle in its development has advanced to this point, that it provides us a lawful remedy for every emergency that may arise. [cheers] I stand here as a son of New England. In every fiber of my being am I a child of the Pilgrims. [applause] The most knightly of all the gentlemen at Elizabeth's court said to the young poet, when he would write an immortal song "Look into thy heart and write." And I, sir and brothers, if, looking into my own heart at this moment, I might dare to think that what I find written there is written also upon the heart of my mother, clad in her snows at home, her voice in this hour would be a message spoken from the land of the Pilgrims to the capital of this nation—a message like that which Patrick Henry sent from Virginia to Massachusetts when he heard of Concord and Lexington: "I am not a Virginian, I am an American." [great applause] And so, gentlemen, at this hour we are not Republicans, we are not Democrats, we are Americans. [tremendous applause]

The voice of New England, I believe, going to the capital, would be this, that neither is the Republican Senate to insist upon its exclusive partisan way, nor is the Democratic House to insist upon its exclusive partisan way, but Senate and House, representing the American people and the American people only, in the light of the Constitution and by the authority of the law, are to provide a way over which a President, be he Republican or be he Democrat, shall pass unchallenged to his chair. [vociferous applause, the company rising to their feet] Ah, gentlemen [renewed applause]—think not, Mr. President, that I am forgetting the occasion or its amenities. [cries of "No, no," and "Go on."] I am remembering the Puritans; I am remembering Plymouth Rock and the virtues that made it illustrious. [a voice—"Justice."] But we, gentlemen, are to imitate those virtues, as our toast says, only by being greater than the men who stood upon that rock. [applause] As this gay and luxurious banquet to their scant and severe fare, so must our virtues, to be worthy of them, be greater and richer than theirs. And as we are three centuries older, so should we be three centuries wiser than they. [applause] Sons of the Pilgrims, you are not to level forests, you are not to war with savage men and savage beasts, you are not to tame a continent nor even found a State. Our task is nobler, diviner. Our task, sir, is to reconcile a nation. It is to curb the fury of party spirit. It is to introduce a loftier and manlier tone everywhere into our political life. It is to educate every boy and every girl, and then leave them perfectly free to go from any school-house to any church. [cries of "Good," and cheers] Above all, sir, it is to protect absolutely the equal rights of the poorest and the richest, of the most ignorant and the most intelligent citizen, and it is to stand forth, brethren, as a triple wall of brass around our native land, against the mad blows of violence or the fatal dry-rot of fraud. [loud applause] And at this moment, sir, the grave and august shades of the forefathers whom we invoke bend over us in benediction as they call us to this sublime task. This, brothers and friends, this is to imitate the virtues of our forefathers; this is to make our day as glorious as theirs. [great applause, followed by three cheers for the distinguished speaker]

Skill in "Setting the Stage"

This speech is deserving of the utmost study as an example of the skillful handling of a difficult situation. Observe the gradual development. He begins with a matter on which all his listeners can agree. He talks at first in a light, fanciful, semi-humorous vein which would please the clever men who were listening. He follows with deftly worded compliments to the different groups among his audience: the Knickerbockers—the native New Yorkers—and the men of German, English, Scotch, French, and Irish extraction. Then he comes back to the Puritans in a statement of the principle of devotion to liberty, on which all Americans pride themselves. Then he points out that the Puritans stood for liberty when guided and controlled by law, and then, and not until then, does he turn attention to the situation of the moment and state the central idea of his speech.

Notice also that Curtis states his central idea only once. That is because, knowing the men he is addressing, he realizes that his appeal will be most effective if merely presented for their consideration without being pushed too far. Instead of undertaking to suggest a possible method for accomplishing the purpose which he advocates, he concludes his oration with an eloquent appeal to the feelings of his audience, to their patriotic devotion to the country's welfare.

Immediate Improvement

In your self-training in effective speaking you will find that attention to determining the central idea of your speeches will be of special help. Some portions of the art of addressing audiences can be learned only gradually. But this habit of taking pains to determine the central idea before making a speech can be attended to at once. Its results will be striking and immediate. If you make your audiences feel, whenever you stand up, that the idea you have chosen to present is interesting and worthwhile, they will listen gladly, no matter how many minor defects of presentation your speech may exhibit.

Chapter 9

DEVELOPING THE PLAN OF YOUR SPEECH

A capable speaker not only has something to say, but he must also know how to say it effectively. The great speakers, such as Winston Churchill, have had something to say, but, in addition, they have recognized that careful study must be given to the manner of presenting a speech.

Like the architect of a building, you must build your speech. The imagination of the architect makes the style of the building. The style conforms to certain rules so that when the building is erected, it can be used for the purpose intended.

An Orderly Sequence of Points

After determining the central idea of your speech, you must consider how to present it fully and with effect to the group of different individuals who constitute your audience. The minds of these different individuals work at different speeds. To make sure that they all grasp your central idea, and at the same time, you need to break it down into steps or sections, which can be presented to the audience one by one in orderly sequence. If you do this skillfully, you can render even an extensive or intricate idea understandable and really interesting.

In conversation such definite progress through the various aspects of the central idea is not usual. It is felt to be too formal. Nor is it necessary, because the listeners can interrupt at any time and make sure of what the speaker means. But when you address a group of listeners, whose temperaments and backgrounds vary considerably, and who are generally, when you begin your speech, in widely differing moods, an orderly development of the thought is indispensable. The purposes are: to make sure of conveying your meaning fully; to present the central idea in its proper perspective; and to render the speech as a whole agreeable to your listeners, easy for them to follow in their thinking.

Always Plan Your Talk

Hence you need a plan. Even when you speak on the spur of the moment you need a plan, sometimes framed quickly but carefully in the few moments between the time you are summoned to the platform and the time you begin to talk. When you have time for systematic preparation, you will of course work out a plan carefully. Some speakers will tell you they never make a plan for a speech, but the statement is hardly valid. The truth is that the *effective* speaker who says he speaks without formally making a plan actually knows his subject so well he has unconsciously planned his remarks. Having talked on the subject many times, he has a mental plan which serves to make his talk a cohesive, logical treatment of the subject. Without a plan you are in great danger of rambling. You may entertain for a while. You may even interest an audience for a short time. But you are not at all likely to cause people to think, or to rouse them to action and get results. The plan will make your talk logical. You will know what you want to say, and you will be able to say it effectively because of your plan. The definite arrangement of your plan will help you to remember.

Stick to the Plan

When you stand up to talk, ideas may come to your mind which seemed to elude you during your preparation. It would be easy to make use of these ideas, but do not succumb to the temptation. If you do, you may find yourself off on a tangent. You may wander away from the subject. In all probability, when you have exhausted the thought that momentarily attracted you, you will experience great difficulty in getting back to your subject. Therefore, always prepare the plan of your talk and stick to it. Your talk will be more forceful and more interesting, which means more effective.

Three Functions of the Plan

The plan is really the skeleton of your talk. The headings or topics which make it up should be in logical sequence. You will divide the material and arrange the portions so that your thought proceeds by a clearly followed line of march. The plan should fulfill the following functions or duties:

1. Convey your central idea fully, giving all that is necessary This includes allowing for and answering by anticipation the questions that may be asked.

2. Give the central idea in the proper perspective, the proper proportion.

3. Present it in a way that will be easy, pleasing, interesting to your body of listeners.

Three Main Stages

In accomplishing these purposes, you will find that your development of the central idea falls into the following three distinct main stages or steps:

1. The introduction
2. The body, or discussion
3. The conclusion

The Introduction

It would be unwise for you to launch immediately into the body of the talk, for you would probably not get satisfactory results. You must first strive to win the attention of your hearers. You desire not their passive attention, but their active interest. Therefore, your speech needs an introduction.

In building this introduction, remember the advice of the poet, Alexander Pope:

> Men must be taught as if you taught them not,
> And things unknown proposed as things forgot.

Do not let your introduction give the impression that you are the teacher and the audience is about to be taught something. Make it fit your particular audience. Use it to awaken their interest and gradually lead into your subject. If you do this skillfully it goes far toward insuring success to your speech.

Personal Introduction

Various methods may be used to introduce your talk, depending on the occasion. One method is the *personal introduction.* Carl A. Gray, president of the Grenby Manufacturing Company of Plainville, Connecticut, began an address before the Economic Club of Detroit as follows:

> I come to Detroit today in humble admiration for the city and you people, who have built so much and do such remarkable things. It is a real pleasure and privilege, I assure you, to talk to you.
>
> I want you to know me, however, in my own guise. I am just a small manufacturer from the little town of Plainville, Connecticut, operating an electro-mechanical factory. I believe in the profit-and-loss system

and want to see it maintained. I am no specialist and haven't any particular brand of economic salvation, except sweating, striving and producing. . . .

I like to be known as a representative of little business, because small business has always been and still is the biggest employer of labor. Two out of three people employed in manufacturing are employed in shops of less than one hundred persons. When you add to this the many small enterprises in other fields, you have eight out of ten people employed in companies of less than one hundred personnel.

I do not minimize the importance to our economy of large companies. Your big companies were once little fellows like myself. They have grown up. Our country would suffer without them. There is no question about it—and I am not just trying to make kind remarks because I'm here in Detroit.

In this instance the personal introduction has a human quality and a frankness which must have won the attention of the audience and prompted them to listen closely.

Two other illustrations of the personal introduction to a speech follow, the first one being from an address by Maurice A. Franks, director and editor of the National Labor-Management Foundation, before the Rotary Club of Jersey City, New Jersey, and the second from a significant address on " 'American', the Meaning of the Word," by Herbert Hoover, former President of the United States, at a celebration of his birthday at West Branch, Iowa:

INTRODUCTION TO AN ADDRESS BY MAURICE A. FRANKS

I am indeed pleased to be back here again, because this appearance means that I have been here "again and again and again."

Since my last visit, I have had an honor bestowed upon me of which I am mighty proud. As an outsider, I had always admired Rotary and all that it stands for. Today, however, I am in a far better position than ever before to appreciate the activities of this wonderful organization, because today I am an insider! As a member of Rotary, Chicago Number One, I am in fact, as I have always been in spirit, one of you —an honor I deeply appreciate.

INTRODUCTION TO AN ADDRESS BY HERBERT HOOVER

I am glad to have your invitation to come again to this Iowa village where I was born. Here I spent the first ten years of my boyhood. My parents and grandparents came to this village in the covered wagon—pioneers in this community. They lie buried over the hill. They broke the prairie into homes of independent living. They worshiped God;

they did their duty to their neighbors. They toiled to bring to their children greater comfort, better education, and to open to them wider opportunity than had been theirs.

I am proud to have been born in Iowa. As I have said before, through the eyes of a ten-year-old boy it was a place of adventure and daily discoveries. The wonder of the growing crops, the excitements of the harvest, the journeys to the woods for nuts and hunting, the joys of snowy winters, the comfort of the family fireside, of good food and tender care.

And out of the excessive energy of all small boys, the evenings were filled with accounts of defeat and victory over animate and inanimate things—so far as they were permitted in a Quaker community.

Indelible in those recollections was a widowed mother, sitting with her needle, cheerfully supporting three children and at the same time ministering to her neighbors. After that came life with Uncle Allan on his farm near this village, with the joys and sorrows which come to every small boy enroute to life's disciplines by way of farm chores. And among them was the unending making of provisions for the next winter. But in those primitive days, social security was had from the cellar, not from the federal government.

You may be surprised if I tell you that at an age somewhat under ten I began here my first national service. By my own efforts I furnished firecrackers required for the adequate celebration of the Independence of the United States on July 4, 1882. To get those firecrackers, I entered into collective bargaining by which it was settled that I should receive one cent per hundred for picking potato bugs in a field in sight of this stand. My impression then, and now is, that it was an oppressive wage rate.

Also, I took part in the political issues of the day by walking beside a Garfield torchlight procession in the presidential campaign of 1884. And by the village flags at half-mast, learned of the assassination of Garfield, with some dim understanding that somewhere in the nation great men guarded its future.

One of the indelible impressions of memory was the original Quaker meeting house. Those recollections chiefly revolve around the stiff repression of the explosive energies of a small boy sitting during the long silences. One time, however, the silence was broken by the shrill voice of Aunt Hannah who was moved in meeting bitterly to denounce the modernistic tendencies of those times. She had firm views on any form of recreation, which included singing in Sunday school.

She closed with a peroration to the effect that if these tendencies persisted that edifice dedicated to God would some day become in fact that place of abomination—a "the-ater." And truly, the old meeting house in its decadent years, having made way for a better edifice, became a movie house. My view is that the abomination part depends on the choice of the film.

And among these recollections was that of a great lady who first taught me in school and remained my friend during her whole long and useful life. Mrs. Mollie Carran.

It was from her that I first heard something about the word American. Many great writers and statesmen have attempted to express what we mean by that word. But there is an imponderable feeling within it which reaches to the soul of our people and defies measure.

A Caution

The introduction to Herbert Hoover's address is an excellent illustration of the effective use of the personal introduction. As a rule, however, the personal introduction should be used with great care. Talking about yourself may encourage apologies, and it is difficult to apologize at length successfully. Attention should rather be directed to the subject. It is not necessary to avoid entirely the use of the pronoun "I." The proper use of the pronoun "I" is not a fault. Merely remember not to overuse the pronoun and never use it in a boastful manner. An audience, like an individual, resents boasting. Modesty on the part of a speaker is an asset. The tone of Herbert Hoover's introduction commands respect for this reason among many others. It is not only earnest, but also genuinely modest, with a touch of humor—an almost unbeatable combination.

Reference to the Occasion

Reference to the occasion is an easy and spontaneous method for introducing a speech. It should be used especially on dignified occasions. Lincoln's Gettysburg speech is a classic example of the introduction which has reference to the occasion. President McKinley, delivering the address at the dedication of the Grant Monument in New York City, began as follows:

A great life, dedicated to the welfare of the Nation, here finds its earthly coronation. Even if this day lacked the impressiveness of ceremony and was devoid of pageantry, it would still be memorable, because it is the anniversary of the birth of one of the most famous and best loved of American soldiers.

The author used the following reference to the occasion to begin an address on "World Trade and World Stability" at Notre Dame University:

This first World Trade Conference at Notre Dame University opens in a strangely distraught world. Men everywhere are struggling with new and powerful forces, for the world is economically and politically disheveled. It has threatened to ride to its doom in a powder cart, as nations have engaged in the cooperative suicide of two world wars. The economic machinery has run down in many nations, and sound business and financial traditions have been destroyed in various parts of the world. Unless there is a release again in these nations of the great fountain of private and free enterprise, the progress of decades may be lost.

It is gratifying that this university has organized this conference to examine one of the most important aspects of contemporary international economic life. Thoughtful men have come increasingly to recognize that in a well-balanced economic order experience must be combined with education. The realism of the market place and the idealism of the classroom must join hands. Education must relate itself intelligently to the fundamental needs of the everyday life of the community and the nation. Out of this union there will come to education, on the one hand, a still richer and more rigid training for young men and women so they may play productive roles in a complex economic order. And to business, on the other hand, there will come that broad education which will steadily raise it to even greater levels of constructive achievement.

It is a privilege, therefore, to participate in this important conference. It is important for two major reasons: first, because world trade is a necessary condition of world stability, and therefore its consideration is worthy of our time and thought; and, secondly, because this conference may well establish a pattern for subsequent meetings here and at other universities where students, educators and business men may join in a fruitful interchange of ideas.

Statement of the Topic

The most logical and the most common type of introduction is that which states the topic to be discussed. It calls the attention of the audience to the subject. It establishes the importance of the topic. You may use this form of introduction with good results on almost any occasion. A notable example of this form of introduction is the beginning of an address in Chicago by Theodore Roosevelt on "The Strenuous Life."

In speaking to you, men of the greatest city of the West, men of the State which gave to the country Lincoln and Grant, men who pre-eminently and distinctly embody all that is most American in the American character, I wish to preach, not the doctrine of ignoble ease, but the doctrine of the strenuous life, the life of toil and effort, of labor and strife; to preach that the highest form of success comes, not to the man who desires more easy peace, but to the man who does not shrink from danger, from hardship, or from bitter toil, and who out of these wins the splendid ultimate triumph.

Frank E. Holman, as president of the American Bar Association, began an address before the Iowa State Bar Association with the following concise statement of his topic:

In these days of confused thinking, when minority pressure groups are trying to change the form and structure of our government it may be worth while to consider for a moment what in the field of law and government may be "Our American Heritage."

Erwin D. Canham, editor of The Christian Science Monitor, began a lecture at Yale University with the following brief statement of his subject:

Let me tell you my thesis bluntly at the outset. It is that the struggle for the salvation of society in our time will be lost unless we in the West—and particularly we in the United States—awaken to and project the fact that we are the great revolutionaries in world history, and that our revolution is basically a spiritual one which we have already proved in action.

The Humorous Introduction

The humorous introduction is much used. It is good for informal, friendly, and festive occasions. It is particularly apropos for after-dinner speeches.

The following examples illustrate the use of the humorous introduction:

From an extemporaneous address delivered at an Associated Press luncheon by General Dwight D. Eisenhower, President of Columbia University

Mr. McLean, my many, many good friends that I am privileged again to meet, and all those others here that I should so like to meet personally, to all of you, greetings.

My first word must be one of apology because, whenever before any professional group a layman is called to speak or to make an appearance, he certainly must do a bit of soul-searching to determine some reasonable excuse. As I see it, the invitation by itself is not enough. Once in a little Kansas town a Californian was coming through and he found it convenient to spend the evening. There was a funeral service going on in the village church and he entered. At one place in this very informal ceremony the minister asked whether there was anyone present who should like to get up and to pay a tribute to the dear departed, and, no one speaking, the Californian took advantage of the opportunity to get up and say:

"Well, I didn't know the deceased and I have never been in the town before. Still I thought it was a good opportunity to describe something of the beauty and the wonderful climate of California."

I am not here, I hope, with such a complete ignorance of your profession as this man exposed as to the town and to the guest of honor at that particular ceremony. I also can claim no possible professional connection with such a distinguished body, a connection which I must admit I think I should rather envy because of the very deep respect that I have for the press and the very deep conviction I have of its responsibilities and its opportunities in the world of today.

Introduction to an address by General Patrick J. Hurley before the Executives Club of Chicago:

I am delighted to be with you on this occasion, and since the chairman has left uncovered only one feature of my performance, I think I'll have to cover it for you. It is true that I grew up in the Choctaw Nation, in Indian territory. Finally when I was still young, one morning I found myself a member of the President's Cabinet, and for Cole County, Oklahoma, that was big stuff.

Well, Christmastime came around and they were putting on a big celebration in Cole County and they asked me to be the principal speaker. The man who introduced me that night told what kind of speaker I am and I'll give it to you. I think he intended it to be complimentary. When I arrived there, the town was in the throes of a "norther," a blizzard. You know, it's away down south, but when one of these "northers" comes down, there is nothing between you and the North Pole but wire fences, and they're down most of the time.

Well, I got out to the schoolhouse, and the moderator was there, and about a dozen other brave souls had come out. The moderator introduced me, and here's what I want you to appraise for me—I want to know just what kind of a compliment he paid me. He said, "A speaker of far less ability than Pat Hurley would have been sufficient for this occasion, but it was impossible to find one."

Now—by way of introduction, also—I'd like you members of the Executives Club to know that my address is written. At one time, you see, when I was a boy out in Indian territory, when I went to work in the coal mines and finally got promoted so I was picking peat, I went to night school. When I married—the most beautiful girl in America—she had been formally educated, so it was incumbent upon me to let her know (modestly, of course) that you could be well educated in night school.

She was accompanying me to New York, where I was going to make one of these speeches, and I read my address to her on the train. I thought when I finished that she would tell me—as a dutiful wife should —that it was remarkable how well I could express myself. You know the way they do. But what she said was this: "Pat, it's really too bad that you couldn't have gone to night school for one more night, to learn to read."

Shortly after Alben W. Barkley was elected Vice President of the United States, he made an address in Chicago in which he used the following humorous story in his introduction:

Now I was under some disturbance mentally as to what I should talk about here today. I am not going to make a political speech. I have never made one here, although it is impossible to discuss anything these days without it having some political implications, in the sense that politics is the science of government; and if I should accidentally or unintentionally trespass upon any political expressions or sentiments, you will understand that I am not talking politics but I am talking about the science of government.

I have not entirely become accustomed to being Vice President of the United States. I don't think the country has either. I always feel some embarrassment in speaking in that capacity because I recall a very, very witty and yet I think sincere remark made to me many years ago by Vice President Dawes when he was Vice President of the United States. You know, he made a great effort to institute some reforms in the rules of the Senate. We have been trying it ever since with not much more success than he had.

But one day he called me up to the Vice President's desk, and he said, "Barkley, this is an awful job I've got."

I said, "What's the matter with it? You still have it. I haven't noticed that you have resigned."

He said, "I can't do but two things."

I said, "What are they?"

He said, "One of them is to sit up here and listen to you birds talk, and I can't reply. And the other is to look at the papers every morning to see how the President's health is."

Forms to Avoid

There is still another introduction sometimes used which might be called the "philosophical." Do not attempt it. The speaker who uses it endeavors to appeal to the ear rather than to the mind. He wants to sound impressive. There are some speakers who imagine that human nature bows down and worships what cannot be easily understood as if it were somehow inspired. They, therefore, talk in such an involved way that they seem to be very learned.

Guard against the dramatic introduction. A dramatic introduction raises your audience to a high pitch of emotion. You make them feel that your entire talk is going to be on the same high plane. After a dramatic introduction, if the body of your talk is ordinary, you will have an anticlimax. Your hearers will have lost interest.

Care in Planning the Introduction

Make your introduction suit your audience and your subject. You are conversing with them. You desire to have them give credence to what you say. Your introduction should lead them to listen with respect and liking. If it reflects your feeling and attitude sincerely and earnestly, it will arouse the interest and attention of your hearers, and lead them to your subject matter.

When preparing a speech beforehand, you may find it best to prepare the introduction *last*. The reason is evident. It is only after you know definitely what the course of your speech is to be, that you determine just how to set the stage and lead up to your central idea.

The Body or Discussion

The body, or discussion, is the principal part of your talk. It is here that you bring out plainly the central idea, the real meat of your address. It is here that you prove your contention, give information, or entertain your listeners. In preparing your speech you may prepare this section of it before you work out the introduction. The procedure on this section is optional. But your first step will probably be to determine your central idea and principal subdivisions.

Planning the Body of a Speech

Let us take a subject and make a plan for the body of a speech. Take, for example, this title:

"America's Pride in her Public Schools."

This phrase would provide a topic for a talk. One need not

grope in the dark to find reasons why we may have pride in our public schools. The plan for a speech on this topic might be:

1. The American government is founded upon the principle of equal opportunity.
2. Equal opportunity necessitates education.
3. Education must be universal among the citizenry.
4. Education must be available to all.
5. America has tried to live up to its ideal of education.
6. The accomplishments of our public schools may be measured in part by the crowded conditions in our colleges.
7. There is much still to be accomplished.
8. Our educators realize their responsibilities and the needs of our public schools.
9. A good foundation has been laid.
10. Our school system is among the best in the world.

Here we have in rough form a plan for the body or discussion of our subject.

When we examine these ten points more closely, we see that their logical relation is shown more clearly if we group them again into four points, as follows:

1. The American principle of equal opportunity demands education.

2. Equal opportunity calls for universal, free educational facilities. The amount of money spent by the various states each year shows to what extent the nation is taking care of the demand.

3. Colleges are demanding higher standards from applicants since they cannot accommodate all who seek to enter. We cannot rest on what we have accomplished. Our educators know that much needs to be done, especially in rural communities, and in the consolidation of school districts. Efforts must be made constantly to raise the educational standards of teachers.

4. Our educational system is merely a foundation, and we cannot rest until every child in this country has a place in a conveniently located competent public school. Our public school system is among the best in the world.

In this grouping, you notice, the first and second of the ten points go into our new first point; the third, fourth, and fifth into our new second point; the sixth, seventh, and eighth into our new third point; and the ninth and tenth into our new fourth point.

Later in the process of preparing the speech, these four points would be filled out with facts and detail ideas. These would have been gathered together, of course, from experience, reading, and conversation. It is imperative that you thoughtfully and conscientiously work to obtain facts, illustrations, and figures that will make clear your central idea, give your audience new information, and buttress your conclusions. You can obtain facts and information of this kind on this subject from your local public library and from the school system in your community. Very few persons will have taken the time to obtain such facts and figures, and you should not find it too difficult to give an informative and worthwhile speech.

The Conclusion

At the end of the body of the speech you need a conclusion. This should be brief, but it has an important function.

To stop short at the end of a detailed discussion which fills the body of your speech would be too abrupt. Good speakers never end their remarks with the bald statement: "That is all I have to say on the matter," or "I think that's all." Instead they add a brief summary of what they have said, or a brief conclusion, or a stirring appeal.

Summary or Restatement

Here are two passages which illustrate the use of a summary or restatement of the chief points that have been presented. The first is the conclusion of an address on "Thrift and Citizenship," by Judge George F. Eyrich, Jr., of Cincinnati.

> . . . This country, in order to continue its matchless progress, must preserve the quality of its citizenship.
>
> The men, or organizations, who develop thrift among the people and give that thrift expression in the form of progress in the community, through the building of homes, are performing a real service to the nation. We believe that our institution is developing stability and love for country among our people and contributing to the happiness of our citizenship. This is a practice of true Americanism in which we find much pleasure in being engaged. It gives us hope for and confidence in the future of our country. No more important or happier service can come to any individual or institution.

Another example of restatement of the main idea is illustrated by the conclusion of an address by John D. Rockefeller, Jr., on "The Personal Relation in Industry."

. . . If I were to sum up in a few words what I have been endeavoring to say to you in regard to the personal relation in industry, I should say, apply the Golden Rule.

Every human being responds more quickly to love and sympathy than to the exercise of authority and the display of distrust. If in the days to come, as you have to do with labor, you will put yourself in the other man's place and govern your actions by what you would wish done to you, were you the employee instead of the employer, the problem of the establishment of the personal relation in industry will be largely solved, strife and discord as between labor and capital will give place to cooperation and harmony, the interests of both will be greatly furthered, the public will be better served, and through the establishment of industrial peace, a great stride will have been taken toward the establishment of peace among nations.

Quotation

A very effective form of conclusion for a speech of serious or impassioned character is a quotation. Henry W. Grady's, "The Old South and the New," delivered at the annual dinner of the New England Society in New York City, closes with two impressive quotations, from Webster and from Shakespeare.

If she does not refuse to accept in frankness and sincerity this message of good will and friendship, then will the prophecy of Webster, delivered in this very society forty years ago amid tremendous applause become true, be verified in its fullest sense, when he said: "Standing hand in hand, and clasping hands, we should remain united as we have been for sixty years, citizens of the same country, members of the same government, united, all united now and united forever." There have been difficulties, contentions, and controversies, but I tell you that in my judgment—

> —opposed eyes,
> Which, like the meteors of a troubled heaven,
> All of one nature, of one substance bred,
> Did lately meet in th' intestine shock,
> Shall now, in mutual well-beseeming ranks,
> March all one way.

Charles L. Anspach, president of Central Michigan College of Education, closed an address at the annual swingout of the college with quotations as follows from Henry Van Dyke and James Russell Lowell:

As a working creed basic to such faith I give you the statement of Henry Van Dyke, "Be glad of life because it gives you the chance to love and to work and to play and to look up at the stars; to be satisfied with your possessions but not content with yourself until you have made the best of them; to despise nothing in the world except falsehood and meanness, and to fear nothing except cowardice; to be governed by your admirations rather than by your disgusts; to covet nothing that is your neighbor's except his kindness of heart and gentleness of manners; to think seldom of your enemies, often of your friends, and every day of Christ; and to spend as much time as you can with body and spirit in God's out-of-doors—these are little guidepaths to peace."

Tonight we toast the future. May you be successful in claiming its promises and in establishing a firm pathway for those who follow. Tomorrow in the words of James Russell Lowell you say:

My golden spurs now bring to me,
And bring to me my richest mail,
For tomorrow I go over land and sea,
In search of the Holy Grail.

Appeal to Feelings

Perhaps the most impressive type of conclusion, when the occasion is important enough to justify it, is the impassioned appeal to the listeners' feelings. Outstanding among the great speeches of the world is the conclusion of Patrick Henry's speech in the Virginia Convention:

It is in vain, sir, to extenuate the matter. Gentlemen may cry, Peace, peace—but there is no peace. The war is actually begun! The next gale that sweeps from the North will bring to our ears the clash of resounding arms! Our brethren are already in the field! Why stand we here idle? What is it that gentlemen wish? What would they have? Is life so dear, or peace so sweet, as to be purchased at the price of chains and slavery? Forbid it, Almighty God! I know not what course others may take; but as for me, give me liberty, or give me death!

By the side of this we may place, as an appeal no less powerful although of a different character, the conclusion of Lincoln's second Inaugural Address:

With malice toward none; with charity for all; with firmness in the right, as God gives us to see the right, let us strive on to finish the work we are in, to bind up the Nation's wounds, to care for him who shall have borne the battle and for his widow and his orphan, to do all which may achieve and cherish a just and lasting peace among ourselves and with all nations.

Chapter 10

SHAPING UP THE SECTIONS OF YOUR SPEECH

IF your speech runs to more than five minutes or so, it is a series of discussions of particular points; that is to say, it is a series of *small* speeches. Each one does its part in carrying along the plan, and thereby developing its central idea. The sections act like the members of a relay race team. Each one takes the token from the one before it and carries it a certain distance, where the next section picks it up.

It is all-important to build these sections carefully. Then the thought of your speech flows on smoothly with steadily increasing power, so that the audience is swept easily into the culmination at the end of the speech, as a railroad train comes easily into the terminal at the close of its run because all sections of the track have been kept clear and in proper condition.

Coordinating the Points of Your Speech

The speaker's skill is revealed especially by his success in shaping the points or sections of his speech. It is here that the inexperienced speaker shows weakness, because he follows the custom of conversation, in which we develop our thought in fragments—dealing with one idea fully and giving the next one just a casual touch. When a person follows this unsystematic method in a speech, where he has to place the individual sections of his speech end to end, the result is inconsistent, jumpy and ineffective. There is no teamwork in his relay team.

But this is a matter which can be fully mastered by study, and easily at that. One reason is that the individual sections are short enough to be handled easily at a sitting. A section will not often exceed 500 or 600 words (four to five minutes' time in delivery). You can lay this out, write a draft, shuffle it, rewrite and polish it at one sitting. Another reason is that it is easy to find model specimens in the speeches of other persons. It is strongly recommended that you study the organization of speeches you hear or read from time to time.

How Many Points?

The number of sections or points in a speech depends on its length and elaborateness. In an address that fills twenty minutes there may be four or five sections. In a speech of ten minutes or less there may be only two or three sections. In very short speeches the introduction, body, and conclusion may each be just a single section. It is probable that most of the speeches for which you will be called on will not have over four or five sections.

Each Section a Miniature Speech

Each of the sections has the function of carrying the central idea forward a certain distance according to your plan. Each one is thus a sort of miniature speech by itself. It has the same three functions as the entire plan: to cover fully the matter which it treats; to present this in proper perspective; and to put it in a way to interest and please, or satisfy the audience. In doing this, each section may even have an introduction, a body, and a conclusion of its own. When you examine one by one the sections of a carefully organized speech, you can generally identify the introduction, body, and conclusion of most of them with little difficulty.

A Speech from Reconstruction Days

Here, for example, is a passage from one of the outstanding speeches of the Reconstruction time, a speech in the United States Senate in 1872 by Carl Schurz, one of the foremost statesmen of the time. He was pleading for amnesty for the Confederate leaders.

> . . . I remember, also, to have heard the argument that under all circumstances the law must be vindicated. What law in this case? If any law is meant, it must be the law imposing the penalty of death upon the crime of treason. Well, if at the close of the war we had assumed the stern and bloody virtue of the ancient Roman, and had proclaimed that he who raises his hand against this republic must surely die, then we might have claimed for ourselves at least the merit of logical consistency. We might have thought that by erecting a row of gallows stretching from the Potomac to the Rio Grande, and by making a terrible example of all those who had proved faithless to their allegiance, we

would strike terror into the hearts of this and coming generations, to make them tremble at the mere thought of treasonable undertakings. That we might have done. Why did we not? Because the American people instinctively recoiled from the idea; because every wise man remembered that where insurrections are punished and avenged with the bloodiest hands, there insurrections do most frequently occur—witness France and Spain and the southern part of this hemisphere; that there is a fascination for bloody reckonings which allures instead of repelling —a fascination like that of the serpent's eye, which irresistibly draws on its victim. The American people recoiled from it, because they felt and knew that the civilization of the nineteenth century has for such evils a better medicine than blood.

Thus, sir, the penalty of treason, as provided for by law, remained a dead letter on the statute book, and we instinctively adopted a generous policy, and we added fresh luster to the glory of the American name by doing so. And now you would speak of vindicating the law against treason, which demands death, by merely excluding a number of persons from eligibility to office! Do you not see that, as a vindication of the law against treason, as an act of punishment, the system of disabilities sinks down to the level of a ridiculous mockery? If you want your system of disabilities to appear at all in a respectable light, then, in the name of common sense, do not call it a punishment for treason. Standing there, as it does, stripped of all the justification it once derived from political necessity, it would appear only as the evidence of an impotent desire to be severe without the courage to carry it out. But, having once adopted the policy of generosity, the only question for us is how to make the policy most fruitful. The answer is: We shall make the policy of generosity most fruitful by making it most complete. . . .

In this passage of 450 words and sixteen sentences, the introduction covers the first two sentences. Sentences three to fifteen are the body. Sentence sixteen is the conclusion.

Study also the excerpt below from an address by General Dwight D. Eisenhower before the American Bar Association and determine the introduction, body, and conclusion in this section of General Eisenhower's address:

I thank you sincerely for the great honor implicit in the warmth of the welcome you have accorded me. Every gathering of Americans—whether a few on the porch of a crossroads store or massed thousands in a great stadium—is the possessor of a potentially immeasurable influence on the future.

Because America has freedom of speech, freedom of communication, the world's highest educational level and untapped reserves of individual initiative, any group of our people, fired by a common purpose, can generate a decisive strength toward its achievement. Some of the most inspiring chapters in our history were written by a handful of our citizens who, joined together to talk out among themselves an idea or a principle, struck a note that revolutionized the world's thinking. That capacity still resides in every gathering in this country.

Those who fear that our people are bogged down in the apathy of regimented thought, have never been privileged to listen to the talk of a squad of soldiers or a gandy-dancer gang on the railroad. Or—for that matter—to a conference of bankers when there was under discussion a topic of vital interest to the future of this republic. Readiness to air a grievance, to propose a remedy, to argue the pros and cons of a plan, is an enduring—and priceless—American trait.

Few groups, however, can have so profound an impact on the course of public affairs as this assembly. Ours is a government of law—not of despotic decree—and you who practice the law have a specialized knowledge and unique influence in human relations. Indeed, without your counsel and advice hardly a single policy decision is reached by any of the forces most potent in the American economy—by labor organizations, by management, by farm groups, by welfare and professional associations, or by government agencies. Your attitude today often foreshadows the facts of tomorrow.

The Introduction of a Section

The introduction of a section has the duty of taking the token from the preceding member of the relay team. The passage in which this is done is often called a transition. General Eisenhower continued the address we have just quoted as follows:

As a consequence, a more than ordinary responsibility is on you to remain free from bias and prejudice when you consider broad social problems. If you are true to your profession and to the responsibilities of your citizenship, you view them within a framework of *three fundamental principles* of American life.

First, that individual freedom is our most precious possession. It is to be guarded as the chief heritage of our people, the wellspring of our spiritual and material greatness, and the central target of all enemies—internal and external—who seek to weaken or destroy the American Republic.

Second, that all our freedoms—personal, economic, social, political—freedom to buy, to work, to hire, to bargain, to save, to vote, to worship, to gather in a convention or join in mutual association; all these freedoms are a single bundle. Each is an indispensable part of a single whole. Destruction of any inevitably leads to the destruction of all.

Third, that freedom to compete vigorously among ourselves, accompanied by a readiness to cooperate wholeheartedly for the performance of community and national functions, together make our system the most productive on earth.

These three principles express the common faith of loyal Americans —the shining guide that, for the vast majority, points always the straight path to America's future. In the industrialized economy of the twentieth century, that path lies down the middle of the road between the unfettered power of concentrated wealth on one flank, and the unbridled power of statism or partisan interests on the other. Our agreement in these three great fundamentals provides the setting within which can always be composed any acute difference.

Yet there are some who build out of catch-words and fallacies a testament of inescapable conflict within our economy. Should misguided or vicious persons lull us into acceptance of this false dogma, the fault—criminal and stupid as it is—will be our own. We will have been victimized by the crude technique of the brazen lie, often repeated. You, of the legal profession, are uniquely fitted to expose this fraud, and thereby prevent senseless cleavage and hostility among us.

Note his transition from the first section quoted to the second section, "As a consequence, a more than ordinary responsibility is on you to remain free from bias and prejudice when you consider broad social problems."

In a speech by Ogden Mills before the New York State Economic Council, the point made in the opening paragraph may be summarized as: "The government has spent a great deal of money, which will have to be met with taxes." The next section begins with this introduction:

No matter who may pay the tax collector in the first instance, ultimately the weight of excessive taxation is borne by the entire nation.

The whole process is exceedingly complicated, but let us try to examine it in the simplest possible terms.

The next section is introduced thus:

If once we grasp the fundamental fact that taxes are paid out of the total current production, problems otherwise obscure begin to take shape.

The next section is introduced thus:

You may feel that I have devoted a great deal of time to establishing a simple and, on the whole, rather obvious fact. But, strange to say, it was the failure of the Administration to grasp this fact that is responsible for both the unemployment and budgetary problems of today.

Passages which mark the transition from section to section are brief, hardly even more than two or three sentences. Sometimes, when the logical relation of the two sections is close, the transition may be only a single clause or phrase. But in all cases the duty of the transition, the introduction to a section, is to give the audience their bearings, to tell them where on the road they are now, and where they are going next. It is like the sign on the lamp post at a street corner.

The Body of a Section

The body of the section develops the idea. In doing this the first consideration, of course, is to make sure of a logical sequence of thought. Each statement is expected to grow out of the one before. Turn back to the passage quoted from Schurz. It will illustrate such sequence.

Sentences three through fifteen, as mentioned above, constitute the body. Sentence three states a proposition which is dwelt upon through sentence nine, and which itself is made up of four subgroups: sentence three; sentences four and five; sentences six and seven; and sentences eight and nine.

Sentence ten, beginning the second paragraph, is another subgroup; sentences eleven and twelve another; sentences thirteen, fourteen, and fifteen still another. Sentence sixteen, as already pointed out, is the conclusion of the section.

Familiar Patterns of Arrangement

You can make it easy for your audience to grasp the logical sequence within the section by utilizing certain familiar patterns or formulas of arrangement. These were worked out long ago. Experienced speakers follow them continually. In fact, even the most unsophisticated listeners are accustomed to these formulas, although they may not consciously recognize them by name.

General Statement Plus Details

One formula or pattern which of course is familiar to everyone is a general statement followed by details. For example, in the speech by Ogden Mills, just referred to, he makes the statement: "As extensive borrowing continues, with no cessation in sight, new dangers arise." Then he adds these details:

Those who are loaning their savings to the government become fearful that the size of the debt may grow so large that the people may be unwilling when the time comes to make the sacrifices necessary to discharge it. Investors become more and more reluctant to lend their savings to the government. The latter, unable either to finance itself through taxation or normal borrowing methods, then resorts to such devices as the manufacture of credit through banking channels. The specter of inflation makes its appearance. . . .

Norman Cousins, editor of *The Saturday Review of Literature,* addressed the Cultural and Scientific Conference of World Peace in New York, and in one section of his address to these representatives from foreign countries he began his remarks with the general statement, "And when you tell the folks at home about democracy in America, give your definition some sense of the stretch and vastness and resonance of the term as Americans see it." He then defined at length and in detail what democracy means to Americans:

Tell them that it is a means to an end and an end in itself; that it gives Americans the right to use it or abuse it; to exalt it or destroy it; that it is as much or as little as Americans want to make of it; as much or as little as they want to make of themselves. Say that it can mean fulfillment or it can mean failure; that it is challenge, a process of reconciliation; that it is adjustment and change.

Say that Americans see it as a chance to see what they can do with themselves, that it is the expression of their faith in themselves.

Say that democracy, in a confined political sense, is majority rule and the preservation of minority rights; but that it reaches out beyond that to a unique blend of negative and positive values. That it is the absence of tyranny, the absence of every arbitrary invasion of the rights of man. That it is a series of magnificent restraints. Point out that the words "no" or "not" are among the most conspicuous in the United States Constitution, and especially in the Bill of Rights. Emphasize that these restraints are directed primarily against government itself.

Say that democracy is an enduring principle—something that liberals can believe in even when conservatives are in power, and that conservatives can believe in when liberals are in power. Say that it means there is enough room in America both for those who believe that President Truman is the greatest living American, and those who believe that ex-President Hoover is the greatest living American—or for those who believe that neither is the greatest living American.

Say that democracy to Americans means the sacred right to make mistakes and the even greater right to try to correct them.

Say that democracy in America comes under the heading of unfinished business and that no one viewing it from the outside should make the error of assuming, because there are imperfections and injustices, that democracy does not exist or that it is enfeebled.

Say that the American people are aware of what remains to be done, and that they believe the answer to an imperfect democracy is not authoritarianism but more democracy.

Say that the Americans believe the human family is greater than any of its self-appointed clans.

Say that democracy must mean intellectual freedom, that it must protect the individual against the right of the state to draw political and cultural blueprints for its painters and writers and composers, or to castigate them, or to enter into those matters of the mind in which the individual is sovereign.

Say, finally, the Americans recognize that great ideological differences separate the people of the world today, but that they are not forgetting for a single moment that peoples are more important than nations, and that what is at stake today is nothing less than the common destiny of man. For we live at a time when the human race has exhausted its margin for error.

Say that America would like to hold out its hand to the peoples of the world by proposing world peace through world law, and that it is doing this not despite the differences that rend the world, but indeed, because of them. For those differences define the problem. The important thing is to keep the frictions growing out of those differences from catching on fire.

Remind your nations and peoples—again in the words of Woodrow Wilson—that the eyes of America are lifted to the great distances of history, and ahead to "the lifting of civilization to new levels and new achievements."

A Caution

In using this pattern, take care to express the details in a way to show plainly their bearing on the main statement. In the examples just quoted this relation is made unmistakable. The relation of the details to the main statement is more easily grasped if each one is stated briefly. If you allow yourself to be carried away by your interest in one of them and talk about it too long, the audience may lose the thread of connection. In that case you lose more than you gain, no matter how interesting your remarks on the one detail may be.

Repetition

Another pattern is that of repetition. You make a statement and then follow it by one or more statements that say the same thing in different terms. In an address to college students on "How to Succeed," Charles M. Schwab once made the statement, "Another important thing is loyalty," and developed it by repetition as follows:

> . . . Now, that is what you boys in universities and colleges learn. You learn loyalty to your Alma Mater. You learn loyalty to your fellow students. You learn loyalty to the friendships that are going to follow you through life. The one thing that you are distinctively in the university is that you are loyal men. Be loyal. . . .

One of the most eloquent men in our history, Robert G. Ingersoll, frequently employed this pattern with striking effect. His fertile imagination and exceptional gift of language enabled him to turn an idea round and round and bring out bit by bit many aspects of it that would not have occurred to those of less observant mind, as in the following:

> . . . Shakespeare was an intellectual ocean, whose waves touched all the shores of thought; within which were all the tides and waves of destiny and will; over which swept all the storms of fate, ambition and revenge; upon which fell the gloom and darkness of despair and death, and all the sunlight of content and love, and within which was the inverted sky, lit with the eternal stars—an intellectual ocean—toward which all rivers ran, and from which now the isles and continents of thought receive their dew and rain. . . .

Contrast

A third formula or pattern is that of contrast. You make a statement and follow it with another which is opposite in meaning or tendency. The contrast serves to bring out more clearly the meaning of the main statement.

During the course of an address on "What Makes America Great?" Colonel Willard Chevalier used contrast repeatedly to emphasize his points as follows:

> Now, *what* was it that has made us that great? As I said before, other countries were as rich as America in coal and iron deposits, but they did not use them. Others had rich deposits of copper and tin, fertile soil, rivers, and forest. Our human resources, the men and women who settled here, were not different from the brothers and sisters they left behind in the old countries. But the British who settled New England and founded America's first industries, who built and sailed our first ships; the Germans who settled in Pennsylvania, the French in Louisiana and Rhode Island, the Poles of our coal fields and steel mills, once they were in this country, prospered and rose to positions they could never have reached at home.

Was it that we had more money for investment at our disposal than the old countries? On the contrary. We were desperately short of investment funds. To build our first factories, to sink our first mines, and to build the railroads that opened up the West, we had to borrow from British, French and German sources. We remained in debt to them up until World War One. Not until after that war did we have a surplus of savings which we could, in turn, export to other countries by making foreign loans.

Was it, perhaps, that this system, which we call "capitalism," had a chance to develop here that it did not have in other countries? I think not. The history of capitalism goes back thousands of years. Ancient Babylon had large business organizations, banks, and insurance companies. Capitalism functioned in ancient Greece and Rome, and in Germany and France in the Middle Ages.

Was it, then, that factory production could develop here faster and better than any place else? England had her industries long before we had ours, and so had France and Germany. As long as four thousand years ago toys were produced by factory methods in the town of Chan-Darn on the Indus river.

Was it, finally, that Americans have had a greater urge to do things, to work hard, to build, and to trade? The slaves that built the ancient pyramids of Egypt, the magnificent temples of Greece and Rome, certainly worked as hard as any Americans ever did. For thousands of years the whip of the slave driver gave people the incentive to work hard. The desire for profits—that too had functioned long before we used it. The incentive of trading profits led the ancient Phoenicians, two thousand years before Christ, to sail their ships halfway around the world; it brought Columbus to America in 1492. The need to provide the necessities of life, the lust for power, the profit motive—all of them had given men incentive to work long before America was discovered.

Natural resources, human resources, funds for investment and strong incentives all played their parts in making America great. But they were nothing new in this world. *The new factor that America had added is individual and personal opportunity; equal opportunity for every individual to shape his life, and to rise as high as he can through his own skill, ability, and willingness to work.*

This pattern of contrast may be used effectively in many ways. Sometimes, it is merely a contrast of words, or of short statements. Sometimes you can make a more elaborate contrast that covers entire paragraphs.

General Statement plus Illustration

A pattern of particular importance for a speaker is that of following a definite general statement with an illustration. One of the outstanding examples of this is the celebrated lecture entitled, "Acres of Diamonds," by Dr. Russell Conwell. Dr. Conwell delivered this lecture many hundreds of times, over many years. Millions of people heard it. With the accumulated profits from the delivery, Dr. Conwell founded Temple University in Philadelphia.

In the text of "Acres of Diamonds" the statements made up hardly more than one-third of the lecture. Nearly two-thirds consisted of illustrations. Dr. Conwell made a statement and followed it with a story—in some cases two stories—which illustrated the idea. The thought or reasoning was accepted with the interesting story. It is an excellent formula for the presentation of ideas to popular audiences. Beyond question, it was the use of this formula which won for this lecture its outstanding success.

Use of a Story

The speech by Charles M. Schwab on "How to Succeed," already cited, offers many instances of the use of this method of development. At one point he says: "Give the best that is in you. Let nothing stand in the way of your going on." Then he tells the story:

> . . . I am going to tell you the story of a man that came to see me in New York, Charles W. Baker, the president of the American Zinc Company, a very good friend of mine. Thirty years ago, as manager of the Homestead Mills, I went to Cleveland to see some plates that were being made. I got there at six o'clock in the morning. . . . When I got to the works I found this young man Baker, a stenographer and employee of the office, who had not been directed to go out there, but who thought when the works manager arrived out there he might want somebody to be on hand to meet him, and he was there, the only one that was there. And when I went back I said to the superintendent: "Watch that young man. When you have a chance give him a chance, because he is in earnest." It wasn't long before Baker got to be his assistant. Later he was agent. Later I made him the general agent of the whole Carnegie Company. Later I made him a partner. . . . That is the story. That one little thing helped him forward. . . .

G. O. Kildow, president of the North Idaho Junior College, used illustrations as follows to emphasize his statements in an address before the state meeting of the Idaho Writers League:

> There is a certain precariousness about being a man poet which is not connected with other types of authorship. In an essay titled "What

Is a Poet," by Mark Van Doren he gives what is supposed to be a popular conception of a man poet. I quote:

"A pale lost man with long, soft hair. Tapering fingers at the end of furtively fluttering arms. An air of abstraction in the delicate face, but more often a look of shy pain as some aspect of reality—a real man or woman, a grocer's bill, a train, a load of bricks, a newspaper, a noise from the street—makes itself manifest. He is generally incompetent. He cannot find his way in a city, he forgets where he is going, he has no aptitude for business, he is childishly gullible and so the prey of human sharks, he cares nothing for money, he is probably poor, he will sacrifice his welfare for a whim, he stops to pet homeless cats, he is especially knowing where children are concerned (being a child himself), he sighs, he sleeps, he wakes to sigh again." . . .

I often visualize mankind as an immense river of humanity, moving with inexorable slowness toward a sort of Utopia where only perfection can exist. This great river is fed by innumerable channels representing all the peoples of the world. Some channels, like clear mountain streams, are composed of people who have found the secret of the abundant life, and rush happily toward the goal of perfection. Other streams, like the clogged rivers of the Missouri valley, are composed of people who know nothing of the abundant life, who move with apprehensive sluggishness toward that which they do not comprehend. Like the individual molecules of water and silt, each person maintains his individual identity. The important thing is that the rate of approach of this vast river of humanity to perfection is in direct proportion to the number of those present who have found the secret of the good life.

At the Olympic Games which were held in London last year, during the relay race, the third runner on the French team dropped the baton as it was being handed to him by the second runner who had preceded him around the track, thereby losing the race. We are told that because of his failure he was immediately overcome by grief, and wept bitterly as he left the track. His failure, he realized, had not only affected himself, but a great many other people. It would be a disappointment to the two men who had preceded him around the track, to the man who would have followed him, to the trainers, the French Olympic team, and of course, to the entire French nation. All of those concerned were linked together in an intangible way, and the failure of one of them to deliver his talents brought failure or disappointment to each.

Remember always when building the body of a section not to allow yourself to run on too long with any one item. It is easy for a speaker to become so interested in this or that detail of a thought that he forgets he brought it in merely to throw light on something else. As a result, he gives it more prominence than he had intended.

The Conclusion of a Section

To round out the section, you need a conclusion. You will note such a section conclusion at the end of the extract given from Charles Schwab. Such a section conclusion will be brief of course—a single sentence or even less than a sentence. It may repeat the main thought of the section, or it may state explicitly that you have come to the end of a topic. Or it may consist of a pointed epigram-like statement which will naturally call for a pause to enable the audience to comprehend it.

Rapid Improvement Possible

Definite attention to the art of building the sections of a speech is often neglected by speakers. The inevitable result is unevenness and incoherence in the progress of their thought. But command of this part of a speaker's task can be surely developed by anyone who will work at it systematically. You can certainly master it, if you will take time to analyze a number of speeches by successful speakers to note their methods, and then to practice applying their methods in speeches of your own.

Chapter 11

GIVING YOUR STATEMENTS LIFE AND POWER

LANGUAGE, which is simply words grouped in definite clear statements or sentences, has power to move the very stones—to change the destiny of nations. The power of language is yours. Learn to make the most of it!

The Power of Vivid Statements

Have you ideas? Your friends and the world at large will never realize it unless you clothe them in language and force men to take note. You use your language to converse. Then use it to enlarge that conversation, and instead of confining to the few the benefits of your thoughts and reasoning, give the larger group in your business, club, church, or fraternal organization, or in your community, an opportunity to appreciate your worth.

You remember the baseball game you attended last year that gave you such a thrill? Next morning you recounted what you had seen to a group of friends. We can hear and see you now. You are telling us that it is the ninth inning. The visiting team is one run ahead. The home team is at bat. There are two men on bases and two out. The local lion walks to the plate, swinging his bat. Now we will see action.

The pitcher hurls the ball. "Ball one," shouts the umpire. Again the ball comes speeding toward the plate. "Ball two!" The pitcher is afraid of the batter. We feel with you that he is going to walk him. Again the pitcher winds up. He sends the ball speeding on its way toward the plate. The batter steps to meet it with a mighty swing—all the force of his muscular shoulders back of it. He crashes his bat into the oncoming ball—BANG—and through space it goes hurtling toward the outfield. With you we are watching it spellbound. We are not paying the least attention to the men on the bases; we are not thinking of the batter. Our minds, by the force of your language, are following the ball and with you we are hoping that its flight will carry it out of reach of the player in right field. It is speeding toward him. We see him leap from the ground to capture it. He fails. It's over his head. It's a three-bagger. Our team has scored two runs and won the game. With you we are taking part in the pandemonium that reigns in the grandstand. With the spectators we are wild with joy.

Language Pictures

Do you realize that on that day, as we listened to you, we were watching that game with you? We were mentally transported to the ball-grounds. We saw the game played, through your language pictures. You were the artist painting motion pictures; not a dead single incident, but incident following incident, alive, thrilling, powerful, effective. You made us see what you had seen, feel what you had felt. We were thrilled as you had been, and you did it all by means of language—by means of definite, vivid, forceful sentences or statements.

Building the Thought-units

Sentences or statements are the thought-units which the mind of a listener or reader picks up. When you told the story of that game, you instinctively composed your statements effectively, because you were stimulated by your recollection of the scene. You arranged the words within them to secure maximum clearness, vigor, and charm. Study of the principles of sentence construction will enable you to achieve in all your talk the same attractive qualities. It is something which anyone can do, if he will put his mind on it.

The trouble is that in most of our talk we give no conscious attention to the way our statements are put together. In writing we work sentences over and over, to make the thought run smoothly and to secure maximum impressiveness. But in talk, as a rule, our words are built together by impulse, or habit. We open our mouths and the words come out, to group themselves into statements almost automatically. Sometimes, as in your story of the ball game, the grouping is just right. Many times, and often on important occasions, it is ineffective. You can improve the effectiveness of your spoken sentences very greatly by a little systematic care. A part of your self-training in effective speaking should be given to this matter.

You need to develop the power of giving your sentences, even when made up on the spur of the moment, definiteness, energy, and exactness. Without aiming at the degree of exactness of written sentences that would make your speech sound artificial, you will try to get rid of inconsistency and carelessness.

Study Sentence Patterns

Most sentences are constructed according to various standard patterns or formulas which have become habitual in our language. Since there is not time, in speech, to stop and plan each statement by itself, the way to improve is by getting a clear understanding of these standard patterns. In this study you should give attention to two aspects of the matter.

First, you should get a clear understanding of the ordinary patterns or formulas that are constantly used in spontaneous conversation: how each of them is composed; what each one is good for; what dangers to guard against with each of them. Then, whether addressing an audience or in conversation, you can trust your mind to frame your sentences spontaneously and at the same time effectively.

Second, you should acquaint yourself with the more elaborate patterns which people employ on exceptional occasions, when expressing weighty thought or when under strong emotional stress. Then, when you find yourself in such a situation, your mind will have something to guide it in the heightened expression which the occasion demands.

Simple Sentences

The basic pattern of English sentences is a single statement made up of a subject plus a verb (predicate) plus an object (or complement):

Henry Brown bought coal.
Summer is hot.

These are called *simple* sentences.

For a question this order becomes auxiliary verb, plus the subject, plus the main part of the verb, plus the object or complement.

Have you bought coal?
Is football exciting?

Of course, it is very uncommon to have sentences in this absolutely simple form. Generally there are modifiers attached to the subject, predicate, or complement.

The great leader successfully accomplished his responsible task.

But in this sentence also there is only a single statement, and it is still a simple sentence. A large proportion of the sentences of conversation follow this pattern. In public speaking they ought to be used more than any other. For in talking to a group of people you should have most of your statements as easy to understand as possible.

Compound Sentences

A second common sentence pattern is made by joining together two or more simple sentences, to form what is called a *compound* sentence. Generally we make use of some word of connection such as "and," "but," or "yet."

The leader accomplished his task *and* received the thanks of his constituents.

Or:

I should like to visit your beautiful city, *but* my present engagements make it impossible.

Compound sentences are used constantly in conversation. In fact, if you listen to anyone relating an experience or urging an opinion, you will probably find the word "and" occurring continually—so frequently as to become tiresome to a listener. This fact suggests a caution in the use of compound sentences in addressing a group. Be careful not to use too many compound sentences or too many "ands." Since the "ands" stand out more in a speech than they do in conversation, too many of them will give your address an effect of formlessness and amateurishness.

Complex Sentences

A third sentence pattern, also used in conversation, but less often than the simple or the compound types, is the complex sentence. This consists of a main clause or statement, and with it one or more subordinate statements. Generally the subordinate statement is joined on by means of a subordinating connection such as "if," "which," "while," "though," or "when."

The great leader successfully accomplished his difficult task *although* he was hampered by circumstances.

Or:

If I did not have other engagements, I would gladly visit your beautiful city.

The complex pattern presents an idea with greater definiteness and precision than is usual with the simple or compound patterns. It is very helpful when you have a thought that is difficult to express. To compose it, however, requires some conscious attention, and for this reason it is less used in spontaneous conversation.

In public speaking you have somewhat more opportunity than in conversation to give conscious attention to the shaping of the sentences, as well as the sections or points. Hence it is possible to make more use of complex sentences. If you use too many, however, you may give your address before an audience an artificial air which will seriously weaken its effectiveness.

Simple Sentences Combined

Study the examples which follow. They are composed mainly of simple sentences, but the second has several complex sentences. You will note how direct and natural they are:

Excerpts from an address to the Graduating Class of Glendale College, Glendale, California, by R. G. McKelvey of Occidental College of Los Angeles.

This is a great occasion. Into it have gone the effort, the anxiety, the trial and error experiment, the hopes and struggles of more than three centuries of American history. Making this occasion possible has cost the sacrifice and devotion of parents, teachers, school administrators, and the scores of thousands of fellow townspeople whose tax tribute created and supports this educational system. From all of them you have taken much. To all of them you owe much. That all which has been given you has been gladly given does not lessen the burden of your debt, a debt which can never be tallied in dollars.

As you go forth from here today to begin the next phase of your plans you should ponder that everyone has an obligation to live his life not merely for himself and for those in his personal circle, but for all those who have gone before, and to the end that all those who come after shall inherit a better world.

You are stewards of a great tradition—the tradition of the precious light of freedom. Freedom didn't just happen. It is the reward of endless struggle. To guard it takes daily vigilance. Through service in the armed forces many of you have had a vital part in keeping freedom's light alive. For many of the world's people, the lamps of freedom have never been lighted. For many others for whom the lamps once burned, although with varying degrees of radiance, the light is out. You have a responsibility for extending the light of freedom at home, and for using your influence to get the lamps of freedom lighted around the world.

I have spoken of your debt. But you are also rich in assets. American is your heritage. Your citizenship in this country is your more priceless possession. The accident of birth has conferred upon you a privilege which has had no counterpart since the days of Rome. That fact weights you equally with opportunity and obligation. As Americans you have the opportunity for a greater freedom of choice than have the individuals and peoples of any other country. But so massive has this nation's power become that your choices will determine the opportunity for choices by peoples in every other land. This creates an obligation that your choices be considered and farsighted. To whom much is given much shall be required.

Our country is not Utopia. Vow with humility and zeal it shall never be less than now. But our country is a place with the tradition that its people shall through common counsel be free both to set objectives and to work toward them. In this you can and must share.

You have the priceless gift of youth. Some day when it is gone you will understand why George Bernard Shaw deplored that such a priceless gift should be wasted on young people.

Youth is a time of dreaming, a time of long, long thoughts. It is a time of idealistic and generous impulse. Often the dream is of a distant day when the dreamer will work miracles. The difference between the dream of one person and the dream of another is less its content than in what the dreamer does about it. The great of this earth, measured by reputation and impact on events, are those who seek to translate the dream into instant reality, but who are not discouraged that progress is slower than vision. For them the time is now, not some remote tomorrow which like a mirage recedes as it is approached. So dream, yes, but be the kind of dreamer for whom the time for action is not some more favorable tomorrow, but for whom the time for action is now.

Don't be intimidated by the fact of youth. Let history encourage you. Alexander the Great, a military hero at eighteen, began his efforts to conquer and control the earth at twenty. At his death at the age of thirty-three, he had exercised dominion over much of the civilized world of his day. For Alexander the time was now. Jeanne d'Arc at nineteen had completed her mission and embraced the immortality of martyrdom. Isaac Newton at twenty-one had contributed importantly to mathematics. At twenty-five he was honored with a professorship at

Cambridge University. Alexander Hamilton at eighteen was famed as an orator for freedom's cause. At twenty he was a lieutenant colonel on George Washington's staff, and Washington's trusted confidential secretary. Lafayette burning to help France and deciding the best way to do so was to weaken England by aiding the revolting American colonies, Lafayette was a major general in Washington's army at nineteen. William Pitt, the younger, one of Britain's greatest statesmen, successfully sought election to Parliament at the age of twenty-one. He became prime minister before he was twenty-five. Thomas Edison at sixteen already had useful inventions to his credit. Winston Churchill, on the eve of going abroad as a foreign correspondent, though not yet twenty-one, gave a farewell dinner party for some of his youthful friends. He proposed the toast, "Those yet under twenty-one who in twenty years will control the British Empire." Henry Luce had already founded his journalistic empire when he was twenty-five. At twenty-nine Earl Warren was deputy district attorney for the important county of Alameda. At thirty-one Harold Stassen was governor of Minnesota.

For each of this company of illustrious names, dreams were incitements to action. For each, the time was now.

Excerpts from an address by Max W. Ball, director of the Oil and Gas Division of the United States Department of the Interior, on "Mineral Resources and Human Resourcefulness."

Geologically, overseas prospects are rosy. Oil is found in sedimentary rocks—rocks laid down under water as mud and ooze and sand, and hardened by time and pressure. Any large area of thick sedimentary rocks is a promising place to look for oil. The earth has many such areas. Some of them have proved highly productive, in Venezuela and Colombia and the East Indies and Mexico and Peru and the Argentine. Others, less productive as yet, may develop great production. The Middle East and parts of Russia may prove the most productive of all. Still other promising areas have not been explored. If all the world—even all the non-Russian world—were open to free enterprise and free interchange of goods, we need fear no shortage of oil for many years.

Politically and practically, overseas prospects are rather gray. The dead hand of nationalization lies on areas of great promise. A certain country has some of the world's largest and most promising unexplored areas, but private enterprise, even the private enterprise of the country's own citizens, is not permitted to explore or develop. Instead of being another Venezuela or perhaps another Iran, the country has a single trifling oil field. Another country with a nationalized oil industry may have ten to fifteen billion barrels of undiscovered oil. To keep step with development in the United States, she should have drilled two hundred times as many wells as she has drilled. Instead of having large volumes of oil to export, as she once did to her great profit, she has scarcely enough for her own needs. In certain other countries, including some of our good neighbors, the door is closed to outside capital.

Whatever success nationalized industry may achieve in other fields, it will not make a success of finding oil. It lacks the necessary diversity of judgment and the ability to take chances.

Finding oil is not an exact science. Using all the geologic knowledge it can muster, it must finally depend on trial and error. Even in the United States, with all our experience and geologic knowledge, only one exploratory well in five is productive; the other four are dry holes. Nearly every present field was overlooked or turned down by many men before someone decided to risk drilling it. Nearly every active oil geologist has located many more dry holes than producers.

Government officials just can not operate that way. No government official would dare to take one long chance after another with public funds, or would last long if he did. I am an oil geologist and a government official; I should know.

All this is hard to understand, for governments are inclined to public operation. They think the business of finding and producing oil is ipso facto productive of huge profits. They think those dreamed-of profits should go to their own citizens instead of to foreigners and capitalists. They underrate the risk that must precede the profits. They underrate the value, and the scarcity, of the huge investments and concentrated experience that make the profits possible. They think, in short, that all they need is a loan to make their treasuries rich from the profits of oil development.

They turn their backs, therefore, on the wealth in dollars and know-how that oil companies are spending in other countries, and on how much those countries are enriched thereby. They turn their faces toward the loans from other treasuries to put or keep them in the oil business.

American oil men are a hardy race. They will keep on knocking on foreign doors, and will enter those that are opened, and once inside will invest huge sums on promises of fair play. But if through the years they find the doors still closed, or having once been admitted find themselves squeezed out, then we need expect little oil from outside our own borders.

You will note also the abruptness of many of these statements. Each one stands out by itself. There is a little pause after each of them. The effect is strong and rugged. However, if an entire address consisted solely of short sentences, the effect would tend to be jerky and unnatural. Consequently, longer sentences are also used to change the pace.

A Series of Compound Sentences

The next example has a number of compound sentences.

Excerpts from an address by Gideon Seymour, vice president and executive editor of the Minneapolis Star and Tribune.

We can see our times in the right perspective only if we look at the world we live in and understand our relation to it; and to do that, we can look backward profitably for a minute at some ancient history which has a parallel today.

The Roman Empire was the first great nation in history, in the modern sense. Tyre and Babylon were great cities, and Greece was a notable confederation of city-states, in loose form, racked by frequent civil war. But Rome came to dominate the known world of its day. It made the rules and supplied the force and the threat of force which introduced stability and progress and higher living standards into the area around the Mediterranean and all of Europe as far northwest as the British Isles.

The time came, about 400 A.D., when the Roman Empire collapsed and disintegrated. It, and the world that lived under its rule, did not recognize or admit for several centuries that it was going or had gone to pieces. Repeated attempts were made to re-establish its authority and its order. But as we look back with our perspective upon history, we see clearly that from 400 A.D. the source of world order, Rome, became impotent; and because no nation or group of nations was able or willing to establish a system of order in the known world, the so-called civilized world descended into what we call in history the Dark Ages. The time of man stood still for a thousand years until, at last, there sprung in northern Italy the blossom of the Renaissance; and out of it quickly grew the age of discovery and exploration which opened the new world. This spurred the religious reformation in Germany and the industrial revolution in Britain. New horizons were opened to man; the spirit of human freedom soared again; and we were launched upon the wave of progress which has carried us on down clear to the twentieth century in increasing knowledge and well-being and peace.

In 1588, barely a century after the Dark Ages ended, Drake and his British fleet defeated the Spanish Armada in the English Channel and Britain began to become a world power—the first authentic world power mankind had known since Rome.

This passage runs smoothly. The individual statements do not stand out so sharply as shorter, more abrupt sentences sometimes do. This compound sentence pattern is often used, both in conversation and in everyday public speaking. You should take care, however, not to use the compound type too constantly. Beware of overdoing the "and" connection.

Complex Sentences Combined

In the next examples complex sentences predominate. You will notice at once the comprehensiveness of the statements.

Excerpts from an address by Dr. Millicent McIntosh, dean of Barnard College, New York City.

Is it our business as educators to grapple with the problems of our generation and to provide a moral synthesis which can guide our students wisely through a mass of contradictory concepts? I believe that this moral synthesis should be a major objective of education but that it can be provided only through freedom of inquiry and discussion, and by the personal idealism of the administrators and teachers who themselves cannot escape the necessity of coming to terms with the major problems of living. In this we are surrounded by a cloud of witnesses: great teachers, from Socrates to Whitehead and Toynbee, who were aware of the moral and spiritual implications of knowledge, and accepted fully the responsibility for passing these on to their students and to the world.

The greatest educational challenge of our time is thus formulated in the necessity of making teaching, on the school or college level, the great function which it has been historically, and which the urgency of our time demands. Graduate schools and colleges which glorify research and publication at the expense of the art of teaching are guilty of a grave and perhaps irreparable sin against civilization. Communities which spend millions for alcohol, cosmetics, tobacco and amusements—and what is left over, for schools—are committing spiritual suicide. We, the educators of America, who meet endlessly to make and listen to speeches keyed to the superficial aspects of our problem, are convicted of letting our world slide into an abyss of technological and moral confusion while we have been concerned with what Professor Howard Mumford Jones calls the "polite fictions of genteel tradition."

William Pitt, in the British House of Commons, replied to Sir Robert Walpole, who had taunted Pitt with youthfulness, with this complex sentence, "The wretch who, after having seen the consequences of a thousand errors, continues still to blunder, and whose age has only added obstinacy to stupidity, is surely the object of either abhorrence or contempt, and deserves not that his gray hairs should secure him from insult."

You may feel that this manner of speaking is less natural than the first two types. In fact, for everyday public speaking, complex sentences are perhaps mainly useful as a change from simple and compound sentences. But in an address occasional complex sentences give the address a smoothness and an easy flow which are desirable.

Practice the Familiar Patterns

You will find it exceedingly profitable to experiment with these three types of sentences, both in the speeches which you have occasion to make and in conversation. By and by, as a result of such experimenting, you will find yourself able to utilize all of them consciously even on the spur of the moment. As you build your ideas together before an audience, you will cast the individual thought in the form of a simple sentence, a compound sentence, or a complex sentence through a swift judgment as to the appropriateness of the particular pattern. That will make your speaking more understandable, more varied and interesting, and on the whole more *effective,* both when addressing groups and in private conversation.

We have been considering the use of sentences with reference to the usual requirements of everyday public speaking. These requirements call for naturalness, directness, simplicity. The sentence patterns that are appropriate even when they are of the compound or complex types are on the whole short and not elaborate. There are occasions, however, when you will wish to employ sentences of a different character, sentences such as you would never use in conversation.

Special Patterns

When you get "warmed up" in an address, when your emotions are roused or your imagination is excited, when you wish to stir the emotions or the imagination of your listeners, you will find yourself prompted to use sentences that are more elaborate and often much longer.

Webster—His Simple Style

Here, for example, are two passages from a speech by Daniel Webster, a plea to the jury in a murder case. They illustrate this difference in form of sentences.

The first extract is from the earlier part of his speech, when he is appealing to the jury's understanding. See how direct and natural the sentences are, nearly all simple or compound, such as he would employ in everyday conversation:

Let me ask your attention, then, in the first place, to those appearances, on the morning after the murder, which have a tendency to show that it was done in pursuance of a preconcerted plan of operation. What are they? A man was found murdered in his bed. No stranger had done the deed, no one unacquainted with the house had done it. It was apparent that somebody within had opened, and that somebody without had entered. There had obviously and certainly been concert and cooperation. The inmates of the house were not alarmed when the murder was perpetrated. The assassin had entered without any riot or any violence. He had found the way prepared before him. The house had been previously opened. The window was unbarred from within, and its fastening unscrewed. There was a lock on the door of the chamber in which Mr. White slept, but the key was gone. It had been taken away and secreted. The footsteps of the murderer were visible, outdoors, tending toward the window. The plank by which he entered the window still remained. The road he pursued had thus been prepared for him. The victim was slain and the mur derer had escaped.

Webster—Appeal to Jury

The second extract is from the latter part of his speech, when he is appealing to the jury's imagination and emotions. These are not the sentences of conversation. Not only are they more flowing and rhythmical, but in several of them the arrangement of sentence elements—subject, predicate, complement—is widely different from that of ordinary conversation.

The circumstances now clearly in evidence spread out the whole scene before us. Deep sleep had fallen on the destined victim, and on all beneath his roof. A healthful old man, to whom sleep was sweet, the first sound slumbers of the night held him in their soft but strong embrace. The assassin enters, through the window, already prepared, into an unoccupied apartment. With noiseless foot he paces the lonely hall, half lighted by the moon; he winds up the ascent of the stairs, and reaches the door of the chamber. Of this, he moves the lock, by soft and continued pressure, till it turns on its hinges without noise; and he enters, and beholds his victim before him. The face of the innocent sleeper is turned from the murderer, and the beams of the moon, resting on the gray locks of his aged temple, show him where to strike. The fatal blow is given, and the victim passes, without a struggle, from the repose of sleep to the repose of death.

Blaine—Simple Narrative

Note also these two examples from Blaine's eulogy on President Garfield, at the memorial ceremonies in Congress. The first is from the quiet narrative of the first part of the speech.

Garfield's army life was begun with no other military knowledge than such as he had hastily gained from books in the few months preceding his march to the field. He knew just enough of military science, as he expressed it himself, to measure the extent of his ignorance, and with a handful of men he was marching, in rough winter weather, into a strange country, among a hostile population, to confront a largely superior force under the command of a distinguished graduate of West Point, who had seen active and important service in two preceding wars.

Blaine—Appeal to Feeling

The second extract is from the famous climax at the close of the address.

Great in life, he was surprisingly great in death. For no cause, in the very frenzy of wantonness and wickedness, by the red hand of murder, he was thrust from the full tide of this world's interest, from its hopes, its aspirations, its victories, into the visible presence of death—and he did not quail. Not alone for one short moment in which, stunned and dazed, he could give up life, hardly aware of its relinquishment, but through days of deadly languor, through weeks of agony, that was not less agony because silently borne, with clear sight and calm courage he looked into his open grave. What blight and ruin met his anguished eyes, whose lips may tell—what brilliant, broken plans, what baffled, high ambitions, what sundering of strong, warm, manhood's friendship, what bitter rending of sweet household ties! Behind him a proud, expectant nation, a great host of sustaining friends, a cherished and happy mother, wearing the full, rich honors of her early toil and tears; the wife of his youth, whose whole life lay in his; the little boys not yet emerged from childhood's day of frolic; the fair young daughter; the sturdy sons just springing into closest companionship; claiming every day and every day rewarding a father's love and care; and in his heart the eager, rejoicing power to meet all demands. And his soul was not shaken. His countrymen were thrilled with instant, profound, and universal sympathy. Masterful in his mortal weakness, he became the center of a nation's life, enshrined in the prayers of a world. But all the love and all the sympathy could not share with him his suffering. He trod the wine-press alone. With unfaltering front he faced death. With unfailing tenderness he took leave of life. Above the demoniac hiss of the assassin's bullet he heard the voice of God. With simple resignation he bowed to the Divine decree.

Impassioned Style

Here are two examples of the elaborate sentences in which the strong emotion of a great occasion clothes itself.

DANIEL WEBSTER

From Webster's oration at the laying of the cornerstone of the Bunker Hill Monument in Boston—his impassioned address to the survivors of the Revolutionary War.

Venerable men! You have come down to us from a former generation. Heaven has bounteously lengthened out your lives, that you might behold this joyous day. You are now where you stood fifty years ago, this very hour, with your brothers and your neighbors, shoulder to shoulder, in the strife for your country. Behold, how altered! The same heavens are indeed over your heads; the same ocean rolls at your feet; but all else has changed! You hear now no roar of hostile cannon; you see no mixed volumes of smoke and flame rising from burning Charlestown. The ground strewed with the dead and the dying; the impetuous charge; the steady and successful repulse; the loud call to repeated assault; the summoning of all that is manly to repeated resistance; a thousand bosoms freely and fearlessly bared in an instant to whatever of terror there may be in war and death—all these you have witnessed, but you witness them no more. All is peace. The heights of yonder metropolis, its towers and roofs, which you then saw filled with wives and children and countrymen in distress and terror, and looking with unutterable emotions for the issue of the combat, have presented you today with the sight of its whole happy population, come out to welcome and greet you with a universal jubilee. Yonder proud ships, by a felicity of position appropriately lying at the foot of this mount, and seeming fondly to cling around it, are not means of annoyance to you, but your country's own means of distinction and defense. All is peace; and God has granted you this sight of your country's happiness, ere you slumber in the grave. He has allowed you to behold and to partake the reward of your patriotic toils; and he has allowed us, your sons and countrymen, to meet you here, and in the name of the present generation, in the name of your country, in the name of liberty, to thank you!

HENRY GRADY

The following is from Henry Grady's address on "The New South," delivered before the New England Society of New York City in December, 1886.

Let me picture to you the footsore Confederate soldier, as, buttoning up in his faded gray jacket the parole which was to bear testimony to his children of his fidelity and faith, he turned his face southward from Appomattox in April, 1865. Think of him as, ragged, half-starved, heavy-hearted, enfeebled by want and wounds, having fought to exhaustion, he surrenders his gun, wrings the hands of his comrades in silence, and lifting his tearstained and pallid face for the last time to the graves that dot old Virginia hills, pulls his gray cap over his brow and begins the slow and painful journey.

What does he find—let me ask you—what does he find when, having followed the battle-stained cross against overwhelming odds, dreading death not half so much as surrender, he reaches the home he left so prosperous and beautiful? He finds his house in ruins, his farm devastated, his slaves free, his stock killed, his barns empty, his trade destroyed, his money worthless, his social system, feudal in its magnificence, swept away, his people without law or legal status, his comrades slain, and the burdens of others heavy on his shoulders. Crushed by defeat, his very traditions are gone. Without money, credit, employment, material, or training, and, he is, in addition, confronted with the gravest problem that ever met human intelligence—the establishing of a status for the vast body of his liberated slaves.

Study Such Special Passages

Examine closely these passages which illustrate the use of elaborate sentences. Read them aloud in a manner that brings out fully their earnestness of feeling and their beauty of fancy. Go back again and again until you become familiar with them. Supplement this by carefully analyzing other speeches you may hear or read. Close examination of many speeches of able speakers will develop your own competence.

Experiment for Yourself

Then, for practice, experiment with working out passages for yourself on subjects that really stir your own feelings or imagination. You cannot produce sentences of the type you have just read on a subject in which you are only mildly interested.

For this part of your self-training, call in the help of pencil and paper. First *speak* your sentences with all the fervor and enthusiasm which the subject arouses in you, and then *write them down* and examine them. This method will enable you to see where to insert expressive words, and how to improve the rhythm and sound in order to give the sentences more fervor and grace.

Sentences of the elaborate type, bear in mind, are to be used sparingly. In most of your speeches it is probable that you will employ them very little, if at all. When an important occasion comes, however, when you feel yourself roused to a pitch of enthusiasm, when you wish to appeal strongly to the emotions of your audience, you will be able to let yourself go without fear of making a false move. The knowledge which you have developed through study of such passages by the masters, and through your own experimentation, will be your guide. It will give your impassioned outbursts not only spontaneity but also beauty and charm.

Chapter 12

GETTING THE RIGHT WORDS

Getting the Right Words

MANY persons shrink from getting up to face an audience because they think they lack words. They believe one must polish up his vocabulary before he can make a creditable speech. That is a mistake. It is true that definite and persistent study of words has an important part in mastery of the art of effective speaking, whether before an audience or in conversation, but it comes later, not at the beginning.

Mental Pictures Precede Words

As a general thing, we do not think about words at all when seeking to express our thought. We all have ideas, the laborer and the executive, the educated and the illiterate. We have mental pictures. They are the remembrance of things that we have seen, experienced or heard. From the storehouse of our memories we draw these mental pictures and express them in statements, sentences. The sentences are made up of words, but we do not think first of the words.

You would not wish to hear a speech by someone who merely spoke words. You can find all the words you wish in a dictionary, but until those words are combined in sentences and used to paint the picture of an idea, they have no real, connected meaning. If, when you had something to tell, you first had to look for words and then had to remember those words before you could relate the incident, your task would be so difficult that you might well be afraid to converse.

Seek First "Fact and Thought"

When you want to relate something to a second person, you fix your attention upon the incident, the imaginary occurrence, or the conclusion you have drawn from some set of facts. The situation is the same when you get up before an audience. Your listeners expect you to say something worth while; do then, what you do in ordinary conversation. Do not think words; get mental pictures. Think ideas and utter them in clear and lively statements. This is nothing new. Far back in Roman times, the poet Horace put this thought in verse:

> Seek not the words, seek fact and thought,
> And thronging in, will come the words unsought.

That is to say, words come to you in conversation without your seeking. One word follows the other without conscious effort on your part. Words should and will come to you in exactly the same way when you are standing before an audience, if you have mental pictures. The stronger, clearer, more distinct the mental picture, the more forceful will you be, the easier it will be to impress your audience.

Don't Worry over Words, at the Start

But your language is defective, you say! You make grammatical slips, at times, in conversation. Has that ever deterred you from talking to a friend? If not, why should it hinder your expression before a group of friends? Is a speech so different from your ordinary conversation? Does it demand different language? Are expressions used in daily life too commonplace for the occasion? Such an attitude is erroneous. You can and will impress your hearers with your ordinary conversational language.

On one occasion, a young man who had heard much about Henry Ward Beecher's prowess as an orator, came to him after he had talked and said, "Doctor, that was a wonderful sermon. I was very much impressed by it, but I was also very much surprised. You made one mistake in grammar." "One mistake?" said Beecher. "My boy, if I made one mistake I made a hundred."

Here is a passage from a speech which Theodore Roosevelt made when saying farewell to his regiment of Rough Riders, after the Cuban campaign. Is your talk likely to be more informal and colloquial than this?

> Now here's a thing I want to warn you against: Don't get gay and pose as heroes. Don't go back and lie on your laurels; they'll wither. The world will be kind to you for about ten days, and then it will say, "He's spoiled by the fame of the regiment in Cuba." Don't think you have got to have the best of everything, and don't consider yourselves as martyrs

in the past tense. A martyr came to see me today. He hadn't had any milk for a whole day. I said to him: "Oh, you poor thing!" and he went away. I hope he felt better. What I want of all of you is to get right out and fight your battles in the world as bravely as you fought the nation's battles in Cuba.

This straight-from-the-shoulder talk from Theodore Roosevelt commanded attention because of its earnest meaning and generous feeling. No one thought of objecting to the informal words. When you talk with sincerity and earnestness, you will be listened to with respect.

Do Not Talk Worse than You Need

Do not think, however, that poor grammar and slang expressions should be consciously sought after and employed. Even if the members of your audience are of the type that habitually uses incorrect grammar and is addicted to the use of slang, studied carelessness is not desirable. Even the immortal Patrick Henry could not win by such an attempt. We are told that on one occasion, when running for office, he addressed a group of rural voters. Knowing the peculiarities of their colloquial speech, he deliberately imitated it and gave the entire talk in the dialect of the neighborhood. He was trying to impress them with his democratic attitude. He failed. He lost their votes. Their intelligence was insulted and their pride hurt. They knew he was insincere in that speech. They had come to hear Patrick Henry, not an imitation of an illiterate person.

Use the words, therefore, that are habitual with you, your everyday speech. If they are good enough for ordinary conversation, they are good enough for the time when you stand up to address a group.

Later, Give Attention to Words

On the other hand, after you begin to feel at home before an audience, and especially after you have given some attention to the central idea, the plan, the division or sections of your speech, and the statements, then you should turn your attention to the words. Language that is not fit for your speech at the club, the fraternity, and the business conference, is not fit for conversation. Improve it systematically by reading good books, by watchfulness in conversation, and by the study of the speeches of the most able persons.

There is a right time and a wrong time to take up particular matters or steps. If you turn your attention to words after you have some command of the principles of building and arranging ideas, the problem of an effective vocabularly becomes easier. You will master it, although you may think the process is slow; and your efforts will fit in with and reinforce your work in other aspects of your training.

Two Tests for Words

Consider what words are. They are the bricks, the material, out of which your thought-units, the statements, are built. While, as stated above, they are not as a rule noticed consciously by listeners, it is very important to have them appropriate. The materials you employ in building your thought fabric should pass two tests.

First, they should not attract unfavorable notice. Your talk should not include words that offend the listeners' ears and prompt them to say to themselves: That's not the right word!

Second, they should harmonize with and reinforce the general character of your speech.

Improvement Not Speedy but Sure

You can improve greatly in both these points when once you begin to turn attention to them. On the other hand, the process of improvement will be less rapid than in the matter of the central idea, the plan, the shaping of sections, or even the building of sentences. For the skillful choice of words is a matter of training that takes time. You must develop the habit of noticing words, listening to speeches and to conversation with the special object of noting words that hinder or help the speaker's effect. But gradually you will acquire the habit; and once you have begun it, you will never stop. You will find it increasingly fascinating.

"Dos" and "Don'ts"

In selecting the right words for the speech you are preparing, you should consider what sort of words to avoid and what sort to employ. Consider first the negative side, the words to avoid. You should see that your words do not at any time fall below the standards of correctness that are commonly observed by educated people in careful conversation. Probably the simplest and shortest way to cover this point is by a series of "Don'ts."

Don't Keep On with Bad Grammar

Don't violate the rules of grammar, particularly the common rules which all of us know, though sometimes we forget. Do not say "He come" for "He came"; or "How did they succeed? Pretty good" for "Pretty well"; or "There wasn't no chance of success" for "There wasn't any chance." Such mistakes are evidence of carelessness. You would avoid them in conversation. Watch yourself in the same way when addressing an audience. The errors in grammar which Beecher made now and then were not of this illiterate character but were minor slips in reference or connection which almost anyone will make in the excitement of eager speech.

Don't use slang if you can think of another way to express your idea. With almost anyone, a slang expression will slip in now and then, but as the habit of noticing words grows stronger, you will become aware of good English expressions that are just as vigorous as the slang which you permit yourself in casual conversation.

Avoid Technical Words

Don't use technical words and phrases excessively. All of us are inclined when talking about our special work to employ the special terms of the occupation. They are intelligible to other experts but not to people in other fields of activity. When you need to employ such technical expressions, be careful to explain their meaning.

Don't Use Made-to-Order Phrases

Don't use the usual "made-to-order" phrases that are listed in some books for the use of public speakers. Those phrases are not yours. It is not you that is speaking when you employ them. You would not think much of a painter who took a beautiful painting and, because it had a dash of magnificent red in it, cut that red out of the picture and pasted it onto his own production. It would almost certainly be out of harmony with the rest of his painting. The same is true of the usual made-to-order phrases and sentences. When you make use of one of them, they may differ so from your ordinary speech that your listeners will know they are borrowed.

Avoid the Excessive Use of Big Words

Don't make an effort to use as many big words as possible. Do not, in the misguided effort for precision, allow yourself to imitate the speaker who said:

> There is one delicate point I wish to speak of with reference to old age. I refer to the use of dioptric media which correct the diminished refracting powers of the humors of the eye—in other words, spectacles.

The person who uses as many big words as possible may make the ignorant imagine that he is learned, but he only proves his ignorance to the intelligent people who listen to him. The ignorant person may seek to hide his shallowness in long words and high-sounding phrases, but he is quite certain to fail in his effort.

The Words to Use

The constructive side of your effort to get command of words consists in training yourself to seek out and employ words that are plain and clear, words that have vigor and drive, and words that have color and picture quality.

Develop the Habit of Noticing Words

No one can just pick these words out of a dictionary or vocabulary. You discover them through listening to good speakers, reading their speeches as printed, studying the effects produced upon your mind, and then analyzing their use of language, to trace this effect so far as possible to particular words. It is a slow process. To develop sensitiveness to word values takes time. But it is certain to bring results. When you are once started on it, you will find fresh interest in every speaker to whom you listen. You will enjoy the skillful management of words of the good speakers and you will find yourself thinking, as you listen to or read the speeches of the poor speakers, just how their wording could be improved.

Some Examples

Here are a few passages from speakers present and past, in which you will see definitely how the words which the speaker has employed impart a special, recognizable character to his speech.

Words That Are Plain and Direct

From a speech by Andrew Kaul III, president of the Speer Carbon Company, Saint Marys, Pennsylvania, at the graduation exercises at Saint Marys High School. It has simple words, but it is a strong address.

Many years ago—longer than I care to remember—the big event of my graduation finally occurred, and I was sitting there with you, and a speaker, whose name I forget, was standing here in my place. I have almost forgotten most of what he said, but he did plant one idea which the class didn't like very much at the time and which didn't really impress me until many years later.

Perhaps it was his fault that the most important thing he said—the most valuable idea he gave us—made almost no impression at the time he said it.

This afternoon I am going to try to do better for you than he did for us so that you may get your sights on the right target now—today.

I don't recall the exact words he used, but the idea was simply this: *there is no way in the world by which you can get something for nothing.*

It can be made to *appear* otherwise, but there is no way of escaping the final truth.

It requires just plain *common* sense, which nowadays has become *uncommon,* to figure out that everything in the world *comes* from somewhere, and *goes* somewhere, and there is *always a reason for its coming and going.*

Life always balances its books and demands its price.

The clothes you are wearing today are *where* they are because your father gave up *something else,* to *somebody else,* in exchange.

Everything you have ever had in the past, and everything you will ever get in the future, must be balanced with something else given up in exchange.

That something else will usually be a certain number of hours of your work.

Work is the currency of our economic life—everything we have of a material nature can be measured in hours of work.

And there is no substitute for work: even a thief has to put in hours of hard work for what he gets.

That, in my own words, is approximately what I heard the day I graduated from school.

As I mentioned before, the idea didn't sound very attractive to me at the time, and it probably doesn't sound very attractive to you right now.

All of us dream of a life of ease and comfort: if we didn't we would not be human.

But this dream of an easy life is a very expensive dream: it costs us a lot of time and trouble that we would otherwise not have to go through, and it can slow us down in the job of—digging ourselves a well-earned fox hole—in the economic system within which we are going to live our lives.

You may be saying to yourself: "This old bird is behind the times. The world has changed from the time when everybody had to worry about himself."

And if you *are* saying this to yourself, you can point to a lot of other people in the country—people in high places—who agree with you and disagree with me.

As a matter of fact, I wish that I were *not* right.

I wish that there *were* some way to supply everybody with a decent living without requiring of them a full day's work.

But that law was laid down, not by some human being, but by Mother Nature, and there isn't anything that anybody can do to change it.

We, in America, do not live better because of some magic system: *we live better because we do more work—because we produce more of the good things that make life better.*

There *is* one form of work—a *hard* form of work—*that any generation can duck out from under* if the people decide that that's what they want to do.

You can duck out from under the work of making your own decisions and from thinking your way out of your own personal problems.

Every generation can always find politicians who are eager to take these problems off their hands and do their thinking for them.

In this way they can reach out for the kind of security that promises something for nothing.

But as I said before, *everything you get in this world is balanced by something you give up,* and in order for you to get this relief from worrying about your personal problems there is naturally something that you have to give up.

That something is your freedom.

Now what good is your freedom to you?

In a way freedom seems to be a burden because it forces you to be self-reliant and to make your own decisions.

In another way freedom is a blessing, because it enables you to be yourself, *whatever that self may be.*

But in the sense I am using the word today, freedom pays off in dollars and cents—in more prosperity and better living.

A More Difficult Passage

The following excerpt from an address by Dr. Henry M. Wriston, President of Brown University, Providence, Rhode Island, was delivered at a Providence College commencement. The remarks of Dr. Wriston before this college audience are properly a little more involved than those in the preceding high school commencement address, but they are equally effective. Some of the words are more difficult, but they are suitable to his audience.

There is another aspect of wisdom of which I would speak. . . . Wisdom is not easily acquired. "For at the first she will walk with him in crooked ways, and will bring fear and dread upon him, and torment him with her discipline. . . . If he go astray, she will forsake him, and give him over to his fall." Patience is necessary, but industry is even more so. Industry is an important constituent of wisdom, yet the virtue of hard work is selling at a serious discount in the public schools of America.

So meanly do we regard our children that one of the commonest assertions is that the disciplines which have so long charmed the minds of men are "too hard." Schools doubtful of their own programs, schools crowded with students kept there against their wills by the law of the land, schools under political pressure to "pass" their students, schools suddenly supersensitive to the psychological dangers involved in the concept of failure have tended consistently to substitute less and less arduous and infinitely less significant materials of instruction. It is a self-defeating program, if wisdom is our goal.

It has been preached for twenty-five years now that the failure of the student is the failure of the teacher, as though failure were not one of the common, one of the inescapable experiences of life. "Passing the buck" for failure from the student to the instructor establishes an escape mechanism that will exact a dreadful toll in years to come. Learning by industry and by foresight to escape failure is one of life's greatest lessons, and to short-circuit that lesson by abolishing failure by edict is to give a false definition of success and to lend an illusion of achievement where none exists. Such a course of action, whatever the motive, must put industry at a discount, just as blaming things on "society" relieves the individual of his sense of personal responsibility.

No one wants to abuse the youth of today, but we are in far more danger of killing them by mistaken kindness than by overwork. Much of course can be done by modern devices to facilitate instruction. But when the last movie reel is put back in its tin box and all the sugar coating has been sucked from the pill, the process of learning will still be difficult. Whoever pretends that it is easy is cheating our youth. Any procedure which miscalls failure by the name of success does not advance, but prevents, education. Any refusal to make a boy face ideas, because ideas are more difficult to grasp than facts, results in simply stuffing him instead of educating him. Any pretense that the material can really be "correlated" outside his own mind misleads him.

Learning, the use of the mind, is hard work. It requires industry of a courageous kind. I have seen many a boy who would sweat all summer building roads quail before a book. But books must be faced; and even worse awaits. What is there must be remembered and reflected upon until it is no longer a piece of a book stuck into the mind, but until the ideas are digested and become an integral part of the mind, just as food well digested becomes part of the body.

Plain Words, with Feeling

There is a different kind of simplicity in this passage from an address by the late Senator Robert M. La Follette, a brilliant speaker. Here the words are short, and almost all of them are familiar to everyone. But they are not literal. They are full of emotion, full of pictures. For most everyday public speaking this style of words, with its warmth and humanness is especially effective.

. . . The youth of today are facing life amidst years of depression. They are without the alluring prospect of opportunity and adventure characteristic of the old frontier conditions. Is there for them any new frontier as challenging as the old?

I believe that there is such a frontier. Indeed, there are frontiers on every hand, requiring for their conquest all the oldtime courage and intelligence—frontiers ready to yield the oldtime satisfaction of achievement. We are dwellers in a continent still unfinished. We have yet to learn how to use to the best advantage the vast resources which nature offers. When we see the tragic effects of a great drought, or of the floods which sweep down our rivers, when we note the dust storms, the eroded and treeless hillsides, we realize that we do not yet know how to make the best use of the very fundamentals of existence—soil, water, plant and animal life. . . .

Examples of Color Words

In the next two examples the words are very different. They are chosen throughout to touch the imagination of the listeners and work upon their feelings. To do this well is not easy. It calls for a thorough knowledge of the meaning and the suggestions of words, for deep sincerity, and for sure taste. Most of us will probably have few if any occasions to use speeches which are so much devoted to the emotions. The examples are taken from two of the greatest orators of our history.

Martial Words

The first is from the famous address by Wendell Phillips on Toussaint L'Ouverture, the negro leader who won independence for Santo Domingo. In this, you will notice it is the warlike, martial emotions that the speaker seeks to arouse. Almost every sentence contains words which would quicken a listener's pulse.

. . . I am to tell you the story of a Negro, Toussaint L'Ouverture, who has left hardly one written line. I am to glean from the reluctant testimony of his enemies, men who despised him because he was a Negro and a slave, and hated him because he had beaten them in battle.

Cromwell manufactured his own army. Napoleon, at the age of twenty-seven, was placed at the head of the best troops Europe ever saw. Cromwell never saw an army till he was forty; this man never saw a soldier till he was fifty. Cromwell manufactured his own army—out of what? Englishmen—the best blood in Europe. Out of the middle class of Englishmen—the best blood of the island. And with it he conquered what? Englishmen—their equals. This man manufactured his army out of what? Out of what you call the despicable race of Negros, debased, demoralized by two hundred years of slavery, one hundred thousand of them imported into the island within four years, unable to speak a dialect intelligible even to each other. Yet out of this mixed, and, as you say, despicable mass he forged a thunderbolt, and hurled it at what? At the proudest blood in Europe, the Spaniard, and sent him home conquered; at the most warlike blood in Europe, the French, and put them under his feet; at the pluckiest blood in Europe, the English, and they skulked home to Jamaica. Now, if Cromwell was a general, at least this man was a soldier. . . .

Words of Pathos

The next example is from Colonel Robert G. Ingersoll's famous "Vision of War" delivered at the reunion of the Grand Army of the Republic. Here the appeal is to the emotions of pathos and sorrow. Robert Ingersoll was a master of language, and this address illustrates the power of highly emotional words.

The past rises before me like a dream. Again we are in the great struggle for national life. We are with the soldiers when they enlist in the great army of freedom. We see them part with those they love. Some are walking for the last time in quiet, woody places, with the maidens they adore. Others are bending over cradles, kissing babes that are asleep. Some are receiving the blessings of old men. Some are parting with mothers who hold them and press them to their hearts again and again, and say nothing. And some are talking with wives, and endeavoring with brave words, spoken in the old tones, to drive from their hearts the awful fear. We see them part. We see the wife standing in the door with the babe in her arms—standing in the sunlight sobbing. At the turn of the road a hand waves; she answers by holding high in her loving arms the child. He is gone, and forever.

We see them all as they march proudly away under the flaunting flags, keeping time to the grand, wild music of war—through the towns and across the prairies—down to the fields of glory, to do and to die for the eternal right. . . .

It is helpful to study such masterful examples of emotional wording. It is not a style which you will wish to employ in your own addresses. It is too far from the tone and atmosphere of most occasions, and to do it well takes the skill of an expert. But to practice imitating such emotional passages in private on subjects that really appeal to your own feelings will quicken your sensitiveness to the power of words and indirectly enrich your everyday speaking.

A Style to Study and Imitate

Sometimes it is very effective to talk in terms of vivid but simple illustrations. Note how well Newton D. Baker, a member of the Cabinet of Woodrow Wilson, used this method in the following passage from one of his addresses.

As you read and reread this passage aloud you will realize how full of meaning it is, how clear and direct in wording, and yet how *easy* and *natural.* It sounds like a man *conversing* with his audience. There is appeal to the feelings and the imagination, but you are never taken out of the atmosphere of friendly, easy conversation.

. . . I amuse myself sometimes by imagining that I am suddenly summoned into a room and introduced to Thomas Jefferson or Benjamin Franklin and am told by the person who summons me that Thomas Jefferson or Benjamin Franklin, as the case may be, has just arrived without any knowledge of the years since he left this earth, and that I am entrusted with the task of taking him out and introducing him to modern society. I am always curious to find what my own notion is: as to whether it would be harder to make Thomas Jefferson feel at home in the life we live than it would be if somebody were to take me back to his day, with all that I have and all that I depend on now, and I were to try to live the life he lived. I confess I have never been able to solve that enigma to my own satisfaction. I rather think that Jefferson or Franklin could more easily adapt himself to our life than we could adapt ourselves to their lives, and I suspect the reason that I think that is this: that education has become a very different thing from what it was in their day. . . .

In Jefferson's and Franklin's day it was possible, practically, to cover the compass of available knowledge and so to have one's sympathies catholic, one's curiosity as broad as the field of attainable knowledge. If Franklin were to come into this room at this minute and we were to try to introduce him to the electric light, it would only be a distinguished descendant of his kite string and so we shouldn't puzzle him very much. He would find soon that it would be very easy to adapt himself to the extension of knowledge in modern times—not acquire, probably, the technical facts that a highly trained specialist nowadays has, but to adapt himself to their use and to reconcile them to the rest of the knowledge he had and was acquiring because of the catholicity of his taste and the universality of his sympathy and curiosity. . . .

Ways to Improve

Here are three definite suggestions of ways in which you can improve your command of words for effective speaking, in addition to listening closely to speakers, and examining their printed speeches.

REVIEW A BOOK ON GRAMMAR

First, take some of your leisure moments to review systematically a book on grammar and a good book on English composition.

PRACTICE WRITING

Second, form the habit of taking a little time, day by day, to write your thoughts down. Take five minutes and put on paper what you think of the weather, or business, or languages—any subject you like. Put it down as though you were talking, not as though you were writing. See where you have made errors, and the next time you can spare five minutes, write again. See whether you cannot do better this time. This will aid in your conversational expression. You want to improve that expression, not merely for the time when you address an audience but for every time you talk, whether you are portraying ideas for one or for a hundred listeners.

USE THE DICTIONARY

Third, when you read, have a dictionary and a notebook handy. When you find a word whose meaning is not clear to you, look it up immediately. Put it down in the notebook, then go back to your reading. You will know how the word fits in with the context. Do not forget, however, that you have jotted it down. Refer to the notebook to recall the word. Make use of the word when occasion offers in your conversation. Make it your own, part of your vocabulary. You will be enriched by its use.

You cannot buy, borrow, or steal language. The only way to get it is by practice. You can enjoy yourself greatly in the practice. Language has no owner until you come along and claim it. You may look at the rich man's mansion and the look is all that will be yours. The ideas and language of the greatest minds, however, are yours to use, to take and possess as your own, and there will be none to dispute your ownership.

PART III

Improving Your Delivery

Chapter 13

IMPORTANCE OF CARE FOR DELIVERY

THE preceding chapters have discussed the problems of effective speaking from the standpoint of subject matter. We have considered how to determine the ideas you wish to convey and how to formulate them correctly and intelligently in language. But that is only a part of the problem of effective speaking. To get your idea into the mind of the other person, you must tell it to him so that he can hear. That involves problems of delivery—the actual physical presentation of the message to the hearer.

Care for Delivery Essential

These problems of delivery are almost as important as those of formulating the thought in language. Your message must be conveyed to other people by means of certain physical mechanisms—your voice, your looks and movements. If you fail to use these mechanisms skillfully you do not get your message through. If you give attention merely to planning the arrangement and wording of your ideas and stop there, you make the same mistake that Robinson Crusoe made when he built his boat in a forest and found, when it was completed, that he could not get it down to the water.

A great many people make this mistake. They have a message to communicate. They are in great earnest. They give the utmost care to determining what they want to say so that it will be accurate and complete. They develop it in orderly, logical form. They work over the statements and wording. And then they assume that all they need do is get up and talk, without considering the problems which are involved in the physical act of talking. Some of the most prominent of our public men have been utter failures on the platform because they seemingly could not master, and apparently would not try to study, the problem of delivery.

Waste from Carelessness

The radio people have learned that if you want to send a message effectively through the microphone, you must adapt yourself to certain conditions of radio talking. Otherwise, you get in your own way. The same thing is true in all talking, whether you are addressing an audience or conversing with an individual. You may not realize the fact because you have never given attention to it, but it is nevertheless true.

There is a remark of George Bernard Shaw which is very much to the point. Some years ago he made a series of phonograph records for an English association for the improvement of English speech. In one of these records, he said, "When I have to address an audience of a thousand people, I direct my voice so that everyone in the room can hear me easily. But when I talk to my wife across the breakfast table, she says to me, "Don't talk with your mouth full, and don't turn your face away, I can't hear you."

Practically everyone is constantly lessening the effectiveness of his talking, whether to audiences or in conversation, by failing to consider the problems of delivery. If you fail to consider these problems, you will not be clearly understood when you address other people. What you say may be irritating because it is clumsily transmitted. Or, you may not be heard at all.

Profit from Care for Delivery

On the other hand, if you do give attention to the matter of delivery, you can increase immensely the effectiveness of what you have to say. The tone of voice in which you utter a remark, your looks and movements while speaking, may reinforce powerfully the thing you are saying. Indeed, to a large extent, the delivery will often serve to convey the idea even without words. Years ago there was a famous Polish actress, Modjeska, who was accustomed to demonstrate this very fact. She would recite the multiplication table or the alphabet in Polish or French and move the audience to tears and laughter. The sounds meant nothing—the mere sounds. Her delivery, her manner of uttering them, however, conveyed emotion and even to a degree, ideas.

While this instance is extreme, you undoubtedly know of many cases in which a person has had his message in very poor shape from the standpoint of logic and language, and yet has conveyed it most powerfully because of his command of the mechanisms of delivery.

Very likely you have yourself been a victim in such a case. Some time or other you have attempted to present a matter, in which you had the facts clearly on your side, and then found yourself utterly defeated by some clever opponent, who had neither logic nor clarity of statement, but whose delivery impressed and charmed the listeners.

You Have the Power

Yet the mechanisms of delivery are at your disposal also. If you give attention to them, develop them, you can use them as effectively as that opponent did. But, whereas he had only the delivery without the substance behind him, you can give your audience the truth and drive it home by proper use of the art of delivery. For these mechanisms are not the special property of any few gifted individuals. Intelligent cultivation of the powers and faculties which you possess will render your talk immensely more interesting and more forceful. This is a contest in which the person who desires can win. Work at the techniques of delivery is certain to bring results. However inexpert you may be at the beginning, you can develop skill, power, and grace.

In succeeding chapters the mechanisms of delivery, what they are, and the principles that govern their effective use are explained. Directions and exercises are given by means of which you can learn to use them effectively yourself.

Don't Talk to Yourself

Consider, to begin with, a point that has been stressed so far in these chapters, that effective speaking is a matter of concentration upon the listener. To express your thought means to get it into the mind of the other person, to tell it so that he can grasp it. Unless you do that, you are not expressing your thought at all. You are merely talking to yourself. We have all heard people who do no more than that. They remind one of the individual who imagined he had formulated a theory as hard of comprehension, by the ordinary man, as the Einstein theory of relativity.

He was walking along the street, mumbling to himself, when an acquaintance stopped him and after bidding him the time of day, inquired why it was that he so often seemed to be talking without apparently having a listener. "No listener?" he said. "I have the most interested listener in the world. In the first place, I am talking to a gentleman, and in the second place, I am talking to the only individual in the world who understands my theories. I can appreciate myself if others do not."

That man was, frankly, talking to himself. Many a person does virtually the same thing without realizing it. However deeply interested a speaker may be in himself and his own ideas, he cannot convey that interest to other people unless he directs his attention toward them. This principle applies in the matter of determining the thought and of formulating it in language. Certainly it applies to the way you utter your words and what you look like when you are talking.

Appealing to Eye and Ear

In talking you must present your thought to the listener through the medium of his senses, his eyes, and his ears. Therefore your talk must be audible; you must be heard easily. If he has to strain his ears to catch what you are saying, he will grow physically weary however wonderful your thought may be. When he gets tired, he will stop listening. Beyond a doubt, also, he will have missed a part of what you are trying to say. Further, your talk must be in a form which is pleasing to his ears and eyes, so that he enjoys listening. All of us have had to listen to people whose voices were so harsh or whose appearance while talking was so grotesque that we were constantly repelled. In this case also, no matter how wonderful the thought may be, the speaker's clumsy presentation is constantly building resistance for him.

The Mechanisms of Delivery

For effective speaking, we need to use with constant skill the voice, the muscles of articulation, and the entire body.

All of us employ these mechanisms constantly in daily life. Sometimes, when we are at our best, we do it very skillfully. When we are in the grip of some strong emotion, so that our whole attention concentrates upon carrying our meaning to the listener before us, our physical apparatus becomes a perfect medium of transmission. Nature steps in and takes charge and we "speak out what is in us." As has been said, we may do this when we are thoroughly angry. We do it—sometimes at least—when we are in love. We do it when we are possessed by a real feeling of enthusiasm or pity.

But most of the time we lack any such complete control and coordination of our delivery apparatus. As George Bernard Shaw said whimsically of himself, "In periods of relaxation when we are not on duty, we are careless." The result is that our command of the techniques necessary for effective use of our delivery apparatus is unreliable, uncertain. For really effective speaking, you need to develop the same sure control of your apparatus which is possessed by the expert golfer, swimmer, or runner. By that is meant a control so complete and intelligent that it has become automatic and will function without conscious attention.

Developing Control

It is entirely possible to develop such control of your delivery apparatus. When that has been done, you can safely give your full attention either before an audience or in conversation, to the formulation of your ideas. You can do this because you know that your apparatus can carry through physically whatever ideas you wish to present. This is the case with every great actor. The actor has acquired such control of his voice, his looks, his movements, that his whole person is a well-tuned instrument which can express fully every shade of thought or feeling which he desires. But this skill is by no means confined to professional actors. There are instances beyond number of men and women in business and professional life who have attained very nearly the same perfect poise and effectiveness in delivery.

A Y.M.C.A. Leader

Years ago, a thoughtful but rather timid young man took charge of the Y.M.C.A. in a small college. No one certainly thought of him as a good speaker. His voice was light, his delivery hesitating. He could not build ideas together convincingly. But he was devoted to his work. It was necessary for him to address audiences, and little by little he learned to do it better. Thirty years after his unpropitious beginning, he had represented his organization in every quarter of the globe. He had addressed audiences of every character. He had become a man of the world with a voice of melody and power, a grace of posture and movement and sure persuasiveness in the presentation of his ideas.

A Business Man

Another instance is that of a young business man who took up the study of public speaking through a home study course. He had a good mind, but his delivery was utterly dull and wooden. His voice was harsh, his face about as expressive as a cigar store Indian. This man also, however, found it necessary to address audiences, and he was willing to learn. Gradually his stiff and wooden personality became supple and expressive. He became a most impressive speaker. His determination and his seriousness of nature reare unusual, but the stiffness is gone. He is able at any moment to relieve the tension of a situation with a touch of fancy or humor.

A Club Woman

Still another instance is that of a woman who in her early married life became interested in women's activities. She had unusual powers of analysis and organization, but she could not talk in public. In fact, she talked very little at any time. She was utterly averse to fluent expression. As time went on, however, it became necessary for this reticent woman to stand up more and more often and say what she thought, and little by little her original shyness and hesitation disappeared. Anyone who heard her on the public platform in recent years would suppose that the perfect poise and fluency which she manifests had been a matter of course with her always.

What these, and hundreds of others have done, you also can do. The following chapters will help you.

Removing Defects Important

We shall consider specifically the main aspects of delivery—voice, enunciation, and the silent expression of looks and movements. All of them are essential in fully effective speaking. You need to develop your voice in order to be heard. You need to gain control of the muscles of articulation so that you can utter the words distinctly and with correct pronunciation. You need to learn how to hold yourself and how to move when addressing an audience, so that you will not weaken the effect of your thought by an awkward appearance.

Gaining New Power

But with respect to all these features of delivery, the chief purpose is not to remove defects but to gain added power for effective speech and leadership.

Consider the matter of voice. If you use your voice properly, the sound of your talk has the charm of music. People will enjoy listening to you aside from their interest in what you may have to say. Even if your voice is today harsh, or broken, or breathy, it is entirely possible for you to make it an instrument of beauty.

With respect to enunciation, you need to be able to form the different sounds distinctly in order to make yourself understood, for you are conveying not sounds merely, but words which represent thoughts. If you can obtain full control of the muscles of articulation so that your utterance is clear and graceful and delicate, your enunciation acquires a positive, persuasive value. Precision and delicacy of utterance suggest to the listener that there is precision and delicacy in the action of your mind. And since enunciation is entirely a matter of muscle action, it is possible for you—for anyone who will work at it—to learn to utter the words you speak with perfect distinctness. Within a few months, your enunciation will improve to a degree that you might have thought impossible.

Finally, with respect to your looks and movements—your posture and gestures. Before you have begun to present a single thought the other person has sized you up through his eye. If it is a pleasure to look at you, that fact alone will powerfully reinforce whatever ideas you wish to express.

Preserve Your Individuality

In working at the problems of delivery, bear in mind that there are two great factors involved. The first factor is your own individuality. You are different from everyone else in the world. You talk with full effectiveness when you express your ideas in your own way. Therefore, never mimic anyone else, no matter how much you may admire his manner of speaking. Study and analyze the secret of his power or charm, but do not just copy the features you admire. Begin with your own thought. Realize it. Consider what it means. Then try to tell it to the particular listener you wish to reach. Take time in your private moments to practice, to rehearse little speeches. You may practice in front of a mirror so that you can see what you look like. You may utilize a phonograph or a dictaphone so that you can hear how you sound to other people. But in all your practicing and self-training, be sincere, throw yourself into the thing you are saying. Picture clearly in your mind the persons you wish to address, and then concentrate your thought upon them. In that way, you will develop a style of delivery which is your own.

Avoid Eccentricity

On the other hand, remember that you are a human being. Your voice, your body, are like those of other people. Just as you must move like other people when walking, running, or swimming, so in your talking you must necessarily follow the general customs of other people. There are limits to the free play of anyone's individuality. If you fail to observe them, you will fall into the error of that poor soul described earlier in this chapter. You will be talking to yourself. Effective speaking, you must not forget, means conveying your message to other people. Mastery of the art of delivery consists in learning how to manage your physical apparatus so as to make the fullest impression on the eyes and ears of others.

Study of delivery can begin at once. Your progress may for a while appear slow because it involves change of muscle habits. Like a setting-up drill, it involves getting rid of the old habits of slouchiness and carelessness, and implanting those of poise and coordination. But gradually, and surely, mastery will come. Month by month as you go on with this practice, you will find your powers of delivery responding more readily and with more steadiness to your demands.

A Fascinating Study

This study of delivery will be increasingly fascinating. When a person begins to train himself in effective speaking, he begins to concentrate upon the matter of formulating ideas in language. He relies upon appeal to the listener's mind by means of words and statements. Then as he grows more expert, he comes to realize little by little that much of the work of conveying ideas can be done more effectively through features of delivery. A look, a tone, a movement of the head may convey a thought more powerfully and far more swiftly than the most cogent verbal statement.

Chapter 14

BUILDING A GOOD VOICE

TO make your delivery effective, you must be heard. To make yourself heard, you have at your command the most marvelous musical instrument known to man. Power or weakness, heroism or cowardice, enthusiasm or dejection, hope or despair, every emotion or passion, every mental or physical state can be graphically portrayed by the voice. With your voice, you can run the gamut of the emotional experiences of mankind.

Making Yourself Heard

But to convey the expression of them, you must be heard. Can you do so? You can shout, of course, but to shout for any extended period of time is impossible. Your voice would become husky. You would suffer from irritation of the throat. You would be uncomfortable and so would your listeners. Shouting is out of the question.

Great speakers do not shout. If they did, they would not be great speakers. During the Civil War, Henry Ward Beecher went to England to stimulate enthusiasm for the cause of the Union. The sympathies of England were with the South. Sympathy for the Northern cause must be created. When he faced an audience at Liverpool, he found those present tumultuously hostile. Did he attempt to shout them down? No. His manner was quiet and tranquil; his voice was soothing, conversational and friendly. Because of that very quiet and friendly attitude, he was heard. He won his audience. Had he tried to outshout them, he would have failed.

Resonance the Secret

Beecher never shouted in his speeches. A great speech would lose some of its value if the speaker did nothing but shout. Your ear will help you to understand how easily the quiet voice can get results, provided it has *resonance.*

Wendell Phillips, who was a powerful speaker, held great audiences spellbound, stirred them intensely, moved them to action, but he never shouted. Most of the time, we are told, his voice was that of a "gentleman conversing." Neither did William Jennings Bryan shout. Nor Franklin D. Roosevelt. Nor Glenn Frank. All these men developed in their voices the invaluable quality of *resonance.*

Resonance May Be Developed

Often, when the remark is made that a certain individual has a very resonant voice, the implication is that resonance is something with which only the favored few are endowed by nature. That is not true; anyone can develop it. We want to get the most out of our efforts. Where resonance is lacking in the voice, effort is being wasted. In salesmanship, in social conversation, in contact with groups of people, large or small, the pleasant voice is a decided asset. For a voice to be pleasant it must be resonant. What your own voice needs is *resonance.* This chapter will show how to obtain it.

Necessary Condition—Mental Alertness

Before we begin, however, there is one thing you must learn, one habit you must begin to develop. That is the habit of mental alertness when talking. How does the individual with a tired, anemic, or lazy voice impress you? Either he lacks energy or he is suffering from some physical or mental ill. A healthy, resonant voice demands *mental wakefulness.* One cannot sleep and expect to keep others interested. If the speaker is healthy, virile, wide-awake physically and mentally, his voice will show it.

Open Your Mouth

Further, do not be afraid of your voice. There are many people, even professional men, teachers, and preachers, who have never used a full round tone. Whenever they talk, the sound of their voices is dull or pitched in a high tremolo. The voice seems to be squeezed out with force. Why? Not because they lack ability nor because they are afflicted with physical defects. The reason is that they have the habit of the lazy lower jaw. Some individuals never open their mouths fully except when eating. The lazy lower jaw, begotten from the habit of tightening the jaw muscles and endeavoring to talk through clenched teeth, prevents the voice from having fullness and robs it of resonance.

Therefore, open your mouth when you talk. A trained singer may be able to produce a wonderfully pleasant high note through almost closed lips, but never through clenched teeth. Moreover, the sound made by the singer is merely a sound. If he wanted to make it an understandable word, he would have to open his mouth.

What Resonance Means

Why is it necessary to open your mouth when you talk? The answer brings us to the explanation of the meaning of resonance, how it is produced, why it is lacking in some voices, and how it can be obtained.

Fullness plus Carrying Power

When we hear a sound that carries over a distance, retaining its fullness of quality, we say that sound is resonant. A shrill, harsh, high-pitched sound carries, but it is not resonant. It is merely piercing. *Resonance implies fullness with carrying power.* This is true whether the sound be made by the human voice, by a musical instrument, or by a simple tuning fork. We will take the tuning fork as an example of sound and resonance, and from it explain how this quality is attained by the voice.

A Matter of Vibration

By striking a tuning fork, the prongs are caused to vibrate. This vibration gives forth a faint sound which we detect by holding the fork close to the ear. If we want the sound to be louder, we shall have to reinforce it by giving it power. Strike the fork again and place the base of it on a wooden table. The vibration of the prongs sets up a sympathetic vibration in the wood of which the table is made. The sound now has become louder and has more of a ring to it. If, instead of a table, you placed the fork on a box, the sound would have still more volume. Place it on the bridge of a violin, and the sound that in the first instance was merely faint, can now be heard in any part of a large room.

Resonators

The table gave it carrying power; the box gave it greater volume; and the violin gave it not only carrying power, but fullness. The vibrations of the prongs of the fork were communicated to the bridge and through the bridge to the body of the violin itself. The wood in the instrument and the air inside of it vibrated in sympathy with the fork.

If you had a series of tuning forks, each one of a different pitch, your violin case would reinforce the sound of some one of them better than that of the others. Each sound can best be made resonant by some special size or shape of resonator. The correct resonator of our tuning fork will obtain for us the greatest power from the sound of the vibrating prongs.

The Resonators of the Human Voice

The human voice is something like the tuning fork. For prongs, we have vocal cords. The effect we obtain from striking the tuning fork is obtained in the voice by vibrating these cords with breath. The vibration of these cords alone gives us a very feeble sound, just as the sound from the tuning fork was feeble. We must use resonators to reinforce the sound. But nature has endowed human beings with variable resonators. That is something of which no musical instrument yet devised by man can boast. The resonators for the voice change with the tone. They assume the shape that will give perfect resonance to the sound we are making at the moment. They change, therefore, with every tone of voice.

If you wish to develop your voice, so that it has the full carrying quality that marks the voices of good speakers, do not think of the vocal cords; think of resonators.

As soon as the vocal cords start vibrating, the sound caused by this vibration is reinforced by a series of cartilage rings, located just above the cords in the larynx itself. It is given further power at the back of the throat in the nasopharynx. The sound, then, as it were, is split into two streams, one to find further resonance in the nasal cavities back of the nose and in the head, known as the sinuses, the other part enlarged in the mouth cavity.

Avoiding Nasal Quality

Interfering with this passage of the sound causes improper voice production. Cut off the mouth cavity and allow the sound to travel up to the sinuses only and you have *nasality*—a heavy, thick, clouded tone of voice. Cut off the sinuses and allow the tone to be reinforced only by the mouth cavity and you have what is known as the *nasal* tone. Both will result in lack of resonance. The nasal voice may carry but its high, shrill quality will not be pleasant. It has no body. It lacks fullness. The sound, to be correct, must come from the nose and mouth at the same time. If you doubt this, hum quietly any note. Keep the lips loosely closed. You will get the sound through the nose without a nasal quality. While humming, open your mouth and you will get the same tone of voice with more fullness and power. Both the nasal and mouth cavities are combining to make the voice pleasant, resonant, full.

A Helpful Exercise

A nasal tone, or nasality, may be caused by tongue obstruction, stiffened throat muscles, malformed soft palate, or a diseased growth in the nasal cavities. To overcome the defect, if it be due to the soft palate, the following exercise will help. Take a small hand mirror and allow the light to shine upon it. Open your mouth fully to enable you to see, by the light reflected from the mirror, whether or not the opening at the back of the throat forms a perfect double arch. If one side is drawn down while the other is high, or if the opening is small, you need exercises which will build up what are called the pillars of the fauces—two muscular arches which support the soft palate. This exercise will not take much of your time, but it must be practiced consistently. At first, do it before a mirror, so that you can see what is happening at the back of your throat.

Another Exercise

Open your mouth fully and pant like a dog. You will notice in your mirror that the uvula—which is the little point of flesh hanging in the center of the soft palate—will begin to swing back and forth. This exercise of the uvula will build up the muscular walls and raise the soft palate to its proper position. Do this for not more than a minute or two at a time. But do it repeatedly, through the day, whenever you think of it.

Let us return to the tuning fork. When you strike a tuning fork, the sound given forth is a simple sound. If, however, you strike two tuning forks of different pitches at the same time, by vibrating together they cause the sound to be complex. Now your voice—every human voice—gives forth only complex sounds. Every tone produced by the voice is made up of a number of different vibrations which are called the fundamental tone and the overtones. This variety of tone gives the voice not only its carrying power but its pleasant quality. That is what makes harmony of voice. Your voice, therefore, is always producing complex sounds. This adding of tones is done in the resonators.

Think of Head Resonance

When you think of voice, think of it as though it were up in your head and not in the throat. You cannot control the vocal chords or the resonators. In other words, you cannot think of placing these organs in a certain position and have them assume that position. Instead of thinking of the position of these organs, the trained singer must think of *tone,* and the vocal chords automatically take the proper position for beginning that tone. The resonating cavities assume the form to give that particular tone beauty and carrying power. This is true with both the singer and the speaker. Let the tone rise up into the head. Feel the vibration at the back of the nose. Feel it on the roof of the mouth just back of the teeth at the same time. When you have this feeling in both places at once, you are vocalizing correctly and your voice will have sufficient carrying power for all the demands you can make upon it.

An Exercise on "NG" Sounds

The following exercise will help you. In practicing it, be careful not to put any tension on the muscles of the throat or jaw. Do not stiffen the tongue. Spread the nostrils to prevent tension of the upper lip. Now practice syllables or words ending in "ng" such as "ming," "wing," "sing," "thing," "ring," and any others of which you can think. In pronouncing them, endeavor to feel the vibration back of the nose and back of the upper teeth on the hard palate. Practice this in a monotone; that is, do not vary the sound. Use the same tone throughout the entire exercise. Learn from this the correct feeling that should go with voice production. Practice will implant right habits, and correct habits will give you results.

Apply the same method to sentences and short passages such as the following, in which the sound of "ng" is prominent:

> Once upon a midnight dreary, while I pondered, weak and weary,
> Over many a quaint and curious volume of forgotten lore—
> While I nodded, nearly napping, suddenly there came a tapping,
> As of some one gently rapping, rapping at my chamber door,
> "Tis some visitor," I muttered, "tapping at my chamber door—
> Only this, and nothing more."
>
> —From "The Raven," by EDGAR ALLEN POE

And there was mounting in hot haste: the steed,
The mustering squadron, and the clattering car,
Went pouring forward with impetuous speed,
And swiftly forming in the ranks of war;
And the deep thunder peal on peal afar;
And near, the beat of the alarming drum
Roused up the soldier ere the morning star;
While throng'd the citizens with terror dumb,
Or whispering, with white lips, "The foe! they come! they come!"

—From "Childe Harold's Pilgrimage," by LORD BYRON

Treat these passages as exercise material, reading them aloud. Bet ter yet, memorize and recite them, day after day. Whenever you repeat them, sound the "ng" syllables, wherever they occur, with extra fullness and care.

Now take another step by applying the same treatment to printed speeches you read, and to ordinary prose. Apply it to pages of this chapter. Turn back and read aloud short passages on the preceding pages, featuring the words containing "ng" syllables.

Exercise on "N" Sounds

Then, after working on the "ng" syllables for some time, include those in which "n" sounds are prominent: "nine," "name," "known," "neither," "dinner," "send," "honor," and other words you can add to the list. In making these sounds also, one tends to speak with resonance.

Practice such passages as the following:

Sink or swim, live or die, survive or perish, I give my hand and my heart to this vote. It is true indeed that in the beginning we aimed not at independence. But there's a Divinity which shapes our ends. The injustice of England has driven us to arms, and, blinded to her own interest for our good, she has obstinately persisted, till independence is now within our grasp. . . .

I leave off, as I began, that live or die, survive or perish, I am for the Declaration. It is my living sentiment, and by the blessing of God it shall be my dying sentiment, independence *now,* and independence forever.

A man's country is not a certain area of land,—of mountains, rivers, and woods,—but it is principle; and patriotism is loyalty to that principle. . . .

So Nathan Hale, disdaining no service that his country demands, perishes untimely, with no other friend than God and the satisfied sense of duty. . . . So, through all history from the beginning, a noble army of martyrs has fought fiercely and fallen bravely for that unseen mistress, their country.

Fight on, thou brave true heart, and falter not, through dark fortune and through bright. The cause thou fightest for, so far as it is true, is very sure of victory. The falsehood alone of it will be conquered, as it ought to be: but the truth of it is part of Nature's own laws, co-operates with the World's eternal tendencies, and cannot be conquered.

Passages in which "n" sounds are prominent are more common than those which feature "ng" sounds. You will find examples everywhere—on many pages of this book, for instance. It will be beneficial to you to look for them in written speeches by reading a passage slowly aloud and *listening* to discover the presence of the "ns."

Effect on Your Speaking

Gradually, as you continue this practice and experimentation, you will find yourself giving slightly more prominence to the "ng" and "n" sounds in your own talk, all of it. This will not be enough to make your talking sound affected; the truth is that in the past you have probably been unduly suppressing these sounds. What may appear to you to be emphasis upon them is only giving them their proper attention.

These simple exercises, if you keep on with them faithfully, will help you greatly to develop resonance in your voice in all your talking.

Practice Singing

Practice singing. Singing is one of the best possible methods of beginning the development of the speaking voice. The notion which some people have that they cannot sing is an absurd one. Just as anyone who can walk can also run, so anyone who can speak can sing. We are not thinking of singing solos, but of producing singing tones. You can do that.

Therefore, practice singing a few words, any tune you think of or no tune at all, just a sort of chant. Do it gently, without any effort whatever, just producing the feeling that you had when practicing on the "ng" sound. Begin to notice the mouth and jaws of other people as they sing or speak. You will soon learn to tell whether they have muscular freedom. When you go to a movie, watch the actors in the picture as they speak or sing. If the voices are pleasant, you will notice the loose lower jaw.

The use of the voice in speaking is just the same as the use of the voice in singing. The real difference is mental and not physical. In singing the artist must be as familiar with tone thoughts as you are with ideas. The singer thinks tones; the speaker thinks the idea. The voice of the speaker automatically takes on the tones that will best express the idea. That tone, however, will be resonant and pleasing if the voice is allowed freedom of action. The clearer the idea, the clearer and more forceful will be the vocal picture of it.

Replacing Bad Habits with Good Ones

Nature endowed each one of us, except in rare instances, with a perfect sound mechanism. Each of us has a pleasant voice. The only thing that can obstruct it is wrong habits. These wrong habits very often come from imitation. A child constantly coming in contact with people who have harsh, disagreeable, nasal, or throaty voices, will acquire by imitation the habits that will give it the same defective voice. The child coming in contact with people who have agreeable, pleasant voices will, of necessity, have a pleasant voice. We learn through imitation; we imitate sounds as we imitate actions. Our pronunciation of words is at first imitation. The voice with which we pronounce those words is again imitation of that with which we have become familiar.

You have a good instrument with which to produce sound. If imitation has led you to perform on that instrument in an incorrect fashion, practice can correct the habits which interfere with its full musical quality and resonance. Do not forget that vocal sound production is a mental rather than a physical action. When talking, therefore, concentrate upon the idea, the mental pictures you wish to express and not upon the mechanism with which it is to be made vocal. In other words, do not think voice when you are talking; think ideas.

Reading Aloud

The "ng" exercise in this chapter for practice will help free your voice. *Repeated practice begets habit.* Do not, of course, think about the "ng" exercise when you are talking to a friend, a business prospect, a group, in your business, your club, or your lodge. That exercise is merely for private practice.

On the other hand, you can use this exercise very profitably when reading aloud. Having the words on the printed page before you, pronounce them so that you will get the sensation of vibration in the resonating cavities, as described above.

Singing in the Bathroom

Do you sing in the bathroom? Many of us do. Many men find that the bathroom is the only place in the house where they can sing and shout without being afraid that their families will think they have gone crazy. Individuals who seem to be without any vocal powers ordinarily, have remarkable resonance of voice in the bathroom. We love to hear the sounds we can produce then. The voice seems to have a ring to it. It has power. We are thrilled by its remarkable qualities.

The presence of water and metal piping aids in giving carrying power to sound. The acoustic properties of the room are good. But more than that, you are usually relaxed. This is the chief reason for the good quality of the sound, when you give yourself a bathroom operetta. The muscles that aid in the production of sound are loose and free. Therefore, we are pleased with the sound. *We feel we have a pretty good voice. We have. All of us.* Practice bathroom singing by all means. Vary it occasionally and change from singing into speaking. Make a bathroom speech. Recite a piece of poetry and get the same resonance in the voice that you experience in singing. It can be done. By listening to yourself talk, you can prove to your entire satisfaction that your voice has resonance. It will carry. It has power if you allow it to be free.

Training the Ear

Listening to yourself talk will help to train the ear. Listen to good speakers. Listen to good singers. Watch the muscular movement of the lower jaw, the throat, and the distended nostrils. Watch, while you listen to the beauty and resonance of their tones. Then listen to yourself and recognize the quality of your voice. You can tell whether its production is full, whether it has carrying power, and whether it is flexible.

Making the Voice Flexible

Flexibility of voice is necessary for beauty. A singer who attempted to render a selection which demanded the repetition of a single note throughout the entire song would give his hearers a decidedly unpleasant sensation. Savages call that singing; civilized people call it monotonous. Tones must be varied in speaking, just as in singing, if they are to give us any pleasure. Variations of tone are what keep sound pleasant. You do vary your tones when you converse. Singing will help you to bring out this variation. Listen to yourself sing; listen to yourself talk.

First-Aid Advice

You may be thinking perhaps, that all this practice is very well for the future, but you wish to talk today—tomorrow. You may have a business interview this afternoon. There may be a meeting tonight at which you wish to talk. You wish advice that will help you right now. Well, then, go ahead and talk. Use the voice which you now have; just be careful that you open your mouth when you talk. You do not need much practice to make that a habit. Opening the mouth will allow the sound to come forth without being obstructed by your teeth.

And one other first-aid suggestion! You are standing up, and about to talk. Whether or not you will be heard will depend upon where you are *sending* your voice.

Throwing Your Voice

There are fifty men in the room. You are standing in one corner; one of your fellow members is in the opposite corner. Can you make him hear you? Certainly you can. Look at him and talk *to him*. If you do that your voice will carry. He will hear you and everyone else in the room will be able to hear. Your voice will carry to each individual. Once you have the feeling of how your voice is traveling to that far corner, you need not keep looking in that direction. You can change your position. You can look at some other person in the room. You will be able to continue with the same resonance in your voice.

Use the Lower Tone

But remember, do not shout. Do not shriek. If you do, you will tire quickly, and your hearers will tire even more quickly. Do not pitch your voice way up to high C; bring it down low. Contrary to popular practice, the lower tones, provided they are not forced, have the greatest carrying power. When we say low tone, we do not mean a basso profundo. Use the natural lower or middle tone of your voice. It will then be more flexible, more pleasant, and will give ease to your speaking. You will not tire quickly. Shouting does not produce volume. It defeats the very purpose for which it is used. The sound of the tuning fork cannot be given greater power by striking it more forcefully. Shouting means forcing the voice. This very forcing tightens the throat muscles and obstructs resonance.

Your Tone Has Personality

Do you think your voice is not as pleasant as it should be? Does it seem harsh or nasal? Do not let that keep you from making a start. Very few speakers have perfect voices. We demand a smooth, pleasant, full-rounded voice from the professional orator. We expect that he has had the necessary training over an extended period to give him a professional voice. But the business man faces no such severe standard. One asset your voice has right now. It has personality. It expresses *you*. Your friends and acquaintances can recognize you from your voice. When you call someone on the telephone, the person at the other end of the wire salutes you by name as soon as he hears you speak.

Correct use of your voice, with practice of the exercises described in this chapter, will help to give it a pleasant personality. Therefore, set about improving your voice. Improve it every time you express yourself; in conversation; in your business interview; in your utterance before a group. Then the quality of your voice, the tones you use to express your ideas, will help you to convince, to sway, to lead.

"Lift Up Your Voice; Be Not Afraid"

The thought of this chapter may well be summarized in the words of the Prophet Isaiah: "Lift up your voice, lift it up, be not afraid."

In other words, use your voice freely. It has personality. It has resonance which will manifest itself if you relax. It will answer your demands.

Use the middle tones. Open your mouth. Talk to the man at the far corner of the room.

Do not think about exercises while conversing or addressing an audience, but think the idea. Meanwhile, in your private hours, practice the exercises faithfully.

Chapter 15

BREATHING

THE voice demands adequate breath. Without breath as the motive power, it cannot function. We have used the tuning fork to illustrate voice production. By striking the fork we made the prongs vibrate and give forth sound, and we compared the vibrations of the prongs to the vibrations of the vocal cords. But in the human voice it is breath which sets the cords in motion. The sound is made by the vibration of the edges of the cords between which the breath is flowing.

Breathing Generally Automatic

We hardly ever think about the way we breathe. In relation to life generally, and except in connection with the use of the voice in singing, speaking, and in some athletic activities, breathing is an automatic physical action. It was started as a reflex action at the moment of our birth. When air is exhaled from the lungs, it is done by muscular action. The air forced from the lungs, causes a partial vacuum. As we were taught in physics, "Nature hates a vacuum." So fresh air rushes into the lungs to restore the supply. The blood demands oxygen, and by inhaling fresh air we supply it. But we do not, normally, think about regulating breath or breathing any more than we think of regulating our heartbeats.

Conscious Control for Public Speaking

On the other hand, while the heartbeat is automatic and cannot be affected by will, it is possible to modify and guide our breathing by will, and for the purposes of effective speaking it is necessary to do so. That is what we are to consider in this chapter.

This discussion of breathing, however, applies mainly to public speaking, addressing audiences of some size. Ordinary speech—ordinary conversation—does not call for any conscious control of breath.

In Conversation, Breathing Is Automatic

You leave your office and on the way out meet a friend. You greet him with "How do you do?" No thought is given to the matter of breath. You express your sentiments because the very fact that you see your friend and wish to greet him is the inspiration which carries with it sufficient breath power to say the words which convey your greeting. The breath is there. You always have enough breath to express your ideas, provided your ideas are clear, if you know what you want to say. When conversing do you recollect ever having to halt in the midst of a statement to replenish your breath supply? We all make pauses in conversation, but not for the purpose of breathing. Our pauses help to convey our ideas. In these pauses we do inhale a supply of fresh air, but this is done without any conscious effort.

In fact, we can talk with a very small reserve supply of breath. Prove it to yourself. Exhale as much breath as possible. Now, without inhaling, say four or five words. You may feel uncomfortable for the moment, but you can talk although your voice will not have its usual power. The only time your breath is insufficient in conversation is when you are laboring under intense excitement, after you have taken strenuous exercise, or if you are suffering from some physical ailment.

Deep Breathing for Public Address

For singing, however, for many forms of physical exercise, and for public speaking it is necessary to acquire and maintain a degree of conscious control over breathing. At least it is necessary to acquire the habit of breathing in a certain way. The right kind of breathing, that is, deep and full, is very closely allied to the health of the individual. Good health, as stated in the last chapter, is necessary for a vigorous voice. It is just as necessary if you wish your expression to be vivid, forceful, and entertaining. Poor health means lack of vigor. When vigor is lacking, expression tends to be insipid.

The Mechanism of Breath

To make it possible to produce the kind of tones described earlier, you need to give some consideration to the physical mechanism which controls breath. The bagpipes, the musical instrument of the Scotch—we may call it a musical instrument through courtesy since even the Scotchman acknowledges that when playing the bagpipes he must walk up and down in an endeavor to get away from the noise—is played by inflating a bag with air. By pressure of the arm, the air is forced out into horns. This forcible expulsion causes the reeds in the horns to vibrate, thereby making sound.

Action of the Lungs

The human lungs are like that bag. They are filled with air by the act of inhalation. The air rushes into the lungs, causing them to fill up the space known as the thoracic cavity. By contraction of the muscles of this cavity, the air is expelled between the vocal cords. These two muscular tissues have come close together and have been stretched for the purpose of making sound. They have assumed the position for the sound demanded at the moment. The stream of air or breath comes between the vocal cords steadily and easily. As a result, they vibrate and emit one note or a succession of notes. The bags or lungs that hold the air to vibrate the cords must not be cramped. Correct breathing demands, therefore, that the lungs have the largest possible space in which to expand. This means that all the diameters of the chest must be used to enlarge the thoracic cavity.

Expanding the Lungs

The lungs must be given the opportunity to extend downward. This necessitates the stretching of the muscular wall, called the "diaphragm," which separates the chest from the abdominal cavity. The lungs must also expand to either side. To give them the room for this expansion, the muscles between the ribs, called the "intercostals," must extend the ribs outward. Further, to enlarge the cavity toward the rear, there must be an expansion toward the back which calls into use the dorsal muscles. Finally, the lungs must expand upward and for that purpose the chest must be lifted. This does not, however, call for raising the shoulders.

Raising the Chest

Diaphragmatic breathing, which is dwelt upon very greatly in the training of singers and speakers, is only part of the movement necessary for correct deep breathing. Practice breathing consciously, then, in such a way that you will make use of all the movements mentioned above. Most important of all, *raise the chest in this practice of breathing.* Get the habit of keeping it raised even when the breath has been exhaled. This upholding of the chest can and should be done by muscular effort. It does not demand a great amount of air in the lungs to act as a prop. The habit of keeping the chest raised will lend support to your voice. The sound that is reinforced in the resonating cavities will be given added fullness by the vibrations communicated to the chest, thereby adding to the power of your voice.

A Well-Developed Chest

Voice resonance, which we discussed in the preceding chapter, has its foundation in the chest cavity. A well-developed chest, which means greater lung capacity, is necessary for a good voice. You will be able to state your ideas more effectively. Your voice will be adequate, so that you can be heard. Further, the raised chest is an asset in any line of endeavor. When you feel discouraged, when you feel depressed, raise your chest and drink in encouragement. Note how the depressed feeling vanishes. The raised chest gives the speaker an appearance of confidence and authority which will aid in making him effective.

Accordingly, here are a number of exercises which are designed to develop lung capacity and thereby add to the resonance of your voice.

EXERCISE I

Before getting up in the morning, remove your pillow and, lying flat on your back, place one hand on the lower ribs, the other lightly on the abdomen. Relax. Give up your whole weight to the bed. Now, inhale through the nostrils slowly, evenly, and deeply, while mentally counting one, two, three, four, etc. While inhaling, notice (a) the abdomen gradually expanding, (b) the sides extending through the expansion of the lower ribs, (c) the rise of the chest as you inhale. *The shoulders are not raised.* Hold the breath while you mentally count four (four seconds), then let the breath go suddenly, and notice the collapse of the abdomen and lower chest. Remember, *the inspiration must be slow and deep, the expiration sudden and complete.* Practice this preliminary exercise for not more than ten minutes each morning for a week. The second week hold the breath six seconds, instead of four, and gradually increase the time. *Do not overdo it.*

While the exercise may be taken at first in bed, this is but a preliminary to similar practice standing in easy poise.

Give the throat and trunk perfect freedom; dress the neck and body loosely; stand erect, evenly upon the balls of the feet; the body straight but not strained. Place the hands on the hips, so as to free the chest from the weight of the arms. Raise the back of the head slightly without bending the neck. This will straighten the spine, raise the chest and bring the *abdomen backward* into its proper place.

EXERCISE II

Inhale as in I; hold the breath four counts (seconds) or more; then vigorously expel the air in one breath through the wide open mouth. Vary this exercise with the next.

EXERCISE III

Inhale very slowly and steadily through the smallest possible opening of the lips, while mentally counting; hold two to four counts; then expel the air in one quick exhalation through the wide open mouth.

EXERCISE IV

Place the hands against the sides, thumbs well back; take, through the nostrils or the slightly parted lips, six short gasp breaths, *moving the ribs out at the side* with each breath. Hold the breath two counts, and exhale through the mouth with six short puffs, *drawing the ribs in at the side* with each puff.

EXERCISE V

Inhale as in I, while mentally counting, one, two, three, four, etc., until the inhalation seems complete. Hold the breath four or more counts; then exhale through the nostrils slowly and smoothly while counting to the number reached in the inspiration. The number of counts can be gradually increased. Do not force the increase. Practice these exercises with an open throat; let the breathing muscles control the outgoing air.

EXERCISE VI

Inhale through the nostrils quickly, deeply and forcefully (one count); hold two counts; exhale through the nostrils as slowly as possible while mentally counting, one, two, three, four, etc. With practice you will be able gradually to increase the number of counts for the exhalation.

EXERCISE VII

For quick refreshment after fatigue, and for use always at the close of your exercises, inhale slowly through the nostrils a full breath; hold two to four counts, then purse the lips tightly and expel the breath in small puffs of air, puff one, hold two counts, puff one, and so on until the exhalation is complete. This has been called ventilating and sweeping the lungs. This simple exercise is of great value.

If you have not at present a good lung capacity, these exercises will help your development. If, before expressing yourself, and during your talk, you had to inhale consciously, you would probably crowd the lungs to their full capacity. Lack of breath gives you an oppressed feeling; and oversupply of breath will give you a choked feeling. Do not, except in exercising, endeavor to *take in all the breath* which your lungs are capable of holding. Doing that will not make expression easier.

But get the habit of taking good, deep breaths, at all times. This habit will stand you in good stead in speaking and in improving your health. Effective use of the breath in speech must be based upon this habit.

Now let us consider the matter of using your breath in producing tones, for public speaking or singing.

In producing tones you drive out the breath across the vocal chords, thus causing them to vibrate. Take, therefore, this exercise:

EXERCISE VIII

Breathe deeply, and drive out the breath steadily and firmly, as you mentally count one, two, three, etc., in Exercises V and VI. Now, however, count aloud instead of mentally. This will give you practice in sounding several *different words* with the chest raised. Now sound the following short sentences in the same way:

As if it were but yesterday, you recall him, the Massachusetts soldier.

He had but just turned twenty. The tint of youthful health was in his cheek.

He knew nothing of the web and woof of politics, but he knew the needs of his country.

His ideal was Philip Sidney, not Napoleon.

Do you ask who he was?
He was in every regiment and every company.
He sleeps in every Massachusetts burying ground.

You will be sounding each of the words *with solid breath support;* that is, the impulse to breathe out will come from deep in the lungs, particularly from the diaphragm.

Further, the words will come out, not jerkily, one by one, but steadily, evenly. If you were to force out the breath too vigorously—a hard separate push on every word—that would produce tones that would be strained, choked, and comparatively weak. Let the breath *flow* out steadily but easily.

Do Not Drive Out All the Air

Also, you will not try to drive out all the air that is in your lungs. The lungs should remain half-filled with air, even at the close of the sentence. While it is not possible to drive out all the air from your lungs, it is possible, if you are not careful, to exhaust it to the point of oppression. Do not endeavor, at any time, when talking, to exhaust your breath power. Lack of breath will take the force out of your voice. Talking to an audience will exhaust you quickly if you are wasting breath. This waste of breath is usually caused by trying to force the voice. Force does not mean power; it only means wasted effort.

Half-empty lungs lower the pitch of the tone, lessen the resonance, and weaken the voice, causing the last word of the sentence to die away and become inaudible. Do not force your voice and in that way waste breath. There must be enough breath in your lungs to produce the full, proper vibrations, both for the beginning and the end of your sentences.

An Exercise on Entire Passages

Now apply the same method to an entire paragraph or group of paragraphs. For your convenience, places to pause for breath have been marked in the extracts here given. You will find that even elaborate passages such as the following can be uttered with ease, if the speaker has steady control of his breath.

The first is from a famous speech by Edmund Burke in the British House of Commons.

I impeach Warren Hastings, Esquire, of high crimes and misdemeanors.

I impeach him in the name of the Commons of Great Britain,/ in Parliament assembled,/ whose parliamentary trust he has betrayed.

I impeach him in the name of the Commons of Great Britain,/ whose national character he has dishonored.

I impeach him in the name of the people of India,/ whose laws, rights and liberties he has subverted,/ whose property he has destroyed,/ whose country he has laid waste and desolate.

I impeach him in the name,/ and by virtue of/ those eternal laws of justice which he has violated.

I impeach him in the name of human nature itself,/ which he has cruelly outraged, injured and oppressed,/ in both sexes,/ in every age, rank, situation and condition of life.

The next is from Webster's Reply to Hayne, in the United States Senate:

When my eyes shall be turned to behold for the last time the sun in heaven,/ may I not see him shining on the broken and dishonored fragments of a once glorious Union;/ on States dissevered, discordant, belligerent:/ on the land rent with civil feuds./ or drenched, it may be, in fraternal blood!/ Let their last feeble and lingering glance rather behold the gorgeous ensign of the Republic,/ now known and honored throughout the earth,/still full high advanced,/ its arms and trophies streaming in their original luster,/ not a stripe erased or polluted,/ nor a single star obscured,/ bearing for its motto no such miserable interrogatory as "What is all this worth?"/ nor those other words of delusion and folly,/ "Liberty first and Union afterwards,"/ but everywhere,/ spread all over in characters of living light,/ blazing on all its ample folds,/ as they float over the sea and over the land,/ and in every wind under the whole heavens,/ that other sentiment,/ dear to every true American heart/—Liberty *and* Union, now and forever, one and inseparable!

The third is from a Decoration Day Address by Justice Oliver Wendell Holmes of the United States Supreme Court.

To the indifferent inquirer/ who asks why Memorial Day is still kept, we may answer,/ it celebrates and solemnly reaffirms from year to year/ a national act of enthusiasm and faith./ It embodies in the most impressive form our belief/ that to act with enthusiasm and faith is the condition of acting greatly./ To fight out a war,/ you must believe something and want something with all your might./ So must you do to carry anything else to an end worth reaching./ More than that,/ you must be willing to commit yourself to a course,/ perhaps a long and hard one,/ without being able to forsee exactly where you will come out./ All that is required of you is that you should go somewhere as hard as ever you can./ The rest belongs to fate.

The last is from an address by Owen D. Young at the dedication of the Harvard School of Business.

Here in America, we have raised the standard of political equality./ Shall we be able to add to that, full equality in economic opportunity?/ No man is wholly free until he is both politically and economically free./ No man with an uneconomic and failing business is free./ He is unable to meet his obligations/ to his family, to society, and to himself./ No man with an inadequate wage is free./ He is unable to meet his obligations to his family, to society, and to himself./ No man is free who can provide only for physical needs./ He must also be in a position to take advantage of cultural opportunities./ Business,/ as the process of coordinating men's capital and effort in all fields of activity,/ will not have accomplished its full service/ until it shall have provided the opportunity for all men to be economically free./

Breathing Points in a Passage

In uttering impassioned or earnest passages such as these, you will need to give some attention to the places to pause for breath. If you try to utter too many words in one breath your voice will be strained and weak. If you stop too frequently for breath, your speech will be jerky, perhaps somewhat incoherent. You will find it both interesting and profitable to analyze various speeches you may have the opportunity to read. Reading aloud, with proper enthusiasm and expression, the speeches of men and women who are expert in the art of public address will train your own ear, and guide you in building your own speeches in word groups that are easy to speak with expressiveness.

For, of course, the purpose of analyzing the speeches of other people is to guide you consciously or subconsciously in the composition and delivery of your own speeches.

Too Rigid Control Unwise

If this book were intended for *singers,* we might spend a great deal of time on the subject of consciously controlling breath. The singer in this practice must give great attention to this point, because in singing he will, at times, have to hold a tone from fifteen to twenty seconds. In speaking, however, we do not hold one tone for any length of time. We use sounds that are almost like the staccato notes in singing. We do not dwell on any one note. In addition, the singer is expressing ideas and emotions that have been set down by the composer. He is an interpreter and on that account his art calls for a mechanical precision, a practiced inspiration and expression of the voice. The greater his art, the less apparent is the mechanical aspect of his rendition, but this must always be the foundation.

You as a speaker will not be doing a mechanical thing. You will be expressing your own ideas. You will be clothing these ideas in your own words. Your voice will give color to that which you say. The color you use will best express what *you* think. As a speaker, whether in conversation or in everyday public speaking, you need pay comparatively little attention to the breath, sentence by sentence.

Avoiding Breathiness of Tone

The danger of thinking about breath when talking is that you are apt to expel too much of it. This not only forces the tone but also causes a defect which in a singer is called "breathiness of tone." In the speaker or conversationalist, "breathiness of tone" can mar his talk. Listen to some of the radio speakers and you may get an example of it. Notice how disagreeable and distracting to the listener is the speech which makes audible the exhalation and hurried gasps for breath.

Singing instructors who follow the old Italian method of teaching use a candle flame to show how little breath should be expended in vocalization. In singing before a lighted candle, they say, with the lips fairly close to the flame, there should be no flicker or wavering of the light. Try it. Hold a lighted candle before your lips and sing the vowel "E"—as in the word "men." Do not forget while doing this to get the feeling of vibration back of the nose and just back of the teeth in the hard palate. If your singing causes the flame to waver as though in a draught, you will be expending too much breath on the sound.

When you are speaking, you naturally will have to pronounce consonants. If you try speaking before a lighted candle, the flame will flicker because of the explosive quality of some speech sounds. Only when singing vowel sounds can the candle test be used.

Breathing through the Nose

You very often hear it said that "we should always breathe through the nose." Ordinarily this admonition should be followed. The nose acts as a sort of filter to catch dust and germs, which if inhaled through the mouth, might cause irritation. When you are talking, however, whether in ordinary conversation or when you are endeavoring to impress a group, *it is not always possible to breathe through the nose.* If, at such times, you attempted to inhale through the nose exclusively, you would distract your hearers. You would call attention to your periodic closing of the mouth and your drawing in of air through the nostrils. We should, ordinarily, from habit, breathe through the nostrils, but when talking or singing, we may have to breathe through the mouth.

If you have difficulty in breathing through the nose, the cause may be some defect or growth in the nose or nasopharynx, unless you are suffering from a head cold. Such obstruction not only impedes breathing and affects the resonance of your voice, but impairs your health. Your remedy is to see a good physician.

A Summary of Suggestions

Now to sum up what has been said about breathing. Proper breathing is essential to effective speaking, for without it you cannot produce good resonant tones.

For the speaker, the thing to do is to acquire the *habit of deep breathing at all times.* Then his voice will always be firm and resonant. Take the utmost care to acquire this habit in your breathing all day long, whether talking or sitting silent at your desk.

When you speak, whether before an audience or in conversation, start every word from the diaphragm; have firm breath-pressure behind it. But do not make hard work out of your breathing, even when you have to address a large audience in a large room.

Filling your lungs to their utmost capacity or overcrowding them with air has a bad effect upon the sound of your voice. There must be a free but not forcible flow of air past the vocal cords. As has been said earlier, if you would produce your voice sounds correctly, you must do so with ease. The same can be said of breath; it too must be easy. If the breath is forced to burst forth from the lungs, the sound of the voice cannot be correct because ease is absent. Such force expresses overanxiety. A salesman usually fails to sell when he is overanxious. He oversells himself or his product. Overselling is as bad as underselling. Neither method obtains results.

In silent breathing, inhale and exhale through the nose. In talking, inhale through the nose or the mouth, whichever at the time comes most easily with the expression. Do not think of breath when you talk. Know what you want to say and you will have the breath to say it. Rest a bit, that is to say, compose yourself, before getting up to address any group. Wait a moment or two before you start speaking. A few deep breaths will help you. Put yourself at ease, relax, then you should not suffer from lack of breath.

In short, breathe deeply but quietly, and your voice will have resonance. You will also have power to utter all your words with distinctness. You will be able to speak with clear enunciation.

Chapter 16

SPEAKING DISTINCTLY

MANY of us are careless with our speech. We are more than careless; we are slovenly. It is necessary for one who would make himself easily understood to be careful of his enunciation, or the shaping of sound into language.

Care for Enunciation All-Important

All expression has for its object, understanding. You have ideas to express but mere sound cannot communicate them. A daub of paint on canvas does not make a picture. The painting must be shaped before it can express what the artist has in mind. So with vocal sound. Sound may be pleasant but have no meaning, or sound may be mere noise, so far as meaning is concerned. The sound of your voice should be pleasant, but it should be more than sound. It should be speech. As speech it must convey ideas. Care in enunciation is absolutely necessary.

When you talk to an individual face to face, carelessness in enunciation may not always hide your meaning, but when you stand up before a group to talk, then indistinctness may cause misunderstanding and loss of interest.

Mumbling Suggests Ineffectiveness

For the speaker, the business man or woman, or the individual who wishes to impress others, careless enunciation is a handicap.

We always tell young men that to present a good appearance, they must be neatly dressed. Neatness in dress becomes a habit with us, an everyday habit. We do not reserve it for special occasions. We know that neatness counts. Is it not rather a shock to you when you meet a well-dressed, attractive individual who by his very appearance seems to be worthwhile, who impresses you when you first meet him, to find that the neatness is all outward show? If his speech is careless, slovenly, are you not prone to feel that carelessness in this regard betokens mental slovenliness?

Clear Enunciation an Asset

The world today demands clear-cut distinct speech. It has become conscious of distinctness. The radio demands clear, crisp enunciation. The talking motion pictures have made the actor and actress attend schools of enunciation. Our schools, recognizing this demand, are giving more and more attention to neatness of oral expression.

When you talk on the telephone, are you easily understood? You cannot be if you are indistinct in your speech. When you converse with your friends or acquaintances, do you dress up your speech with as much care as you would exercise in the spelling of words in a letter? You wish to raise yourself in the estimation of your customers in business, or your clients or patients in your profession. Therefore, learn to talk distinctly. The stenographer in an office could give much better service if those dictating to her enunciated clearly. Clear enunciation will help your voice. It will promote care in every other use of language. Listen to good speakers. Listen to radio speakers; judge their good and bad points in regard to distinctness. Then watch your own speech and guard against defects which you find in others.

The Fault of Dropping Syllables

One of our great faults in America is the dropping of syllables. Some people talk almost like the man in the following story:

An Englishman visiting this country said to a doorman at a hotel, "I think it will rain today, don't you?" The Englishman was much puzzled by the reply. He went over to another man standing near by and said, "I say, I just asked that doorman over there whether he thought it would rain today and he said, 'Little dogs it will and little dogs it won't.' What did he mean?"

The man called to the doorman, "Say, Sam, what did you say to this gentleman?"

The doorman said, "He asked me if I think it's goin' to rain today. I said, 'Pups it will and pups it won't.' "

The Fault of Clipping Words

Very few of us would distort "perhaps" into "pups," but the carelessness of some individuals in clipping and telescoping their words often makes spoken language almost as ludicrous. We say "com'ny" for "company"; "his'ry" for "history"; "p'rator" for "operator"; "pop'lar" for "popular"; "Jeff'son" for "Jefferson"; "Constootional" for "Constitutional." A few years ago James M. Cain quoted in the New York *World* the following specimen of the careless utterance into which even lawyers sometimes slip:

"Now genlemen of the jury, you've just heard the opening stament of the proscution, and I want to say before I go any fuyther you won't hear no such stament from me, no such truly remarkable stament, I may say, because in all my espeernce at the bar I don't think I ever heard such a grossly ezaggerated, such a unnessarly harsh, such a thurly ridiclous distortion of a simple set of facks as my friend of the proscution has just given you genlemen. No, my friends, I shall confine myself to a plain stament of what we hope to prove, of what we will prove, I think I may say, I'm confident to the complete satsfaction of you genlemen, and beyond all reasonable doubt, and avoid distortion and personalities and misrepassentation of any kind whatsoever."

If you are guilty of such carelessness, (and which of us isn't?) watch your speech. Compare your speech with the clear, distinct, crisp diction of such masters as the late George Arliss. His pronunciation of syllables and words made his wonderful voice more entrancing; or listen to Lionel Barrymore, with the art of speech so well developed that what was art seems art no more but the beautiful expression of thought and emotion as nature intended.

Sometimes careless speakers omit a syllable in the following words:

February	boisterous
government	comfortable
misery	difference
memory	interesting
desperate	library

When a long "o" as in "no" occurs at the end of a word like "borrow," do you pronounce it "borra"? Do you say "tomorra" instead of "tomorrow"? Watch carefully all such words as narrow, fellow, follow, shadow, window, meadow, yellow, swallow, and piano.

Running Words Together

Furthermore, you may pronounce every syllable in a word, and still not be understood. The reason will be that you run one word into the other. Do you make an entire sentence sound like one word? Doingthisintheprintedwordwouldmakereadingdifficultand understandingdoublyhard. This sentence is hard for the eye to read. If you speak it the way it is written, it is just as hard to understand. Much of the speech we hear is just like that sentence. Talking too quickly makes it difficult for people to understand. Separate your words. This does not mean that you should make an appreciable pause between each word. Pronounce distinctly and crisply one word before enunciating the next. Make each sound distinct and clear-cut.

Do Not Mumble

Mumbled sound very often causes the speaker to have his statement misconstrued, as happened in the following case.

Three ladies overheard Mrs. Smith make a remark to her husband. In discussing what they had understood, Mrs. A. said, "They must have been to the zoo, because I heard her mention 'A trained deer.' "

Said Mrs. B., "No, no. They were talking about going away and she said to him, 'Find out about the train, dear?' "

"I think you are both wrong," Mrs. C. interrupted. "It seemed to me they were discussing music, for she said, 'A trained ear' very distinctly."

A few minutes later Mrs. Smith herself appeared, and they told her of their disagreement.

"Well," she laughed, "that's certainly funny. You are poor guessers, all of you. The fact is, I'd been out to the country overnight, and I was asking my husband if it rained here last evening."

You want your hearers to understand what you have to say. You want to impress them with your ideas. If you mumble, you cannot expect that they are going to be interested or that you will impress them. Mumbling is caused, like poor voice, by the lazy lower jaw. Open your mouth and you cannot *mumble.*

Distinctness and Carrying Power

Distinctness of enunciation not only makes speech understandable in conversation but it aids your voice. It helps the carrying power of your voice. Albert J. Beveridge said that:

Wendell Phillips seldom spoke in any voice but a conversational tone and yet he was able to make an audience of many thousands hear him distinctly. . . . It is probable that no man ever lived who had a more sensuous effect upon his hearers than Ingersoll. In a literal and physical sense, he charmed them. I never heard him talk in a loud voice.

In referring to Henry Ward Beecher, he says:

A gentleman who heard that speech (in Liverpool) told me, notwithstanding the pandemonium that reigned around him, Beecher did not shout, or speak at the top of his voice a single time during that terrible four hours.

Phillips and Beecher, like most great speakers, had in their voices a peculiar power of penetration. This power is really a coupling of a resonant voice and distinct enunciation. Therefore, learn to be careful of your enunciation at all times—in conversation—in your business—when you get up to talk to a group.

Producing the Sounds Accurately

What must you do to acquire distinctness? It involves giving definite attention to the way you produce the individual sounds which make up words. Most of us never receive definite instructions in this matter. Our methods of enunciation are picked up in childhood from those around us and as a rule we modify them only slightly in later life, and then very unsystematically.

But you can easily change all this if you wish. Enunciation is a matter of using certain muscles, particularly of the tongue and lips. To produce a certain sound or a combination of sounds, you move these muscles in a particular way. It is possible to analyze this muscle movement as definitely as the movements of the typist's fingers on the keyboard. If you will put your mind on this matter and be careful and persistent, you can render your utterance perfectly distinct within a few months.

The Individual Sound

The English language as spoken today, contains a number of different sounds. These are represented in the written language by the twenty-six letters of the alphabet. All these sounds are produced by adjusting the position of the mouth to modify the tone as produced in the throat. Speaking distinctly means making the definite sounds accurately and completely. Indistinctness means failure to place the mouth in the proper position for the various sounds, either assuming an absolutely wrong position, or assuming the right position imperfectly.

Getting the Right Muscle Active

For example, the sound of long "e" as in the words, see, week, me, is produced by drawing the lips back sideways without dropping the jaw. The tongue is up almost at the roof of the mouth. Try saying "see," "me," "week," in this position and you will be surprised to find how clear they are. On the other hand, to produce the sound of "oo" as in book, good, would, and the sound of long "o" as in go, row, crow, you must pucker the lips almost as when whistling. If you take these respective positions carefully, you are certain to make the sounds with accuracy.

But you will find that many people attempt to say "me," "week," "see" with lips rounded or puckered. On the other hand, they attempt to say "go," "crow," "row," "book," with lips pulled back sideways. That show of carelessness blurs your enunciation and makes it difficult for people to understand.

Learning the Right Positions

Practice. Read aloud. Stand in front of a mirror and watch your lips as you speak a sentence or two. If your lips are rigid or form a straight line, you cannot be distinct. If you hold the corners of your mouth so they are tightly pressed together, allowing the lips to change formation only at the center, you are not talking correctly. If your tongue is stiff, if you fail to shift it quickly and deftly to form the different sounds, not only will your words be indistinct, but your voice will have a poor quality. You will be causing tension and, as you remember, tension retards resonance. Practice in front of a mirror will let you see exactly how you are saying things. By watching the movements of lips and tongue, you will know where to apply correction.

Principles for Guidance

The following general directions will help you: (1) Open your mouth; keep the jaw loose *always*. This keeps your articulation apparatus pliable, ready to assume whatever positions are required. (2) Pay attention to your lips. Train them to be sensitive and mobile, that is, movable, so they produce with exactness the sounds in which the lips have a part. (3) Pay attention to your tongue. Train the tongue to be both mobile and firm, thereby producing with exactness, the sounds in which the tongue has a part.

Here are some specific suggestions with regard to the various sounds.

Vowels and Consonants

The individual sounds in our language—about fifty altogether—fall into two great classes; consonants and vowels. The vowel sounds, of which there are about twenty-five—the various forms of a, e, i, o, u—are sounds in which the tone is produced in the throat and is modified without being checked by changes in the position of the tongue. We shall speak of the vowels later. The other sounds, called consonants, also number about twenty-five.

The Consonants

The consonants are sounds which are produced by stopping or checking the tone by means of the tongue or lips. The individual consonants are represented by the following letters:

b, d, f, g, h, k, l, m, n, p, r, s, t, v, w, y, z

Besides these (and the vowels mentioned above), the written alphabet contains the following letters:

c, which is used in writing to represent sometimes s and sometimes k

j, which is used in writing to represent the soft sound of g

q, which in combination with u, is used in writing to represent the sound kw

x, which is used in writing to represent the sound of ks

Lip Consonants

Some of these consonants are made with the lips: p, b, m, f, v, w, and the combination wh. To make these lip sounds distinctly, press the lips tightly together. If you take pains to localize the sensation in the center of the lips just in front of the upper teeth, you will be sure of getting these sounds correct.

Here is a list of words for p: paper, peeper, piper, pippin, pepper, popper, puppy, pope, pupa.

Make up similar lists of words for the sounds of b, m, and the other lip sounds.

In connection with the lip sounds, remember that the words should seem to be formed by the upper lip and come out through it. Then it will be easy to pronounce distinctly. In this way, the words will be formed outside the mouth and will be readily heard. Give this method a trial and you will agree with this statement.

Tongue Consonants

The sounds which are the chief source of inexactness in English are those made with the tongue. Here is a list of the tongue sounds. They fall into three sub-classes.

Those made with the tip of the tongue: t, d, n, l (and the combination th).

Those made with the middle of the tongue: k, g (and the combination ng).

Those made with the sides or edge of the tongue: s, z, j (or soft g, and the combination ch).

Making the Tongue-Tip Sounds

The tongue tip sounds are the ones that give most trouble. People do not make them firmly or exactly. This is the cause of most indistinct speaking. If you will take care always to press the tongue tip tightly against the upper front teeth, you will make these sounds correctly and distinctly.

If you learn to produce these tongue tip sounds accurately, you will go far toward solving the problem of indistinctness, for your muscles will automatically adjust themselves to the requirements for other sounds.

Here are some trial words for the tongue-tip sounds. Practice uttering the words of each line on a single breath, emphasizing slightly the particular sound which is featured.

1. tightly, total, tainted, tutor, tea, tarter, tittle, tattle, tut-tut, tottered, tattered
2. adding, deadly, dowdy, dude, dyed, dated
3. lily, lilac, little, linen, lowly, lonely, lately, lightly, latterly, learning
4. nine, ninny, neatness, known, none, nutting, natal, nudity, nattily

The Vowel Sounds

In producing the vowel sounds the tone is not broken or stopped as with the consonants. Instead it is modified or shaped by changes in the position of the tongue and lips to make the vowels accurately.

These are the principal vowel sounds:

"e" as in week, "a" as in and, "a" as in at, "a" as in ah, aw, "u" as in up, oh, and oo

and the diphthongs:

"oi" as in oil, "ou" as in out, and "i" as in ice.

Positions of the Vowels

A good way to learn to make the vowels accurately is to practice them in a series arranged according to the position of the lips and tongue.

Thus "ee" is made with lips drawn back sideways and the tongue almost at the top of the mouth—weep, mean, seen, keen, lean.

With "a" as in aid, the lips are not quite so wide and the tongue is a little lower.

With "a" as in at, the lips are not quite so wide and the tongue is still lower.

With "a" as in arm, car, father, the jaw is dropped and the mouth opened wide, and the tongue rather low.

With "ah," the lips are somewhat puckered.

With "oo," the lips are puckered closely, almost as in whistling.

A Vowel Exercise

As an exercise, run through the series from e to oo: e, a, ah, aw, oh, oo, shifting lips and tongue from point to point. Practice this exercise regularly a few minutes every day. You will find that the practice will help you in two ways. First, it will make your articulation apparatus, tongue and lips, more flexible and sensitive. Second, it will train your ear, so that you will notice more closely the sounds you produce and thereby produce them more accurately.

Combination of Sounds for Practice

For further practice, here are a number of words giving combinations of sounds. Sound the words of one group one after another on a single breath. If some groups are too long to be uttered in a single breath, omit some of the words.

1. Beetles, breach, deep, means, reaped, reasoning, shrieking, smeared, spheres, weird
2. Brink, built, fiddle, pickles, ribbons, slip, swift, winked
3. Bled, breadth, glen, helps, length, meddled, pledged, quenched, stress, themselves, trees
4. Claim, fate, glade, played, prayed, quaintest, ranges, snails
5. Act, apt, cattle, dazzle, facts, happen, landed, rash, tackle
6. Barn, charged, garb, hearth, hearts, scarf, scars
7. Blithe, crimes, fires, isles, knives, lines, wilds, wives, writhe
8. Blotted, bottled, from, gloss, plotting, propped, rotten, solved, spotted
9. Claws, dawdles, faults, flaws, fraud, stalks, wards, warns
10. Bounds, clownish, crowded, crowned, drowned, ploughed, snout, sounds, towns

11. Cubs, interrupt, loved, loves, lungs, muddles, plus, puffed, shrubbery
12. Boilers, coiled, coins, foiled, jointed, hoists, loyal, poisoned, royally
13. Bones, crows, growing, oaten, opened, posts, robed
14. Brook, crook, looking, nooks, rooks
15. Bloom, boots, gruel, loosened, moors, proved, trooping, wound
16. Duties, feuds, fumes, mules, rebukes, stewed, tunes

When practicing these exercises observe four rules:

1. Open the mouth.
2. Go slowly.
3. Sound every part of each word.
4. Bite on the last letter.

Do Not "Er"

Be careful, however, when you pronounce the consonant at the end of a word that you do not follow the consonant with a vowel. Do not say, for instance, "worda" or "word-uh" for "word"—"eacha" or "each-uh" for "each." Heed the advice of Dr. Oliver Wendell Holmes:

> And when you stick on conversation's burrs
> Don't strew your pathway with those dreadful urs.

The "ur" and "ah" at the end of a word may become an actual speech defect, like stammering or stuttering. It very often occurs where the individual is speaking words instead of expressing thoughts.

Whispering

Whispering is an exceedingly fine exercise for practice in clear enunciation. In whispering you are forced to make careful use of the lips and the tongue. Whisper some short sentence or paragraph so that you can be heard and understood at the other end of a small room. The passage should be brief because you may find that this practice may make you somewhat dizzy. That is a sign for you to rest.

Regularity of Practice

Remember, with all these exercises, that a little time spent every day is sufficient. But work at them every day. Bear in mind that if you have faults of speech, you have made them habitual by a lifetime of practice. The only way in which you can correct them is by practicing steadily, little by little, until you have replaced the careless old habit with a new habit of accuracy. But when once the new habit is rooted, you will never lose it. After that, distinctness of utterance will be automatic, without your having to think about it.

One word of caution here. You do not want to seem stilted in your language. You do not want others to feel that you are assuming distinctness of speech in order to show off. Speak clearly but never affectedly. Keep your utterance both distinct and natural. It can be done.

Drill on Sentences

You will find it both interesting and profitable to follow your drill on single sounds and single words with sentences or paragraphs. Here are a few sentences with which to begin this more advanced drill in enunciation.

As a vessel is known by the sound, whether it be cracked or not, so men are proved by their speeches whether they be wise or foolish.—DEMOSTHENES

Freedom of religion, freedom of the press, and freedom of person under the protection of the habeas corpus, these are principles that have guided our steps through an age of revolution and reformation.—JEFFERSON

Personal liberty is the paramount essential to human dignity and human happiness.—BULWAR

No free government, or the blessings of liberty, can be preserved to any people but by a firm adherence to justice, moderation, temperance, frugality, and virtue, and by a frequent recurrence to fundamental principles.—PATRICK HENRY

Few men are lacking in capacity, but they fail because they are lacking in application.—CALVIN COOLIDGE

It is cynicism and fear that freeze life; it is faith that thaws it out, releases it, sets it free.—DR. HARRY EMERSON FOSDICK

Words without actions are the assassins of idealism.—HERBERT HOOVER

New ideas can be good or bad, just the same as old ones.—FRANKLIN D. ROOSEVELT

It is not the crook in modern business that we fear, but the honest man who doesn't know what he is doing.—OWEN D. YOUNG

Victory, simply for the sake of achieving it, is empty.—ALFRED E. SMITH

No man, who continues to add something to the material, intellectual, and moral well being of the place in which he lives, is left long without proper reward.—BOOKER T. WASHINGTON

The danger is, when liberty is nibbled away, for expedients, and by parts.—BURKE

God demands of those who manage the affairs of government that they should be courageously true to the interests of the people, and the Ruler of the universe will require of them a strict account of their stewardship.—GROVER CLEVELAND

No government is respectable which is not just.—Without unspotted purity of public faith, without sacred public principle, fidelity, and honor, no mere forms of government, no machinery of laws, can give dignity to political society.—DANIEL WEBSTER

Let us have faith that right makes might, and in that faith, let us to the end, dare to do our duty, as we understand it.—LINCOLN

Talents are best nurtured in solitude; character is best formed in the stormy billows of the world.—GOETHE

Fear is not in the habit of speaking truth; when perfect sincerity is expected, perfect freedom must be allowed; nor has anyone who is apt to be angry when he hears the truth, any cause to wonder that he does not hear it.—TACITUS

The first and last thing which is required of genius is the love of truth.—GOETHE

Perfect wisdom hath four parts, viz., wisdom, the principle of doing things aright; justice, the principle of doing things equally in public and private; fortitude, the principle of not flying danger, but meeting it; and temperance, the principle of subdoing desires and living moderately.—PLATO

If we work upon marble, it will perish; if on brass, time will efface it; if we rear temples, they will crumble into dust; but if we work upon immortal minds and imbue them with principles, with the just fear of God and love of our fellow-men, we engrave on those tablets something that will brighten all eternity.—DANIEL WEBSTER

When I consider the wonderful activity of the mind, so great a memory of what is past, and such a capacity of penetrating into the future; when I behold such a number of arts and sciences, and such a multitude of discoveries thence arising, I believe and am firmly persuaded that a nature which contains so many things within itself cannot but be immortal.—CICERO

"Impossible"—never let me hear that foolish word again.—MIRABEAU

Never is the deep, strong voice of man, or the low, sweet voice of woman, finer than in the earnest but mellow tones of familiar speech, richer than the richest music, which are a delight while they are heard, which linger still upon the ear in softened echoes, and which, when they have ceased, come, long after, back to memory, like the murmurs of a distant hymn.—HENRY GILES

Sheridan once said of some speech, in his acute, sarcastic way, that "it contained a great deal both of what was new and what was true; but that what was new was not true, and what was true was not new." —HAZLITT

A wise man reflects before he speaks; a fool speaks, and then reflects on what he has uttered.—DELILE

When God lets loose a great thinker on this planet, then all things are at risk. There is not a piece of science, but its flank may be turned tomorrow; nor any literary reputation, nor the so-called eternal names of fame, that may not be revised and condemned.—EMERSON

Weaving the Sounds Together

To give yourself further training in properly weaving together individual sounds, practice the following extracts:

From Chauncey M. Depew, American lawyer and United States senator who was a notable after-dinner speaker.

We stand today upon the dividing line between the first and second century of constitutional government. There are no clouds overhead, and no convulsions under our feet. We reverently return thanks to Almighty God for the past, and with hopeful promise march upon sure ground toward the future. . . .

The spirit of Washington fills the executive office. Presidents may not rise to the full measure of his greatness, but they must not fall below his standard of public duty and obligations. . . . With their inspiring past and splendid future, the people of these United States, heirs of a hundred years, marvelously rich in all which adds to the glory and greatness of a nation, with an abiding faith in the stability and elasticity of their Constitution, and an abounding faith in themselves, hail the coming century with hope and joy.

From Dr. Charles R. Parkhurst, American clergyman who attacked political corruption.

People say, you can't do anything. You can. One man can chase a thousand; we have the Almighty's word for it. I have done it. I am not bragging of it, but I have done it. And any man can do it, be he Catholic, Republican, or Democrat, if he has the truth on his side, dares to stand up and tell it, and when he has been knocked down once, gets up, and goes at it again. One man can chase a thousand. Let our earnest, fiery citizens once get but an inkling of what citizenship means, in its truest and innermost sense, and there is no wall of misrule too solidly constructed for it to overthrow; no "machine" of demagogism too elaborately wrought for it to smash. There is nothing that can stand in the way of virtue on fire. A fact you can mistake, a principle you can put under a false guise, but a man you cannot down; that is to say, if he is a man who has grit, grace, and sleeps well o' nights.

If any one wants to do something for his town or city, and asks me what he shall do, I answer; Get the facts; state them; stand up to them.

From Charles James Fox, famous English statesman and orator, 1749–1806.

"But we must pause!" What! must the bowels of Great Britain be torn out—her best blood be spilled—her treasures wasted—that you may make an experiment? Put yourselves—oh that you would put yourselves in the field of battle, and learn to judge of the sort of horrors that you excite! In former wars a man might, at least, have some feeling, some interest, that served to balance in his mind the impressions which a scene of carnage and death must inflict.

If a man had been present at the battle of Blenheim, for instance, and had inquired the motive of battle, there was not a soldier engaged who could not have satisfied his curiosity, and even, perhaps allayed his feelings. They were fighting, they knew, to repress the uncontrolled ambition of the Grand Monarch. But if a man were present now at a field of slaughter, and were to inquire for what they were fighting—"Fighting!" would be the answer, "they are not fighting; they are *pausing.*"

"Why is that man expiring? Why is that other writhing with agony? What means this implacable fury?" The answer must be: "You are quite wrong, sir; you deceive yourself—they are not fighting—do not disturb them—they are merely *pausing!* That man is not expiring with agony—that man is not dead—he is only *pausing!* Lord help you, sir! they are not angry with one another; they have no cause of quarrel; but their country thinks there should be a *pause.* All that you see, sir, is nothing like fighting—there is no harm, nor cruelty, nor bloodshed in it whatever; it is nothing more than a *political pause!* It is merely to try an experiment to see whether Bonaparte will not behave himself better than heretofore; and in the meantime we have agreed to a *pause,* in pure friendship!"

And is this the way, sir, that you are to show yourselves the advocates of order? You take up a system calculated to uncivilize the world—to destroy order—to trample on religion— to stifle in the heart, not merely the generosity of noble sentiment, but the affections of social nature; and in the prosecution of this system, you spread terror and devastation all around you.

From Clarence Manion, dean, College of Law, University of Notre Dame.

American constitutional government was not designed to be a glorified and powerful source of bounties, blessings, and order. In the American system, God alone is the power, the glory, and the source.

After God, man is next in the American political lineup, while government is third and last in the procession.

In the American system government is a mere hedge against the possibility that men will use their freedom to injure other men.

How could such a weak, divided, and subdivided government as ours be expected to keep order? The answer is that the founding fathers did not expect it to do so. James Madison, the so-called father of the Constitution, made this very clear when he expressed the determination, "To rest all of our political experiments on the capacity of mankind for self-government."

"What is government itself," he said, "but the greatest of all reflections on human nature? If men were angels," he concluded, "no government would be necessary."

This is simply the converse of Jefferson's famous dictum that, "Those people are governed best who are governed least—for from this it certainly follows that those people are best who require the least government.

Thus the men who designed the American constitutional system distrusted government as much as they trusted their own ability to govern themselves under God's commandments. They realized that the survival of our system would depend upon the strength of individual character rather than upon strong and streamlined government. They gambled upon the sustained quality of virtue in the average American citizen and this historic bet paid off at the astounding odds of more than a million to one.

Our glorious history shows that a free, conscientious, and virtuous citizenry, under a strictly limited government, can produce the most lavish material civilization that the world has ever seen, along with a constantly increasing standard of living for the individual citizen that is the envy of all mankind.

Today, the fate of civilization everywhere depends upon the sustained strength and solvency of all that is implied in the expression, "The United States of America."

From Harold F. North, Industrial relations manager, Swift and Company, Chicago.

A generation ago the books of Horatio Alger were read by almost all youngsters. His books were many, and each was a simple example of how to achieve success. Each was a consuming inspiration and for many youngsters pointed the way to great personal achievement. Oftentimes I ask myself these questions—Who killed Horatio Alger? What was wrong with his idea of "work and win"—or the story of "rags to riches"? Since when can we afford not to exalt the simple virtues of—honesty, patience, reliability, energy, ambition, and above all personal sacrifice? These virtues are the only sure way to success. Why do fond and well-meaning parents struggle to educate their children and explain their sacrifice with the statement "I don't want my children to work as hard as I do for so little"? I keep asking myself, "What is wrong with dignified manual work?"

Why is it that people put so much emphasis on financial status and achievement as *the* "yardsticks" for determining man's success in this life? Why is it that so many people look with pity and disdain upon the fine men and women who day after day gloriously manifest the real virtues of toil and personal sacrifice to produce the necessities of life for us, or to educate our children, or to minister to our physical and spiritual needs, or to enter honestly into a career of government service.

Fortunately for us, the question—"Opportunity or Security?" is not an "either or else" matter. Opportunity is the doorway to a better life—it provides the satisfaction that is found in serving mankind, it is the foundation stone of genuine security. Opportunity is the very essence of Freedom—the "possession of a self-determining power," a right and a freedom to do things—freedom to do what one chooses as long as it does not interfere with the rights of others. Unfortunately for all of us, security has come to mean for many people today Freedom from Care, Freedom from Want, and even Freedom from Work. *This* is a false security that can be supported only by conquest or confiscation—and where, in justice, are the worlds to conquer.

The Value of Enunciation Drill

And now, supplement the practice passages given you in this chapter with others, selected by yourself. Select passages in books, and in printed speeches and sermons, which particularly appeal to you because of their thought, feelings, and stimulating expression. Use these for drill in enunciation. Read them aloud, day after day. Memorize some of them and recite them in your bathroom concerts.

Such work will help you in various ways. It will supple up the articulation muscles of tongue, lips, and cheeks, and the increased dexterity and control will carry over into your own talk, whether before an audience or in conversation. It is readily possible to learn to speak with perfect distinctness. In addition, such practice will give you glimpses into the devices by which expert speakers give their speeches the color, fire, and enthusiasm from which their power comes.

Chapter 17

PRONOUNCING CORRECTLY

TO speak in a way to be clearly understood, either in addressing a group or in conversation, you need to give attention to both enunciation and pronunciation. However, the problems in connection with the two are different. Enunciation is a matter of distinct utterance; the problem it presents is that of getting full control of the muscles of articulation so that you can utter with precision the sounds you desire to produce. Pronunciation is a matter of sounding the words you use in the manner which is accepted as correct. We speak of *distinct* enunciation but of *correct* pronunciation.

Pronunciation a Matter of Accepted Custom

Words are signals. To be understood you must make the signals in the manner which is familiar to the persons you are addressing. It is possible to enunciate words with perfect distinctness and yet pronounce them in a way to be unintelligible to the persons you are addressing. Correct pronunciation means sounding words in the manner which is familiar or satisfactory to your hearers.

There is of course no positive law in the matter. There is no authority or court anywhere, not even the dictionary, which has the power or the right to say you must pronounce the words of our language in this way or that. It is all a matter of custom. But custom is all-powerful. If you pronounce words in a manner that is strange to the persons you are addressing, they will not understand. Or perhaps, if they make out your meaning, they will think you ignorant or eccentric. In that event the effectiveness with which your message is conveyed is lessened.

Slips in Pronunciation Noticed

You will find, also, that people are quick to notice variations from pronunciation standards. It often happens that serious defects in a speaker's arrangement of ideas, in his voice, or enunciation will pass without conscious notice on the part of his listeners, although of course they have a powerful subconscious effect. But if he pronounces a few of his words in an unusual manner, the same listeners may note the fact and comment regarding it.

Therefore, you need to watch your pronunciation, to make sure that it conforms to accepted standards, that is, to custom.

Alertness Required

This requires alertness. Yet it presents no serious difficulty, if you go about it in the right way. Beyond doubt, you already pronounce most words in the manner that is accepted by the people you address in conversation or in everyday public speaking. To guard yourself against slips in the case of the other words is a matter of getting an understanding of a few general principles and then of developing the habit of alert listening to the way other people pronounce words.

National Standards

The term, "standard of pronunciation," has several different meanings. There is first of all the general national standard. Every language has its own general scheme or pattern for sounding words. A foreigner who has not mastered the general pronunciation scheme observed in English is instantly recognized as French, German, Italian, Spanish, Japanese, even though he uses English words fluently and grammatically.

There is a story of a French clergyman who undertook to preach a sermon in English to a large group of English-speaking visitors. He had learned English from dictionaries and grammars. He began by announcing his text, which sounded to his English listeners like this: "Kah ze leeaw sha's ee skay, or ze leopar ee spoh?" You may imagine that they were mystified. Gradually those among the audience who knew a little French made out that the scripture text he was expounding was the familiar verse: "Can the lion change his skin, or the leopard his spots?"

The Frenchman had been applying to the English words the French pronunciation scheme, which of course did not fit.

Learning the American Accent

Every foreigner is in danger of doing something of the kind. A foreigner, who wants to master English, to use it with full effectiveness in conversation and in everyday public speaking, should concentrate first of all upon getting the "American accent." He should listen carefully to the people about him and pick up the general tune or pattern of the way they sound their words.

One of the best aids he might find would be to study public speaking with some American friends. Practicing exercises such as those in this book, reading aloud also the selections from speeches given in this book, or memorizing and reciting them, and listening to his friends' rendering of the same passage should help him greatly to familiarize his ear with American pronunciation.

The attention given in this book to voice production and enunciation should be of great indirect assistance, for it will render his ear more alert and sensitive to the way the people around him talk.

Standards of Locality

Then there is the pronunciation standard of locality. This is a very real matter. Many words are pronounced differently in New England, in Pennsylvania, in the South, and in the West. Each of these sections, and even regions within a section, has a recognizable pronunciation scheme of its own. Even the first words of a stranger may indicate the section of the country from which he hails.

These sectional peculiarities do not, as a rule, interfere with effectiveness of speech. You do not need to work to get rid of them, as the foreign-born citizen needs to work to get rid of his foreign accent. No one would suggest that the Bostonian change his speech to conform to the New York pronunciation, or vice versa. The Southern voice is often appealing in its beauty. The bluff heartiness of the Westerner's speech suggests vigor and energy. Your ordinary pronunciation of the words that you use every day, so long as it is not contrary to the best usage in the locality in which you live, is the pronunciation you may find it best to use.

Modifying Your Local Accent

On the other hand, you may prefer not to be labeled always as a Southerner, Westerner, New Yorker, or "Man from Maine," the moment you open your mouth. The wise course, as in the case of the foreigner, may be to listen and imitate the people about you, whether you are a Northerner who has moved to the South, a New Englander in the West, or a Southerner residing in New York or Chicago.

By developing a sensitive ear, you will find your speech gradually adjusting itself almost automatically to the neighborhood where you happen to be. But do not yield to the impulse to accentuate your sectional characteristics and keep yourself different. Remember the old saying, "He who learns another language opens to himself another world." In a degree that is true of the adjustment to another section.

Standards of Good Taste

What is commonly meant by correctness of pronunciation is conformity with good taste, with the custom of intelligent educated people. This is recorded in our dictionaries. You wish to talk in the manner followed by such people. You should therefore keep a dictionary at hand, and make a habit of consulting it systematically to check the pronunciation of every word you meet which is at all unfamiliar.

The Dictionary

Dictionaries do not make good usage, they record it. The publishers of our large dictionaries maintain large staffs of experts who constantly observe the custom of the public, particularly the intelligent and educated portion of it, to note how these people pronounce the words in their talk. If these editors find that the current pronunciation of a word on the part of the educated public has shifted, the next edition of the dictionary takes note of the fact. Sometimes common usage moves faster than the dictionary. Dictionaries, it may be repeated, do not make pronunciation; they merely record the verdict given by the custom of careful speakers.

An Indispensable Guide

But the dictionary is of course an indispensable guide to tell us what is good current usage for most words. You should own a copy of a good standard dictionary. All of us have a double vocabulary. One vocabulary is made up of words with which we are thoroughly familiar, which we use continually in our conversation, which come to our lips spontaneously on all occasions. The second vocabulary is that of words whose meaning we recognize but which are not sufficiently familiar to be used in conversation. We are not sure of the pronunciation of many of the words in this second group. Probably we have never taken the trouble to look them up in the dictionary.

Some Words to Look Up

Here are a number of words which we may not use every day but for which we have occasional need. You will find it profitable to look these up systematically in your dictionary and copy down the pronunciation given for them. Learn the meaning also if you do not know it.

acoustics
acumen
adobe
advertisement
agile
ague
algebra
alma mater
alpine
alternate
alternately
ambiguity
amendable
anti
antipathy
apropos
architect
au revoir
auxiliary
avoirdupois
awry
aye

bacillus
bade
bass
baton
bestial
biography
bitumen
bivouac
blatant
bona fide
bouquet
bourgeois
bravado
brochure
bronchial
brusque
buffet
bureaucracy

caisson
calliope
carte blanche
casualty
cello
charge d'affaires
chary
chic
chimney
circuit
circuitous
clangor
clique
coadjutor
column
comptroller
condolence
conduit
connoisseur
consummate
corral
coupon
creek
cuisine
culinary
cupola

dahlia
decrepit
demise
demoniacal
demur
depths
desperado
dietary
dilettante
dishabille
dogmatic
donkey
drama

eczema
egregious
either
eleemosynary
enema
enervate
ennui
en route
entente cordiale
equitable
excursion
exemplary
explicable
exquisite
ex tempore

facial
facsimile
falcon
fetish

fiancé
fiduciary
figure
financier
finis
forehead
foyer
fragile
fricassee
fungi

gape
garrulous
genealogy
genuine
gibberish
gibbet
gist
government
granary
gratis
grievous
gyroscope

habeas corpus
hearth
heinous
herculean
heroine
horizon
hypocrisy
hysterics

ignoramus
illustrate
immobile
implacable
importune
incognito
incomparable
indictment
indigenous
indisputable
indissoluble
inexorable
inexplicable
infinitesimal
ingenue
inhospitable
insatiable
internecine
inveigle
irascible
irrelevant
irreparable
irrevocable

jocund
jugular
juvenile

kaleidoscopic
kiln

lamentable
languor
laryngoscope
larynx
legend
leisure
leonine
liaison
library
lithographer
livelong

maintenance
mandamus
maniacal
massacre
measure
medieval
mediocre
menu
mercantile
mischievous
misconstrue
molecule
momentous
municipal

naïve
nape
naturalization
nausea
negligee
nomenclature
nominal
nothing

occult
often
orchestra
orchid
ordeal
oust

panegyric
papyrus
parabola
paresis
parliament
pathos
patron
peremptorily
pharmaceutic
pianist
piquant
placable
plebeian
posse
potato
precedence

precedent
preface
premier
presage
presentiment
prestidigitator
prestige
prima facie
process
prodigy
progress
pronunciation
pumpkin

quay
quietus
quoit

recess
recluse
recognize
recourse
recreant
regime
rendezvous
reparable
reptile
research
resource
retail
revocable
romance

sachem
sacrifice
saline
salutary
sanguine
scenic
schism
secretary
seismic
senile
short-lived
sinecure
sine die
slough
sonorous
status
subtle
succinct

tenet
thyme
tiara
tomato
toward
truculent

ultimatum
unctuous
untoward
usurp

vagary
valet
vase
virago
virile
virulent
viva voce
vizier
vizor
voluntary

zoology

Some Troublesome Words

There are some words which many persons find difficult to pronounce. You will notice in the dictionary that the words are syllabized. When the pronunciation or accent of a word troubles you, separate it into syllables. Pronounce each of the syllables first individually, then joined together, and you will find that the difficulty will be ended.

Stress the First Syllable

In the following words the accent should come on the first syllable. Many persons stress the second syllable, incorrectly:

ab′-ject
ad′-mirable
ad′-versary
a′-lias
al′-ter-nate
ap′-plicable
brig′-and
chas′-tisement
com′-batant

com′-parable
com′-promise
con′-trary
con′-versant
cor′-net
dec′-ade
def′-icit
des′-picable
des′ultory
dis′-putant
eq′-uipage
ex′-igency
ex′-tant
for′-midable
har′-ass
hos′-pitable
im′-pious
in′-famous
in′-fluence
in′-terested
in′-teresting
o′-vert
pos′-itively
pref′-erable
pri′-marily
rep′-utable
res′-pite
syr′-inge
the′-ater
trav′-erse
trib′-une
ve′-hement

Stress the Second Syllable

In the following words the accent should be placed on the second syllable:

ab-do′-men
ad-dress′
a-dept′
a-dult′
al-ly′
an-tip′-o-des
clan-des′-tine
con-do′-lence
de-fect′
de-tail′
de-tour′
do-main′
en-tire′
fi-nance′(also fi′-nance)
gri-mace′
in-quir′-y
ly-ce′-um
mu-se′um
ob-lig′-a-to-ry
pe-can′
pre-ced′-ence
pre-tense′
py-ram′-i-dal
re-cline′
re-coil′
re-me′-di-able
ro-bust′
rou-tine′
trous-seau′ (also trous′-seau)

Look Up This Special List

Here is a list of words whose pronunciation may give you difficulty. In some cases even the authorities may differ regarding the correct pronunciation. The wise course is to look up the words in your dictionary and use the pronunciation given. If you do not know the meaning of a word, take time to familiarize yourself with it and make up sentences containing the word.

acclimate
aggrandizement
alternate
aspirant
brooch
brusque
chivalric
cliché
confiscate
contemplate
contour
cursorily
debut
decorous
demonstrate

dishabille	illustrate	patron
envelope	misconstrue	pianist
envoy	naïveté	prestige
equanimity	orchestral	quinine
extant	patriot	route

Standards of the Occasion

There is still another standard to be allowed for in your pronunciation as a practical matter. That is the nature of the occasion. In casual conversation you do not give words precisely as you do on a formal occasion, or in an address to a large audience. Queen Victoria, it is reported, said of her prime minister, Mr. Gladstone, "He talks to me as if I were the House of Commons!" What she may have meant was that Gladstone was using in his conversation with his sovereign the extra-careful utterance, or pronunciation, which he would use in a public speech.

Many of us have had a somewhat similar experience. To be addressed in informal conversation with the extra-precision of a public address is decidedly vexing. On the other hand, when a speaker employs on the platform the slurred and lazy pronunciation of casual conversation, his speech is felt to be unsuitable. It shows an attitude of carelessness which is unfitting to the occasion.

Familiar Words to Watch

You will find it definitely worthwhile to watch your pronunciation of the following familiar words:

of	for	catch
from	them	and
was	can	because

When addressing an audience be careful not to say:

uv	fer	ketch
frum	thum	'un or 'nd
wuz	kin	becuz

Minor Syllables to be Watched

Another aspect of the same point is the pronunciation of unemphatic syllables. The following are cases to watch:

abate	agree
about	alert
adorn	

Be careful not to say: uhbate, uhbout, uhdorn, uhgree and uhlert.

With the following:

be-lieve	be-fore
be-come	be-gin

Be careful not to say: b'lieve, b'come, b'fore, b'gin.

With these:

de-bate	de-fer
de-cide	de-gree
de-test	

Be careful not to say: duhbate, d'cide, d'test, d'fer, duhgree.

With these:

ef-fect	ef-front
ef-face	ef-ficient

Be careful not to say: ee-fect, ee-face, ee-front, ee-ficient.

With these:

pre-dict	per-form
pre-fer	per-haps
pre-side	per-mit
pre-sume	per-plex
pre-vent	per-tain

Be careful not to say: per-dict, per-fer, per-side, per-sume, per-vent, pre-form, pre-haps, pre-mit, pre-plex, pre-tain.

And with these:

po-lice	po-lite
po-lit-i-cal	

Be careful not to say: p'lice, p'litical, p'lite.

Improvement a Gradual Process

Do not be discouraged if you find yourself for a time making slips in pronunciation. Improvement in this point comes surely but gradually. In proportion as you acquire more fully the habit of listening to the way others talk, your ears will become more sensitive, and your articulation muscles more agile. Then you will adjust your way of sounding words, almost unconsciously, to the general custom of the persons with whom you are talking and with correct usage.

Chapter 18

SILENT EXPRESSION

AN able speaker not only has a good voice and good enunciation and pronunciation, but he also speaks with his whole body, his spirit, and his personality.

Expressive Looks and Movement

You wish to impress others with an idea in which you are deeply interested. You wish them to accept your thought. Expressing it vocally will give them the idea, but the picture you paint on your hearers' minds with your voice alone may be faint and indistinct. You need to reinforce it by utilizing the resources of *silent expression,* the expressive power of looks, posture, and movement. All good speakers do this. Here is an inspiring passage which you will find it worth while to read aloud carefully to yourself. You will find yourself prompted to vary not only your voice but your *manner* also. Watch your own manner, as you read, and you will detect at least some of the changes in look and in bearing with which you are prompted to accompany these remarks of Dr. Marsh.

A passage from a baccalaureate address by Daniel L. Marsh, president of Boston University.

I have lived a fairly long and exceedingly rich life. I have been privileged to transmute knowledge into wisdom in the alembic of experience. If you were to ask me for an outline of my philosophy of life, I could give it to you in five points of fellowship which a wise individual may have with abundant living.

The first point is expressed in a quotation from James Whitcomb Riley. In Riley's poetry, the vicissitudes of weather stand for the vicissitudes of life, fair weather representing the pleasant and prosperous things, and rainy weather the unpleasant and adverse things. In his quaint Hoosier dialect Riley makes the farmer say:

> "It hain't no use to grumble and complane;
> It's jest as cheap and easy to rejoice.—

When God sorts out the weather and sends rain,
W'y, rain's my choice."

This is a philosophy of contentment, based upon a firm faith in the overruling Providence of a good God.

The second point is the dictum of Saint Paul: "We know that all things work together for good to them that love God." This means that I need to be sure of only one thing, and that is that I love God. To love God means more than mere conformity to some ritual or the repetition of some creed—it means that I make my practices square with the will of God, and require myself to keep step with His Commandments against all the forces that oppose me. If I love God, then I can trust Him to make all things work together for good—work together as bitter and sweet work together for bodily health, as sunshine and shower work together for the harvest's fruition. I need not fill up my system with the poison of anxiety and worry. If I aim sincerely to love God, I can trust Him to make things work together for my good. That is, I must trust God as though everything depended upon Him, and I must behave myself as though everything depended upon me.

The third point is expressed in a bit of poetry—hardly more than doggerel—which I picked up in some fugitive way, but which I use almost every day:

For every evil under the sun
There is a remedy or there is none.
If there is a remedy, find it.
If there isn't, never mind it.

That saves the philosophy of contentment from becoming fatalism. Its propositions are self-evident: For every evil—personal, social, economic or international—for every evil under the sun, there is a remedy, or there is none. If there is a remedy, don't fret and fume about the evil: Find the remedy! If there is no remedy, then what is the sense of fretting and fuming? Never mind it!

The fourth point I do not express in a quotation, but in an aphorism of my own. It is this: *If you cannot realize your ideal, then idealize your real.* Henry Ford, when on the witness stand in his libel suit against the Chicago *Tribune,* said: "The idealist is a person who helps other people to be prosperous." J. G. Holland opined that "Ideals are the world's masters," and A. Bronson Alcott, in his *Table Talks,* declared that "Our ideals are our better selves."

Have ideals! Carl Schurz reminds us that "Ideals are like stars. You will not succeed in touching them with your hands; but, like the seafaring man, you choose them as your guides, and, following them, you will reach your destiny." If you are not drawn upward and onward by ideals, I give you up now! But if you have an ideal whose realization is deferred, don't let it make your heart sick! Go to work, and idealize your real. Poet Walt Whitman says that

> Through thy ideal, lo, the immortal reality!
> Through thy reality, lo, the immortal ideal!

Thus the practical idealist will never be defeated. The other evening, Professor Elmer A. Leslie shared with me a dynamic motto which he came upon during his student days at the University of Glasgow, German words by Moses Mendelssohn, as follows:

> Aus der Vergangenheit Schöpfen,
> In der Gegenwart leben,
> Für die Zukunft arbeiten!

The words lose but little of their pungency by being translated into English, thus:

> Create out of the past,
> Live in the present,
> Work for the future!

The fifth point of my philosophy of life is expressed in the immortal words of Jesus: "Whosover would be great among you shall be your servant, and the greatest of all shall be the servant of all." That is, the true standard of real greatness is service to others. Humility is one of the most beautiful of all the virtues; but humility, rightly understood, is simply a disposition to serve. The person who thinks he is too big to serve others is really confessing that he is too little. Jesus performed the most lowly service that one person could render another, and His dignity suffered no abatement in the performance because He was essentially big! If you desire a radiant and wholesome philosophy of life, some rule by which to live that will make life meaningful to you, be sure to enthrone therein the idea and the ideal of service to others.

An excerpt from an address by Dr. William H. Alexander before the Executives Club of Chicago may also be helpful to you.

If I had nothing to believe but what I read on the front page of the papers this morning, I'd wish I didn't have three children to grow up in a world like this.

We're on a train, and the name of the train is the United States of America. We're going ninety miles an hour downhill. The brakes are gone, the train is loaded with dynamite, and there is a cliff just ahead. There are other trains behind us—Europe and Asia—but they won't go over the cliff unless we do.

In the cab of the engine you have a few fellows fooling around with this instrument and that—in a harried sort of way—hoping that they'll hit the right throttle. The windows are so dirty they can't see out of them, and the train goes madly on its way. The fireman is stoking on coal as fast as he can, and most of what he's throwing in there is money. He thinks that's the answer to all our problems.

The train goes faster and faster on its way to destruction. We go on back to the Government car, where a few officers are sorting out packages. Every once in a while, when they think no one is looking, they hide a package under their coats.

We go back to the Labor car, where they are having a meeting. It's a noisy meeting, and they're saying, "We'll fix them back in that club car. We'll blow it up." They don't realize that if they blow it up, the whole train is lost, because it's loaded with dynamite.

You go back to the club car, where you find a few well dressed boys . . . sipping their highballs and smoking long cigars, and they're saying, "We'll starve them out in the Labor car." They don't realize that if they starve them out, the whole train is lost.

Going back to the coaches, the kiddies are running up and down the aisles, throwing orange peelings at each other. A man comes into the car—maybe it's a lawyer, maybe it's a business man, or preacher, or scientist, but someone comes in—and says, "People, be careful. I've been up front, and I know what's happening. This train is going ninety miles an hour downhill, the brakes are gone, the train is loaded with dynamite, and there is a cliff just ahead. For heaven's sake, let's pull together. Let's lean out the windows and throw golf sticks between the brake shoes and the wheels, or do something to slow down this train." They don't even hear him, because they're too busy listening to soap operas on somebody's portable radio, learning that Duz "does everything," or reading pulp magazines, and the only one who does hear is a waiter, and he goes in the dining car, puts on a clean white jacket, and stands on the observation platform, looking at the stars, wondering how soon the end will come. That's not too dark a picture of our world today.

We are in the most dangerous period of mankind's history, and yet I do not come with a discouraging message. . . .

I know that there is one thing more powerful than anything that has been discovered, is being discovered or will be discovered in the laboratory of modern science, and what is that? It's that something within the heart and mind of an individual which, when tied to an eternal truth, results in all of humanity being lifted to a new level. That is the most powerful thing in the world.

Victor Hugo said, "The most powerful thing in the world is an idea whose time has come." And, gentlemen, believe me, the time has come when our best brains must go over into the spiritual foundations that will result in our even being able to keep our world.

Read these remarks of Dr. Alexander aloud and you will find yourself impelled to accompany the words by expressive changes in looks and movements.

The Oldest Language

Now the impulse to accompany the words of talk with expressive looks and movements is universal. Indeed this silent expression must have been the earliest form of language. Certainly it is found among all races. Among many peoples, this silent language of pantomine or signs has been carried to a high point of development.

Still Used and Relied Upon

In later ages, since the development of oral speech, then of writing, and finally of printing, less and less conscious attention has been given to the oldest and most universal language, the language of looks and movements. Hardly anyone today, except the actors on the stage and in the movie studios, studies it definitely. *But we all make use of it, in all our talk.*

Whenever we speak, no matter what may be the subject, the utterance of the words is accompanied by changes in the expression on our faces, and in the bodily attitudes we assume. In ordinary conversation you use your voice by the expression of your face. You gesticulate with your hands. You shift your position. In short, you combine voice, posture, gesture, motion, in conveying your message to your listener's mind. When conversing eagerly you instinctively lean forward; your eyes closely scan the face of your listener; very likely you emphasize your statements by movements of your hand, perhaps tapping the desk or table in front of you.

Suppose an offer is made to you in a business interview which you strongly disapprove. You reject it indignantly. "No!" you say, "I don't want it! I won't have it!" The tones of your voice are positive and your enunciation sharp. In addition, you frown and shake your head. Very likely you make a quick repelling motion. On the other hand, if you are making an offer to someone, inviting him to join you in some project, you smile, you lean slightly toward him, perhaps you extend your hand.

A Running Accompaniment in All Talk

If your interest in the conversation is but slight, you may speak more impassively, perhaps sunk back in your chair, your face and person listless. But there is still a constant change in look and pose, according to the thought which you utter. The fact that in conversation this running accompaniment of silent expression is virtually unconscious adds to its significance in the present discussion. It is evidence of the importance of silent expression in all effective speaking. The truth is that in interpreting the meaning of what people say to us, it is their looks and movements while speaking, along with the tones of their voices, on which we chiefly rely.

Improving Silent Expression

Making your speaking more effective does not involve doing things which are different from what we do ordinarily. It means stepping up the devices and methods of daily life so that they become more powerful and more consistent. That is the case with silent expression. To make your delivery fully effective you need to study this phase of our everyday talk. First you need to get a clear understanding of its principles. Then you should experiment and practice to apply them with greater effect in your conversation and everyday public speaking.

Vigor, Trimness of Bearing

The first point to consider is that when you rise to address an audience, your bearing and posture should indicate health, vigor, alertness. The fact that you are challenging the attention of these other people, asking them to keep still and listen to you, implies that you are in earnest about what you are saying. If in earnest, your whole person will be active and alert. Hence, you will stand erect.

Stand in a position that is easy, but will bespeak confidence. If your idea is vivid enough, you will be so dominated by the idea that you will unconsciously assume a position that is erect and courageous. You will not take a lazy position. You will not half sit on a table, or lean against the wall or a table. If your idea is worth expressing, you will not need a prop to hold you up for the purpose of making your thoughts known.

Stand Still

Do not pace back and forth while you talk. The caged tiger paces back and forth, but you are not caged. Nervous pacing in front of the group you are addressing implies agitation. The pacing speaker distracts his hearers. They feel he is not sure of himself. Stand still. If you have the pacing habit, practice talking in front of a mirror. Make a speech to your reflection. You will have to stand still to do that. Guard against the habit of jarring yourself by raising your body on your toes and dropping onto your heels every time you wish to emphasize a thought. That mannerism will distract your audience. Stand firmly on your feet. If you rock back and forth, bounce up and down, or pace back and forth, you are hindering your expression. Shall you change your position with a change of thought? Surely, but do not move continually. Let your hearers fix their gaze upon you. They will not do so unless you make it easy for them to do so.

What to Do with Your Hands!

In this connection, a word about your hands. Beginners, when they first stand up to express themselves before a group, tend to become conscious of their hands. They often ask, "What shall I do with my hands?" If they were asked in turn, "What do you do with them in conversation?" the answer probably would be, "I don't know, I never noticed."

Of course you never noticed. When you are conversing, you are not thinking about your hands; your attention is on the thoughts you are expressing. When you get up to address a group, do what you do in conversation. Forget your hands. Instead of wondering what you are going to do with them, you will unconsciously make use of them in a way that will aid your expression.

It is a very common failing on the part of the beginner at public speaking, to lock his hands together behind his back. He thinks he can "hold himself up" better. Often he vaguely feels more sure of himself.

Forget Them

That attitude is a delusion, because the holding is really a withholding of part of the physical power which should be put into expression. Your audience will sense it. Your words, your voice, will be somewhat retarded in their expression by the very fact that your hands are hidden and held at tension.

Put your hands in pockets, if you must. But do not do this continually. Any action that is carried on continually through a talk, any posture that is assumed again and again as an habitual action, becomes a mannerism. It detracts from expressiveness. It is like hearing a speaker a number of times and finding him repeatedly making use of the same sentence or the same phrase.

An Expressive Face

Let your feelings show in the expression of your face, as you utter successive ideas. In conversation, as noted already, the expression of a speaker's face is constantly changing. There should be the same slight but constant play of the features when addressing an audience.

Unfortunately, not all speakers remember this. Owing to embarrassment, or to an imperfect grasp of the principles of communication, they actually suppress their natural impulses to silent expression. Who has not heard a speaker begin a speech, perhaps on a subject of great interest to himself and his hearers, with words like these: "Ladies and Gentlemen: I am happy to be with you this evening and I am greatly pleased that you have extended to me the privilege of addressing you."

And how often has the speaker's silent expression given the lie to what the words were meant to convey! Perhaps he looked sad, worried, fearful. His face showed that he was not glad to be there, that he was undergoing an ordeal. Or perhaps his facial expression was cold and he was giving the audience a stony, icy stare. You felt that his words were merely a conventional formula. Conventional expressions are recognized as such and have no effect. They leave the audience cold and unimpressed. In cases like these a speaker's neglect of silent expression greatly weakens the effect of his words, perhaps kills it.

Let Your Feelings Show

If you were to meet a friend whom you had not seen for six months and you greeted him with words of pleasure, your face would show that pleasure. Your eyes would betoken gladness. Your entire countenance would light up. What you implied by the spoken word in your greeting would be emphasized, strengthened, vivified, by the joy expressed in your countenance. In the same way, let your feelings shine out in your face, when addressing an audience.

You can obtain suggestions with respect to mobility and expressiveness of countenance by watching the close-ups in motion pictures. Every emotional experience of the character must be portrayed in the actor's face. But you need not go outside of yourself to learn to express your feelings. As noted above, you use the same aids to expression naturally in conversation. When you are horrified at some tragic happening, your face aids your words in expressing your thoughts and feelings. You do not have to utter a word to show that you are angry. You do not have to cry out when you are in pain. You do not need to sing in order to express joy. Those who come in contact with you will know the emotion you are laboring under by the look on your face. When you get up to converse before a group of people, remember to employ the facial expression of animated conversation. Only in this way will you make the most out of the vocal expression of your feelings and your thoughts.

The Most Expressive Medium

Let your face indicate friendliness toward your audience. Never "look down" on them. A superior attitude is sensed by them from your carriage, voice, look, gesture. If your attitude is superior you can never hope to impress them favorably. They will be antagonistic. Remember that you are standing before them to give expression to your ideas. They are ready to listen, waiting to be impressed. They will help you in your expression if you have the right attitude.

Be sincere and let your sincerity shine out from your countenance. Do not wear a mask when you are talking. Let your feelings shine through with the sound of your voice. Two thousand years ago one of the Latin poets said, "If you would draw tears from others' eyes, yourself the signs of grief must show."

Your Eyes

In particular, remember that your eyes are the most expressive feature of the face. Look at your audience. Do not fasten your gaze on the ceiling or the floor. The individual who does not look you in the eye when conversing with you loses a great advantage. When conversing with an audience, you will suffer a similar loss if you do not look directly at them. Looking over their heads is not looking at them. Look into their faces.

Take care, however, that your gaze is not fastened throughout on one individual. Your audience is like the small group of friends you were talking with after luncheon. There were five of you. You were doing most of the talking. Your eyes were not glued on one individual, but looked at every one of them. The entire group came into the range of the focus of your eyes. So with your audience, look around. Let your gaze take in all of them. Turn to this group and that. Each of your audience will feel you are directing your gaze, and therefore, your remarks to him.

One caution, however, may be useful. Be careful when you catch the direct gaze of any individual, for that may cause you to lose the thread of your discourse. Unless you have your subject so well in hand that you need fear nothing, look your audience in the face but not directly in the eye.

An Example from Dr. Van Dyke

An excellent way to get started in the free use of facial expression is through analyzing and reading aloud passages from good speeches. It exercises you in doing consciously what in your conversation you do unconsciously. Try the following passage from a speech on "The Typical Dutchman" delivered by Dr. Henry Van Dyke, a gifted writer and speaker, before the Holland Society of New York.

What hero, artist, philosopher, discoverer, lawgiver, admiral, general, or monarch shall we choose from the long list of Holland's illustrious dead to stand as the typical Dutchman?

Nay, not one of these men, famous as they were, can fill the pedestal of honor tonight. For though their glorious achievements have lent an undying luster to the name of Holland, the qualities that really created her and made her great, lifted her in triumph from the sullen sea, massed her inhabitants like a living bulwark against oppression, filled her cities with the light of learning and her homes with the arts of peace, covered the ocean with her ships and the islands with her colonies—the qualities that made Holland great were the qualities of the common people. The ideal character of the Dutch race is not an exceptional genius, but a plain, brave, straightforward, kind-hearted, liberty-loving, law-abiding citizen—a man with a healthy conscience, a good digestion, and a cheerful determination to do his duty in the sphere of life to which God has called him.

Tracing the Signs of Expression

In the paragraph preceding this selection, Dr. Van Dyke had mentioned by name a number of the illustrious figures in Dutch history. Now he briefly recapitulates the diversity of their talents to lead up to the point he means to stress, the character of the *average* Dutch citizen. This opening question will be uttered deliberately and inquiringly. The speaker's face and manner will express active desire for an answer.

As he answers his own question in the sentence beginning "Nay, not one," the speaker's face expresses a downright negation, very likely with a shake of the head. He pauses, to let his statement sink in. Then his expression changes to the controlled eagerness of manner of one who has an interesting and surprising fact to impart. As he proceeds working up to a climax, as he enumerates again the many aspects of Holland's greatness, force and posture will express more and more strongly the feeling of enthusiasm. He pauses again, still with the look of eager expectancy. Then, in the closing sentence, he gives the answer, and face and posture express the delight and triumph of one who is telling his listeners something which he knows will please them as much as it does him.

Study this passage. Read it aloud before a mirror. Realize the successive changes of feeling and then let them shine out in your look and bearing. That will bring forcibly to your mind the part which silent expression plays in effective speaking.

An Example from "T. R."

Here is another example, from a speech made by Theodore Roosevelt a number of years ago. Here there are two dominant feelings. First is indignation. As the short blunt statements are uttered the speaker's posture will be erect and tense, and the expression of his face stern. With the sixth sentence, "No good whatever," the feeling of indignation changes to one of eager explanation. The speaker now is trying to make his point clear to those who have been careless in their thinking. Face and body will express an eager mood of "Can't you see?"

The danger is not really from corrupt corporations; it springs from the corruption itself, whether exercised for or against corporations.

The commandment reads: "Thou shalt not steal." It does not read: "Thou shalt not steal from the rich man." It reads simply and plainly: "Thou shalt not steal." No good whatever will come from that warped and weak morality which denounces bribery, but blinds itself to blackmail; which foams with rage if a corporation secures favors by improper methods, and merely leers with hideous mirth if the corporation is itself wronged. The only public servant who can be trusted honestly to protect the rights of the public against the misdeeds of a corporation is that public man who will just as surely protect the corporation itself from vengeful aggression. If a public man is willing to yield to popular clamor and do wrong to the men of wealth or to rich corporations, it may be set down as certain that if the opportunity comes he will secretly and furtively do wrong to the public in the interest of a corporation.

Read this statement before a mirror. Note the impulses to facial expression that come to you and work them out with repeated readings.

Analyzing Speeches Will Help You

Practice of this kind, applied first to these two passages, then to the passages at the end of this paragraph and to speeches you read, will give you a better understanding of how your face changes, naturally, to express this or that feeling. Watching the play of features in the conversation and public addresses of other people will give you further aid. The sensitiveness to facial expression thus developed will carry over, even without your realizing the fact, into your delivery of speeches of your own.

The following passage from an address by Winston Churchill at Massachusetts Institute of Technology may be helpful to you as you read it aloud:

In the first half of the twentieth century, fanned by the crimson wings of war, the conquest of the air affected profoundly human affairs. It made the globe seem much bigger to the mind and much smaller to the body. The human biped was able to travel about far more quickly. This greatly reduced the size of his estate, while at the same time creating an even keener sense of its exploitable value. In the nineteenth century Jules Verne wrote *Round the World in Eighty Days*. It seemed a prodigy. Now you can get 'round it in four; but you do not see much of it on the way. The whole prospect and outlook of mankind grew immeasurably larger, and the multiplication of ideas also proceeded at an incredible rate This vast expansion was unhappily not accompanied by any noticeable advance in the stature of man, either in his mental faculties, or his moral character. His brain got no better, but it buzzed more. The scale of events around him assumed gigantic proportions while he remained about the same size. By comparison therefore he actually became much smaller. We no longer had great men directing manageable affairs. The need was to discipline an array of gigantic and turbulent facts. To this task we have certainly so far proved unequal. Science bestowed immense new powers on man and at the same time created conditions which were largely beyond his comprehension and still more beyond his control. While he nursed the illusion of growing mastery and exalted in his new trappings, he became the sport and presently the victim of tides, and currents, of whirlpools and tornadoes amid which he was far more helpless than he had been for a long time.

Posture and Movement

Before long you will find that the impulse to act out in this way the meaning of your words, by changes in the expression of your face, will go further. It will extend to your entire body. As a matter of fact, you cannot express in your face the signs of eagerness, enthusiasm, triumph—or anger, grief, or shame—without some changes in the poise of your body, without impulses to movements of hands, arms, or body.

Bryan's "The Cross of Gold"

Read aloud earnestly this passage from Bryan's famous "Cross of Gold" speech that won him his first nomination for President. You may find yourself impelled to act out the vehement statements in spontaneous pantomime.

The sympathies of the Democratic party are on the side of the struggling masses who have ever been the foundation of the Democratic party. There are two ideas of government. There are those who believe that, if you will only legislate to make the well-to-do prosperous, their prosperity will leak through to those below. The Democratic idea, however, has been that if you legislate to make the masses prosperous, their prosperity will find its way up through every class which rests upon them.

You come to us and tell us that the great cities are in favor of the gold standard; we reply that the great cities rest upon our broad and fertile prairies. Burn down your cities and leave our farms, and your cities will spring up again as if by magic; but destroy our farms and the grass will grow in the streets of every city in the country!

It Prompts to Gestures

You may be prompted to mark the contrast in the first paragraph by movements of the arm, downward first and then upward. In the second paragraph the bold challenge of the statements is likely to prompt repeated strong movements of the arms, a wide sweep of the arm at the reference to "broad and fertile prairies," a challenging shake of the hand toward the audience at "burn down your cities," and another sweep of the arm with the close of the sentence. That is, you will be making gestures.

The Significance of Gestures

Many beginners at everyday public speaking are troubled about this matter of gestures. Never having given consideration to the nature of silent expression, they think of gestures as something unnatural, something not really a part of their message, but which they have to "put in" every so often.

You can now see clearly that this idea is wrong. Gestures, movements of hands, arms, head, and trunk, are like the little changes in facial expression, the natural and spontaneous result of the impulse to act out the mental picture which you are conveying. Everyone makes gestures, both in conversation and in addressing audiences. Some persons move only slightly, others gesticulate frequently, but no one keeps body and arms absolutely still. When addressing an audience the movements will be larger than in conversation, but they will be just as spontaneous. Certainly, in the early stages of your study of everyday public speaking, do not worry about gestures. When you have the impulse to move hand, arms, or head, yield to it. Watch yourself in the mirror, in studying facial expression, and note what movements suggest themselves in connection with particular ideas or moods. Observe other speakers and note their movements just as you note the play of their features, the tones of their voices, their choice of language.

Be Natural

George F. Hoar, who was a United States senator from Massachusetts, and one of the most impressive speakers of his day, once said: "I believe that the most successful speakers whom I know would find it hard to tell you whether they themselves make gestures or not. They are so absolutely unconscious in the matter."

In other words, these speakers did not make gestures for the sake of moving their arms and hands. They were expressing thoughts, and with the expression came the gesture.

Some General Principles

The postures and movements actually used in gesticulation vary with the individual. For anyone deliberately to work out gestures and "put them in" may be fatal to effectiveness. At the same time, since all human bodies are built alike, there are certain movements and postures which are more expressive and more graceful than others. You do not want to appear awkward. A clumsy or absured posture detracts from the impressiveness of what you are saying.

In the course of ages, certain principles with respect to postures and movements that are effective before an audience have been discovered. It will be well for you to consider them. These are not matters of theory. When you are dominated by your feelings so that you forget yourself, your muscles will automatically move in the ways suggested below. If you continue your study of effective speaking so that addressing audiences becomes a matter of course with you, your gestures will eventually come to follow the lines here indicated. It will save your time, however, to have these principles in mind from the start.

Bold and Free Movements Best

Bear in mind in the first place that when standing in front of an audience, large and bold movements are more appropriate, more natural, than little twitching movements of the hand. A gesture is evidence of feeling or of active fancy. That feeling presumably dominates the entire person. Hence it will manifest itself not merely in the twitch of a hand, but in the sweep of an arm, in the poise of the whole body. A "lukewarm" gesture is unnatural.

The Impulse Travels Outward

In the second place, the impulse to illustrate a point starts in the nerve centers and travels outward to the extremities. Hence, when prompted to use your arm for a gesture, you will move the arm as a whole, pivoting it on the shoulder in a curve, a sweep. During the sweep the hand may be relaxed or even limp. When the gesture reaches the climax, the hand flicks open or the fist clinches. A gesture in which the hand assumes position first and then is pushed out by the arm tends to be unnatural.

Four Common Types

In everyday public speaking, you will be prompted constantly to use the four types of gestures listed below. Each individual will make these in a slightly different way, but the general principles here indicated should be borne in mind.

INTELLECTUAL APPEAL

Most common of all is a movement of intellectual appeal, exhibiting evidence, or challenging consideration of a statement. In this, the open hand is extended toward the audience with palm up. The position suggests, "Here are the facts! Look at them!" If you are standing on a platform, the hand should be tipped slightly downward so that the audience can see the "facts" you are displaying. In this gesture, as in all others, the hand should not fall much below the waist.

POSITIVE ASSERTION

Another movement that is universal is the gesture of assertion, a downward stroke of the arm ending about the level of the waist to emphasize the point. This gesture suggests, "This is true! We must do it!" As the gesture comes to its culmination, the hand may be open, the fist may be clinched, or the hand may be closed except for the forefinger. But always the suggestion is that of a downward blow; not of an effort to exhibit something to an observer.

DISAPPROVAL, REJECTION

A third gesture of emphasis is the movement used to indicate disapproval, repulsion, to suggest, "This will not do! Take it away!" Such an idea may be suggested by a bold sweep of the arm sideways and down, the palm open as if striking the object or idea referred to aside.

A PICTURING GESTURE

Finally, you will often wish to use a picturing gesture to direct the listeners' gaze to some distant object or scene. This gesture takes the form of a sweep of the arm from front to side on a level with the eyes, as if you were sighting along your fingertips to the object on the horizon. In this gesture, the palm is turned away from the speaker and toward the imaginary object referred to. At the climax of the gesture, the hand is open and firm, or closed except for the forefinger.

What has been said above is merely given by way of general suggestion. Try these postures and movements for yourself. Memorize short passages of speeches and see how gestures of the kinds described can be utilized in delivery. Occasional practice in front of a mirror will help you. Observe other speakers and see how their movements exemplify the principles given here.

The speaker's use of gesticulation illustrates strikingly what was brought out earlier. The point was made that there are always two factors in delivery. One factor is the personal taste and impulse of the individual speaker. Since you are different from every other person, your movements will be different just as are your thoughts, and your way of using language. The second factor is that you are a human being, and your body is like that of everyone else. The movements you employ to convey ideas must follow certain lines or they will not be understood; they will not appear natural.

Do Not Move Too Much

Remember, however, not to move too much. Too many motions while talking distract the listeners. In Hamlet's "Advice to the Players" he says:

> Nor do not saw the air too much with your hand, thus, but use all gently; for in the very torrent, tempest, and (as I may say) whirlwind of your passion, you must acquire and beget a temperance that may give it smoothness. . . . Be not too tame neither; but let your own discretion be your tutor. Suit the action to the word, the word to the action.

Do not saw the air or use the hand as an axe upon the chopping block. The up-and-down movement of the arm, the continual repetition of the hand moving horizontally back and forth, from right to left, and left to right, is a mannerism. The habit comes from improper training in the use of gestures. It does not help to impress your idea but distracts and takes away from the vitality of your expression.

If you do not think of gestures or other aspects of expression for themselves, but concentrate upon the idea, your words will suit the thought, and the action will combine with the word to express the thought. The more intensely you feel about the subject on which you are going to talk, the more thoroughly you are convinced of the righteousness of your cause, the surer you are of the need for action, the more easily will you forget words, voice, movement, and have a natural poise which will make your expression not only impressive but artistic.

The Perfect Poise of a Master

This perfect poise, making possible the fullest use of the resources of silent expression, along with those of voice, of language, and of thought, is the distinguishing mark of the speaker of power.

Wendell Phillips was a brilliant speaker. Here is an analysis of his command of the powers of silent expression and of voice, made by George William Curtis, himself an eloquent speaker.

THE ART OF WENDELL PHILLIPS

He faced his audience with a tranquil mien and a beaming aspect that was never dimmed. He spoke, and in the measured cadence of his quiet voice there was intense feeling, but no declamation, no passionate appeal, no superficial and feigned emotion. It was simple colloquy—a gentleman conversing. Unconsciously and surely, the ear and heart were charmed. How was it done? Ah! how did Mozart do it, how Raphael?

The secret of the rose's sweetness, of the bird's ectasy, of the sunset's glory—that is the secret of genius and of eloquence. What was heard, what was seen, was the form of noble manhood, the courteous and self-possessed tone, the flow of modulated speech, sparkling with matchless richness of illustration, with apt illusion and happy anecdote and historic parallel, with wit and pitiless invective, with melodious pathos, with stinging satire, with crackling epigram and limpid humor, the bright ripples that play around the sure and steady prow of the resistless ship. Like an illuminated vase of odors, he glowed with concentrated and perfumed fire. The divine energy of his conviction utterly possessed him, and his

Pure and eloquent blood
Spoke in his cheek, and so distinctly wrought,
That one might almost say his body through

Developing Your Inborn Power

None of us can attain perfection in all aspects of public speaking, but anyone who will apply to his own speaking some of the principles which have been discussed here, who will let his own nature express itself freely, who will think straight, formulate his ideas plainly and vigorously, and then let his feelings express themselves freely in voice and silent expression, will win attention, respect, and admiration. If he has a real message, and will let it shine out through his delivery, he can become an exceptionally able speaker with power for leadership.

PART IV
The Strategy of Presentation

Chapter 19

ENTHUSIASM—THE DRIVING POWER

THERE is an old saying: "The race is not always to the swift." It happens continually that a man who can run well when practicing privately is beaten out by another man who uses his head as well as his legs, who knows when to spurt and when to save his strength, and who takes advantage of special features of the track. The same principles hold true in public speaking.

Putting Your Powers to Use

Your effectiveness depends upon the way you use your mental powers, your expression apparatus, and the resources of language. You must never forget that speaking is a matter of action. It is the actual carrying of a message to the mind of other people so that they pay attention, grasp it, like it, and do what you desire.

Earlier we learned the recognized ways of framing, arranging, and stating the message in language. Then we learned the accepted ways of using the transmission apparatus—voice, utterance, and powers of silent expression. All this is necessary help toward improving the quality of your message and developing the full possibilities of your powers of transmission. It helps you to guard yourself against clumsiness, long-windedness, and other faults. You should master all this technique, just as a runner, no matter how gifted by nature, needs careful training. But the essential matter is the way you utilize ideas and the technique you use before an audience.

Unfortunately, it is possible to become engrossed in the preliminary practice without making it count effectively in actually talking to audiences. You may know speakers who have good ideas and perhaps fine powers of delivery (good voice, clear articulation, expressive face and person), but who are nevertheless ineffective as speakers. They are unable to put their powers to dynamic use, so that people follow them with interest. They lack delivery power. Sometimes they lack tact.

Learning to "Sail Your Boat"

In the succeeding chapters this vitally important matter of "sailing your boat," presenting a particular message to a particular audience, is treated. In some respects it is the heart of your training as an effective speaker.

Three Commandments

There are three commandments which you will find it profitable to observe whenever you address an audience. First, you must have what might be called a sufficient "head of steam" when you get up to speak. You must be enthusiastic, and you must manifest your enthusiasm. Second, you must talk to your listeners, not to yourself. In other words, you must focus attention upon the people you are addressing and their reactions to what you are saying. Third, you must adapt your manner of presentation to the kind of message you have to convey and to the situation. Different kinds of material and different situations require different ways of "propelling" your thought. Further, you must observe the rules of the game. When people gather in a group, as an audience, there are certain customs with regard to the conduct of the meeting which must be observed.

These commandments are absolute; there is no arguing about them. If you obey them, you have an opportunity to win the attention of any audience, and hold it. If you disregard them, your efforts may be futile. You may be unable to propel your message or guide it properly.

Be Enthusiastic and Show It

You must be enthusiastic whenever you speak. Lukewarm speaking, perfunctory speaking, is worse than useless. The very fact that you stand up and ask other people to be quiet and listen to you implies that you are in earnest.

Your message may be a stirring appeal for action, a thoughtful discussion of ideas, or a good-humored chat with a company of friends at dinner; but the people you are addressing must be made to feel that you wish them to hear what you would like to say, that you are deeply interested in talking to them.

In other words, you must show your enthusiasm. Merely exhibiting your thought to them with a detached, "take it or leave it" attitude is not effective speaking.

A Detached Attitude Is Fatal

Years ago, there was a distinguished professor in a leading college who had this detached manner. He taught by lectures. He was deeply interested in his subject and worked up his lectures carefully so far as the substance was concerned. If you paid attention, you received valuable information. But he seemed to care nothing about whether you listened. When the bell rang at the beginning of the hour, he began to read from his manuscript. He read straight through the hour, only pausing now and then to perform some experiment before the class. When the bell rang at the end of the hour, he stopped at whatever point in his manuscript he had reached. He spoke distinctly and correctly. He was a man of intelligence and culture, and his material was clearly and smoothly worded. But his voice and manner did not vary. He might have been an automaton.

This man's course was required in certain departments. But though he was a scholar of some note, very few students came back to take more of his work. His lecture was utterly lacking in enthusiasm.

This detached attitude is not confined to college lecture rooms. A woman on the producing staff of a motion picture studio, went out to address a "better films" association, in a suburb of a city, to tell them the story of the production of a current picture, full of activity and thrills. The material she had to present, the scene she had to describe, was dramatic in the extreme. Her listeners were keenly interested in learning about it. But her presentation was so languid, colorless, and detached that her audience almost went to sleep. She may have been an effective coach for other people, but she was utterly ineffective herself. The thing she was reporting was something in which she was deeply interested, but she failed to manifest her enthusiasm.

What Bryan Did at Chicago

On the other hand, think of William Jennings Bryan at the Democratic National Convention in Chicago in 1896. Bryan was then a young man only thirty-six years old, almost a nobody in that assembly of national Democratic leaders, but he was aflame with enthusiasm. He was bound to reach the minds of those delegates. His enthusiasm gripped them and set them also on fire. It won their acceptance of his platform, won for the dashing young orator the nomination for President, and changed the course of the party's life for years afterward. It is such enthusiasm, manifested enthusiasm, which is the vital element in all effective speaking. It gives driving power to your message.

The Power of Manifested Enthusiasm

It is too easy for us to lose sight of the tremendous power that comes from the manifestation of enthusiasm. We forget that the people we are addressing are not mind-readers. They cannot discover how earnest we are in our thought about a matter unless we reveal our feelings. "Silent waters run deep," says the proverb, but it is only when the river plunges over a ledge in a waterfall that the world can appreciate the power of that moving flood.

"Nothing great," says Emerson, "was ever achieved without enthusiasm." Thought alone is sometimes not enough. Sometimes thought may remain with the individual and never be successfully imparted to the world. Encompass all the knowledge of mankind in the brain of one individual and keep it there and he leaves the world as he found it. But fire that man's brain with enthusiasm, so that he gives the world the knowledge that is his, and the world and humanity may benefit from his thinking and enthusiastically follow the lead of the thinker.

When great thoughts are fired by the torch of enthusiasm, they become actions, accomplishments. As Bulwer-Lytton said, "Enthusiasm is the genius of sincerity, and truth accomplishes no victories without it." Bruce Barton commented that "If you can give your son only one gift, let it be enthusiasm."

Patrick Henry

Enthusiasm has overthrown despotism and built up governments. Would Patrick Henry have had the courage to denounce tyranny and to fling into the face of the British Government the challenge that initiated the American Revolution without the inspiration that must go with enthusiasm? Enthusiasm in the righteousness of the cause he espoused gave him the courage to taunt the powerful enemies of his country. By it he lighted the torch which was destined to sever the allegiance of the colonies to the crown; with enthusiasm he started the conflagration that freed the colonies.

Enthusiasm for Your Own Work

But perhaps you say, "That's fine, but I am going to talk on my everyday profession, my business, things with which I am thoroughly familiar. I haven't the urge that fired Patrick Henry."

Is that true? Is the statement fair to yourself? Far from it. In discussing ways and means to promote your business, in explaining some phase of your profession, in giving voice to your conviction on some local need, you have actually the same incentive for earnest feeling that dominates a great national figure. Enthusiasm, earnestness of purpose, is a mark of every individual who is striving for success. The professional or business man or woman who gets results must be filled with enthusiasm for his or her work. Everyday profession. Everyday business. A life work that permeates your entire being with the urge to action and accomplishment.

Without enthusiastic belief in the ultimate success of his work, Louis Pasteur could never have carried on the research that has made his name famous wherever the study of medicine is known. Do you believe that jurists like Chief Justice John Marshall and Justice Oliver Wendell Holmes and many others that members of the legal profession can mention, could have carried on their work without enthusiasm for it? As a business man, you also are of necessity enthusiastic about your product and the service which your business gives. It takes enthusiasm to sell. It takes enthusiasm to make products. It takes enthusiasm to build. It takes enthusiasm to be a great teacher, doctor, minister, musician.

Revealing Enthusiasm in Your Talk

Accordingly, the first requisite in making yourself an effective speaker is to permit this enthusiasm which you feel to manifest itself freely when you talk to others. If a young man came to you seeking a position with your business, how would you treat him? If he seemed to be a desirable candidate and you needed his services, you would become enthusiastic about your business. You would tell him about the hardships, but the picture you painted would make the hardships less important when viewed in the light of the chances of advancement and the remuneration for accomplishment that would be his reward. When you stand before a group and talk about your profession or your business, let this same enthusiasm be evident.

Do you thoroughly believe in what you are going to say? Have you thought it through so that you are convinced it is correct? Are you sure that those listening to you will be benefited by hearing and accepting your message? If so, let this conviction show in your talk.

Joseph Joubert once said, "No man can give faith unless he has faith. It is the persuaded who persuade." Likewise, it is those who have thoughtful convictions, and enthusiasm over these convictions, who persuade others to their viewpoints.

Club or Lodge Affairs; Public Questions

Enthusiasm enters also into the life of the fraternal order and club. If you are enthusiastic about the ideals of your order, if you have ideas that will accomplish results in a social way for your club, you should and will be able to put that enthusiasm into your address, whether your talk lasts minutes or lasts an hour.

Too little interest is taken by the business man in governmental affairs. When you feel the urge to talk about local, state, or national government; when there is a wrong to be righted; when public opinion needs to be aroused; enthusiasm will help to accomplish it. Whether you are talking about the need for paving certain streets, or discussing the need for the reduction of taxes before the members of your civic organization, your viewpoint will beget enthusiasm in others. That which seemed hard to accomplish will, because of the energy given by enthusiasm, yield to your great enthusiasm. That which you wish to see done will be done. You will accomplish it. Enthusiasm is contagious.

The way you manifest your enthusiasm will vary according to the circumstances, the type of audience you are addressing, and the nature of the particular message you have to present. It will, of course, vary also according to the type of person you are.

In the case of Billy Sunday, his enthusiasm manifested itself in inexhaustible physical energy and dash. With Wendell Phillips, it was entirely different; his fiery thought was delivered in a manner that was quiet, almost like conversation, but with a ring of passion in his tones that gripped the attention of all who heard him.

No Halfheartedness in Good Speeches

If you will analyze carefully the best speeches you hear you will find in nearly all of them clear evidence of the speaker's enthusiasm. These evidences have taken a different form in the speeches of finished orators such as Ingersoll, and Henry Grady; in those of popular leaders such as Lincoln, Bryan, Theodore Roosevelt, Franklin D. Roosevelt, and Alfred E. Smith; in those of leaders in social service, such as Dan Beard, and Helen Keller, and in the speeches of entertainment by Tom Collins. But however the speeches differ, you will find that they have one trait in common —there is no halfheartedness or lukewarmness in them. The speaker apparently puts his whole heart into his talk. He drives at the particular purpose he has in mind with all his energy, whether the purpose is to move the audience to stern indignation, to make them think, or to make them laugh.

This, then, is a major requirement in effective speaking: When you get up to speak, no matter what the situation may be, concentrate your entire energy upon expressing your thoughts without holding back. Then the convictions you have will reveal themselves and grip the hearers. Genuine feeling always commands attention.

The Basis of Enthusiasm—Imagination

But again you may interpose with the question, "How can I acquire this power of giving myself completely to the subject, and concentrating all my energy upon the message?" The answer is: Cultivate your imagination. Get away from the mere details of your message for a while. Stand back and look at it broadly. Consider its significance, its implications. Why, after all, should these listeners pay attention to it? What will they lose if they fail to grasp it? If you do that just before speaking, and if you have prepared your message conscientiously, you will recover the thrill and tingle of interest with which the message first flashed into your mind, and the torch of enthusiasm will be set ablaze. Enthusiasm may be stimulated by imagination. That is true in the world of deeds. Charles M. Schwab said: "A man to carry on a successful business, must have imagination. He must see things as a vision, a dream of the whole thing." Napoleon spoke with even greater positiveness; he said: "The imagination governs the universe."

Vision and Realization

What made radio possible? Knowledge? Yes, knowledge of electricity and communication. But back of that was imagination. Someone dreamed a dream, and scientists in various parts of the world began working on that dream. Radio was born. Then someone's imagination stepped in and made radio the stage from which the speaker and entertainer could move the audience to laughter and tears, to sorrow and joy. Someone's imagination through radio made a neighborhood of the universe.

Every inventor uses his imagination. The business man who walks down Main Street, looks at a building and says, "I think that would be a good place for my shop," is using his imagination.

Dreamers the Architects of Greatness

On the dreams of men of vivid imagination is built the enthusiasm that makes progress possible. Says Herbert Kaufman:

> Dreamers are the architects of greatness. Their brains have wrought all human miracles. In lace of stone their spires stab the Old World's skies and with their golden crosses kiss the sun. The belted wheel, the trail of steel, the churning screw, are shuttles in the loom on which they weave their magic tapestries. A flash out in the night leaps leagues of snarling seas and cries to shore for help, which, but for one man's dream, would never come. Their tunnels plow the river bed and chain island to the Motherland. Their wings of canvas beat the air and add the highways of the eagle to the human paths. A God-hewn voice swells from a disc of glue and wells out through a throat of brass, caught sweet and whole, to last beyond the maker of the song, because a dreamer dreamt. Your homes are set upon the land a dreamer found. The pictures on its walls are visions from a dreamer's soul. A dreamer's pain wails from your violin. They are the chosen few—the Blazers of the Way—who never wear Doubt's bandage on their eyes—who starve and chill and hurt, but hold to courage and to hope, because they know that there is always proof of truth for them who try—that only cowardice and lack of faith can keep the seeker from his chosen goal; but if his heart be strong and if he dream enough and dream it hard enough, he can attain, no matter where men failed before.
>
> Walls crumble and empires fall. The tidal wave sweeps from the sea and tears a fortress from its rocks. The rotting nations drop off Time's bough, and only things the dreamers make live on.

Use This Power in Your Speaking

Therefore, as you plan your speech, call your imagination into play. There is evidence of such play of imagination behind the great speeches of history, the informal but inspiring talks you hear at your luncheon club or convention.

As you reflect upon your idea, in the light of imagination, you will be convinced not only of its value but of the necessity for getting action upon it, for communicating it. You will have the urge to talk. If that urge is for an object as lofty as that which fired the enthusiasm of Patrick Henry, you will rise to the heights of oratory. Those who hear will be challenged to follow you to attain the objective you seek. You may not as yet have all the expert's skill in framing your message. Your delivery apparatus may at present be untrained, awkward, faltering. But if you have the driving power of strong enthusiasm, your speaking will rouse attention in any audience at any time.

Chapter 20

MANIFESTING YOUR ENTHUSIASM

LET us consider in more detail the question of how you can make your enthusiasm show, so that it will be effective. What is involved specifically?

For one thing, remember to put color into your delivery—always. When addressing an audience, you cannot afford ever to speak in a passive monotonous manner. Everything you say in a speech should have a live, individual quality which will catch the attention of those you are addressing.

Each item you present should be significant, should contribute to building up in your listeners' minds your own enthusiasm.

Color through Delivery

This does not mean making every statement noisy or aggressive. It means putting color into your talk. It means skillfully utilizing inflection and emphasis—the manner of uttering the individual words and phrases—in ways that are appropriate to what you are saying and the effect you wish to secure. Few people realize how much the successful conveyance of ideas depends upon the manner in which the individual statements are uttered.

Emphasis and Inflection

Take a very simple illustration, the common phrase of greeting, "How do you do?" Here we have four words whose meaning, you might say, everyone would know. But are you sure? Just what does the sentence mean as you see it on this page? What is behind the greeting? Is it cordial? Is it joyful? Is it mere cold politeness? You cannot tell merely from seeing it in print.

But if you heard the sentence spoken in conversation, you would know at once what it meant. For "How do you do?" takes on a wide variety of meanings, depending on the inflection and emphasis given to the different words as you speak them.

Emphasis and inflection are used by us every time we speak. They color the sound of everything we say. By their variety, they cause the words to reveal the speaker's mental attitude, his thought, and emotion. Insufficient color in speech produces monotony, and that stifles the listener's interest. The speech of spontaneous conversation is not monotonous because the expression of our thoughts is colored automatically by the feelings which dominate us at the moment.

Often Lacking in Public Speech

About the only time we fail to use inflection and emphasis in our talk is when we are repeating an expression whose meaning we do not thoroughly understand, or when we are making a speech without having the driving power of enthusiasm.

Sometimes this lack of inflection, this monotony of expression in delivering a speech, is caused by diffidence. We are afraid, or rather ashamed, to show our emotions. We simply give the word content, leaving the hearer to interpret the words as best he may. This diffidence may possibly be traced back to the schoolroom where, as children, we read monotonously for fear of being laughed at or becoming the butt of the gibes of companions.

Generally, however, the trouble is merely failure to use the appropriate degree of emphasis and inflection. We forget that talking to a group is magnified conversation, and that therefore the emphasis and inflection which are suitable for conversation with a single individual need to be enlarged and magnified, in proportion.

Stepping Up Conversational Emphasis

How can you learn to magnify the inflection and emphasis so they will be adequate and effective in talking to a group? You can take some familiar expressions or statements such as you employ in private conversation and study them. Find out what you do when you give them proper emphasis and inflection in conversation. Then experiment in giving them the degree of enlargement which seems appropriate for the louder tone and slower utterance of public speaking. Consider, for example, the sentence of greeting, "How do you do?" Repeat it four times, emphasizing a different word at each repetition. Notice the meaning when you emphasize "How"; when you emphasize "do"; when you stress "you";

or make the last "do" the word that stands out. You will discover that each of these four words can be variously emphasized to show a number of shades of meaning.

Skillful Use of Contrast

You will not always, of course, pronounce the emphatic word in a louder tone of voice. A word may be made emphatic by uttering it more quietly. Or it may be made emphatic by drawling out the sound, dwelling upon it. Any use of the voice which makes the word differ in its vocalization so that it is more impressive than the other words in a sentence is emphasis. "Emphasis with pencil or etching needle is," said Philip Hamerton, an English artist, "the exaggeration of some point which has powerfully struck the artist, or to which he intends to direct the attention of the spectator." Substitute "listener" for "spectator," then erase "with pencil or etching needle" and insert "by the speaker or conversationalist" and you will have an excellent definition of emphasis generally.

To return to our question, how are you to determine the degree of increase in loudness or sharpness of utterance in the wider range of pitch which is appropriate for the particular speech you are delivering?

Watching the Audience Helps

First of all, remember to look at your audience, as we have already explained, and talk directly to them. Perhaps you can pick out some one of your listeners and talk to that individual. This of itself will help you to give the correct degree of color to your expression. You will tend to make the actual adjustment in volume and intonation unconsciously, because you are thinking of that individual and aiming your remarks at him.

Writing Your Speech for Analysis

You may find it very helpful also to write out a speech you are preparing and then go over it systematically from the standpoint of emphasis and inflection. Read it aloud passage by passage, thinking always of the persons for whom it is designed and their probable reaction. Try different passages over again and again in various ways and note how they sound, until you get an effect that seems to you right for that audience. The value of this exercise lies in its stimulus to your imagination. Be careful not to try to memorize the emphasis and inflection.

Some speakers go so far as to write out their speeches and then deliberately place marks of inflection and emphasis above the different words to be given emphasis in the address. This method may be practical for certain individuals. There is a slight danger that it may be stilted and unnatural.

Prepare the speech thoroughly, study it carefully, and determine beforehand some of the major places where emphasis is required. Your enthusiasm on the platform will naturally help to give emphasis at appropriate places as you speak.

Analyzing Other Speakers

When you are preparing a speech, make it a point to listen to other speakers who may be handling material similar to your own. Note their use of emphasis and inflection. You are likely to obtain some hints which you can apply to your own delivery.

When you listen to speakers on the radio, notice their methods. Some of them utter their remarks naturally, easily, and interestingly. There will be others whose speech will sound mechanical. In some instances the speaker will apply inflection and emphasis in an exaggerated manner, causing you to think of his method of talking rather than of the speech itself. Any inflection, any emphasis, which calls attention to itself is defective, and detracts from expressing your thought.

Motion Pictures

You can learn something perhaps from the movies, even if the picture you see does not give material that closely parallels what you plan to cover. Note particularly the difference in the degree of stress placed on important words and the degree to which the actors' voices range up and down in pitch, according to the different situations and scenes.

The Best Aid—Reading Aloud

One of the best of all aids in preparing good controls for your use of emphasis is that of reading aloud other speeches of a character or style somewhat like the one you are preparing. Working over other speeches to study the use of inflection and emphasis will be helpful in developing your ability to give your own speeches color.

One man who is frequently called on to address business gatherings utilizes this device regularly. When he has a speaking engagement, he makes it a practice, generally the evening before, to take down a volume of speeches, find one that is somewhat parallel in situation or feeling to the one he is preparing, and read the speech aloud, with all the spirit and expressiveness he can command. He finds that this always helps him to make the most of his own material when he faces his audience.

You have at hand, in this book, a collection of excellent excerpts from many speeches. Many interesting passages are in the last chapter of the book. Others are scattered through the earlier pages. Practicing inflection and emphasis with these passages should greatly assist you with your speeches.

Training Yourself in Reading

A word should be said here about your manner of reading for this purpose. It is necessary, of course, to read expressively and with ease. You will get little value from your reading if you merely stumble along uttering the words. To be helpful to yourself, your reading of the other man's speech must bring out fully his thought and feeling. To make sure of getting these you will generally find it wise to go carefully over the passage to be read, beforehand.

Most of us need to read a selection two or three times before we can properly interpret it. The first time you read an article you cannot put the proper inflection or emphasis on the words because you cannot correctly interpret what you read. A second reading will enable you to grasp the thought relations and the author's feeling. Then, having recognized the words and digested the thought, you will be able to express the thought properly by giving adequate color to the words. Practice of this sort is valuable indeed. It helps you to make the very most of your own powers of expression without risk of artificiality.

Incidentally, everyone likes to hear good reading. This practice which you take up merely as a stimulant to the use of your expressive powers in making a speech can be developed into an art that may help you on occasions when you are asked to read a statement or report to a group.

Color Through Form of Statement

The foregoing comments illustrate what can be done for the display of enthusiasm by attention to the details of delivery. What can be done in addition by modifying the methods of formulating the thought, the selection of words and forms of sentence structure, and the types of examples and illustrations?

Dramatizing Your Remarks

When addressing an audience you should make every effort to dramatize your statements, to express them in picture terms. You should work out a manner of dramatization which is appropriate to the kind of situation and audience. All of us do this when we are under the influence of strong feeling. Then we naturally tend to see things concretely, and to put them in picture terms when reporting them to other persons. In ordinary conversation, when not particularly excited, we fail to do this. We just employ the colorless generalized or abstract terms which we employ in our private thinking upon a subject. For public speaking the abstract terms are generally wrong. People need to be addressed generally by means of pictures. You should increase your power of painting pictures in words.

To this end you need to acquire the habit of letting your mind dwell on a point, recalling its graphic details if you are telling of an action, or building up in your mind with similar definiteness what might have happened if the scene is purely imaginary. This means not merely having in mind an idea that pictures for you an individual object or subject. It means giving that subject or object movement–making it grow.

An Auto Trip

You recall perhaps the story a friend told you recently about a pleasure trip that he took with his family. Just the statement, a pleasure trip that he took with his family, gave some kind of picture but not a definite picture. The trip might have been by boat, train, motorbus, automobile, or airplane; the language did not make this clear. Your friend went on to say that he motored from Los Angeles to New York. Still that expression, though it tied down the idea definitely to a motor trip between two points, gave no real picture of the trip. It brought out merely a picture of a straight line passage between the two cities. But when he told you he had purchased a new car in Los Angeles, started on the trip, enjoyed the scenery, and painted some of that scenery in words for you, you began to enjoy the trip with him.

Telling the Story in Pictures

You climbed with him up the mountain roads, and when he told you of a winding road down the side of a mountain, one side a cliff —a rocky wall rising up hundreds of feet—the roadway just wide enough for two cars—the other side of the road an abrupt precipice, the sight of which made one dizzy—you saw the picture of that road. When he related how something seemed to be wrong with the car—it continually veered over toward the edge of the precipice, and it took all his alertness to keep it on the inside of the road—you sat with him at the wheel. You were steering the car with him.

Suddenly the car swung in the opposite direction, toward the cliff. He couldn't hold it back. It crashed into the wall of rock. The wheel had come off. You were with him in his sigh of thanksgiving. You saw the possibility of the car having veered in the other direction. You felt with him the sure destruction that he had escaped. He visualized the experience through which he had passed. His language painted the picture he had in mind. He was living over again that trip and you, because of his pictures, were taking part in the experience with him.

Practice Visualizing

You can do the same thing in your talk to other people, if you will let yourself go. You can make others think through an experience along with you. Practice visualizing in developing an idea. Picture, think, during the time which everyone of us usually wastes, or which we could put to better purpose. When walking home, when riding alone in a public conveyance to and from business, and on the many other occasions during the day when the mind is working but not working purposefully, practice systematic visualization of an idea or an event.

David Belasco, before staging a drama, used to visualize the actions and attitudes of every character in the play. He sat before an open grate fire in his study and pictured in the flames not only the actors and actresses moving across this imaginary stage, but the very stage settings, the draperies, and the costumes of the characters. He saw mentally, before he attempted actually. This unusual power of mental vision that David Belasco possessed was undoubtedly a factor of major importance in making him one of the greatest dramatic directors of his day.

Analyzing Your Speech for Pictures

Do this with portions of a speech which you are preparing: take up one item or detail at a time and work out a little passage, either in your head or in written form. Polish it. Get it as near as you can to a form that satisfies your taste. Then put it aside. As with the matter of inflection and emphasis, the benefit you receive comes from exercising, stimulating, refreshing your memory and fancy, so that when the time comes to face the audience you will have these patterns of pictures in mind, ready for use.

Study Other Speakers

Here again the excerpts of speeches given in this book can be used continually. Look over a passage of a type similar to the one you are preparing. Examine the speaker's powers of picturesque statements, and see what suggestions these passages offer you with respect to the graphic formulation of your own speech points.

Speakers achieve their dramatic effects by widely different methods. The style of Wendell Phillips was very different from that of Alfred E. Smith. The style of Winston Churchill differs from that of Franklin D. Roosevelt. When you are preparing a speech study the choice of language or the building of illustrations in other speeches. Select one of them which embodies to some degree your own manner of presentation, analyze it, read it aloud, and then try clothing your thought in a similar form.

Color Through Use of Humor

One of the most useful aids in obtaining attention, and holding attention if it begins to wander, is the use of humor. When preparing a speech, consider this feature also. It may be desirable for you to open with a humorous story. Or it may be desirable to lessen tension, here or there, by inserting a pertinent humorous comment or remark to illustrate a point. There are, of course, occasions when any introduction of humor would be out of place, but they are comparatively few. Most speeches, whatever the subject, would be improved by a touch here and there of what has been called the "salt" of humor.

A strong point is to be driven home in your talk. You want your hearers to remember it. You impress it upon their attention by telling a humorous story, which makes the point clear. Your hearers chuckle with enjoyment and the story insures that the point will be remembered. Speakers who decry the use of wit and humor in a public address are likely not to be naturally gifted with wit, or not to be skilled in the art of story-telling. Beyond question, wit and humor very often serve to rouse attention in an audience or to keep interest alive.

Using Humor Judiciously

However, these devices should be used judiciously. Lincoln is often held up as an example of the good story-teller. Have you noticed that Lincoln never told a story just for the story's sake? Whenever he used a humorous anecdote, it emphasized or brought out some serious point. Here you have the fundamental rule for the use of humorous stories in speeches. *Never tell a story merely for the story's sake. Use it if it will aid in forcing home or illustrating a point.*

A notable example was given by the late "Jimmy" Walker, once mayor of New York, in recounting his first experience as an after-dinner speaker. He was the last speaker on the program. The man who preceded him was brilliant and witty.

> That speech, as far as the audience was concerned, finished the evening. Chairs were pushed back . . . and goodnights were said. The toastmaster gained attention only with difficulty. "Gentlemen," he said, "we have one other speaker on the program but I am sure he will agree with me that another speech would be an anti-climax. However, we should give him an opportunity to bid us goodnight."

Mr. Walker said he arose, shaking with nervousness.

> "Gentlemen," I said, "it is my hard luck to talk after such a speech as you have just heard. I should have spoken first. That's clear. But we can't all be first. Even the first President of this country wasn't first in everything. He was first in peace, first in war and first in the hearts of his countrymen. But, gentlemen, he married a widow."

That introduction in a very embarrassing situation attracted the attention of the audience. For the next twenty minutes they were kept in good humor by the witty remarks of the man who had cleverly won a hearing.

Learning to Tell a Story

There are men who say they can never tell a funny story. If you feel that way, simply tell your stories as anecdotes. Visualize the situation and just relate the anecdote as a picture from life, as something that happened. You will find that your story will win your hearers' attention, because it illustrates or forcibly brings home your point. You will also find that whatever humor there is in it will make its own impression without your effort. You will discover after a little experience, that you also can tell stories smoothly, that you may enjoy telling them, and that you will give amusement to your hearers.

There is always, of course, the possibility that your humorous story may have been heard many times before. Bear in mind, however, as Carolyn Wells once said:

There are jokes existing today that have existed since time began, and will be laughed at so long as humanity is on earth. They will be welcomed uproariously by each successive generation, and each new dawning sense of humor will respond to them as inevitably as the sunflower to the sun. For, like the sun, they are eternal, and they shine for all.

Good Telling Makes Old Stories New

Indeed, a story may have been heard many times and still be enjoyed. The secret lies in the manner in which it is told. When you tell a story visualize it. Take the following for instance:

A housewife inquired of her maid whether she had seen the merry-go-round which was reported to have been erected in an open square of the town.

"Yes, ma'am," replied the maid. "Dat lazy husband of mine wuz riding on dem wooden horses all yestidday afternoon. I wuz thar when he got off last night and I sez to him, 'Look heah, Jim, yer been ridin' all day and yer spent a dollah, now whar you been?' "

In telling this story, picture the merry-go-round. See it. Hear the music. See the husband, Jim, riding on one of the horses. Picture the enjoyment he is getting. Now picture him getting off the horse to start home. See his wife approach him and hear her upbraid him. If you can picture a story, humorous or not, in that fashion, it may help you to make it alive and interesting. That which you can mentally picture you can more easily tell about.

When telling a humorous story do not join in the laughter. You will get the best results by keeping a sober face. And unless you are a clever mimic, do not attempt to use dialect in your stories. Put the story in plain, everyday English. Most dialect stories are just as funny if told without the mimicry.

Some Aspects of Humor

The humor in your speech may make use of some of the following devices:

THE TRIVIAL, BUT SPECTACULAR, MISHAP. People always laugh when a fat man slips on the ice.

THE DOWNFALL OF FALSE DIGNITY. The snob in the tall silk hat whose dignity is affronted by a batted baseball.

EXAGGERATION, which puts false value on the thing, but emphasizes its real value by contrast.

THE PARADOX. A statement of thought by seemingly irreconcilable opposites, usually followed by an explanation.

IRONY, which, like the paradox, involves opposite statements but also implies an element of ridicule. When Job said in the Bible, "No doubt but ye are the people, and wisdom shall die with you," he stated the contrary of what he meant. That was irony. In Shakespeare's *Julius Caesar,* when Mark Antony said over Caesar's dead body, "For Brutus is an honorable man," it was irony.

SARCASM may have wit in it but it is cutting, bitter, and sharp. Voltaire said, "I know I am among civilized men because they are fighting so savagely." That was sarcasm. Irony might be called light sarcasm.

PARODY is a feeble or ridiculous imitation. The language or style of an author may be mimicked for comic effect. Someone wrote a poor parody for "ham" actors on these lines of Hamlet's soliloquy as follows:

> To be, or not to be—that is the question:
> Whether 'tis wiser to be biffed in the eye,
> By a soft and creamy custard pie,
> Or soaked and assaulted in the ear
> By the abhorrent and decayed vegetable.

Any of these devices may be used to good advantage, but be sparing in your use of the stinging humor called sarcasm. When sarcasm is made personal, the results obtained may be an antagonistic attitude on the part of your hearers. Sarcasm may have its place in a public address. It may be effective in overcoming an antagonist in an argument. But never overdo it. Sarcasm is very often resorted to by men who have no facts to present. They ridicule and by their ridicule hope to carry their point.

Color Through Sincerity

Remember, finally, that your oral expression of ideas can only be worthwhile if it is natural. Naturalness in this connection, as in every form of the art of expression, presupposes thought. The thought must be thoroughly digested before this ease or naturalness can be attained.

Know, then, what you want to say. Say it as you would say it in conversation. Sincerely express your thoughts. Your very sincerity must make for naturalness. If you are expressing your own thoughts, thoughts of whose validity you are convinced, you need not pose or assume an unnatural character. Your emphasis, pause, inflection, will be correct and inspiring. As Lewis Carroll said, "Take care of the sense and the sounds will take care of themselves."

"Eloquence Is Thought on Fire"

Sincerity, honesty, trustworthiness, are necessary in the individual who would address others and make them follow him. Sincerity may be simulated by the speaker who is dishonest in his expression, but his influence can hardly be permanent. His insincerity will be discovered, and thereafter his power will be lost. Whether the listeners can see and hear him as he speaks before them at a public gathering, or if they can merely hear him as he addresses them over the radio, sincerity must be the foundation stone upon which the structure of his thoughts is built. William Jennings Bryan is said once to have stated, "Eloquence may be defined as the speech of one who knows what he is talking about and means what he says—it is thought on fire."

Thought on fire must be sincere.

New Opportunities—Radio Talks

When you talk over the radio, and you may be called upon to do so, your gestures and facial expression will not be seen. Your inflection, emphasis, and pauses will take their place. Through them will shine forth your sincerity. Your hearers will drink in your words and follow your reasoning because, with good judgment as the arbiter, you have weighed your thoughts. If you should speak on television, your gestures and facial expression will be seen and can be used to convey your message with effectiveness.

Speaking has become the school of the nation and of the world. You have the opportunity to aid in clarifying topics in which the public is interested, in influencing men and women for good. It is an opportunity the like of which has never before been offered. Practice so that your influence will count. The ability to speak effectively can be acquired. It is an acquirement rather than a gift. Practice, after careful thought, will secure for you the acquiremen. of effective speech.

Chapter 21

WATCHING YOUR AUDIENCE

AS we have already noted, the first requirement for effective use of your powers in addressing an audience is enthusiasm. But there is a second requirement that is just as important, namely, that the speech be appropriate to the occasion, the situation, the audience. Far too many speeches fail at this point; they do not fit the situation.

Suiting the Speech to the Audience

A good speech is never a mere general statement addressed "to whom it may concern"; it is as individual as a letter. It is a message adjusted to a particular group of listeners at a particular time. No matter how valuable your ideas, no matter how great your own enthusiasm may be, if your thoughts and your manner of delivery are not adapted to the capacity and tastes of the people you are addressing, your message cannot "get over" with full force.

Speakers Who Do Not "Get Over"

We listen to some men talk from a sense of duty. A man who is an expert on some subject may be a speaker of this type. While he is talking his mind seems to be far away, ruminating on something not connected with his statement. He is looking back, as it were, searching his mind. Instead of expressing himself, he is reflecting and searching.

Or we find an individual addressing a group of his subordinates. They listen to him not because of what he has to say but because of his position. He has the facts but has no plan to his talk. He may be enthusiastic, but he gives no physical outlet to that enthusiasm. He is not talking as a man with a message. He fails to impress.

Then there is the speaker to whom we listen because we are courteous. We are charitable. We hesitate to disturb him while he talks. We are too polite to get up and leave. He does not entertain us. He does not instruct us. He is just a voice. Why? He has made no real preparation. His talk is just an aimless ramble. He is like a man telling the oft-repeated story of his boyhood days or his experiences in the wars. Children listen open-mouthed and open-eyed, but adults listen merely from courtesy.

Talk to Your Audience

On the other hand, there is the speaker to whom we listen because of his power. People say of such an individual, "You have to listen to him; he is so interesting." The reason is that he is thinking of his audience and definitely addressing his talk to them.

You do not want to be listened to out of a sense of duty or through mere politeness. You want to make people anxious to hear you. Therefore, as a condition of speaking effectively, focus your active interest on your listeners and present your message in a form which they will like, and which will require no deliberation by them to find out what you are trying to say. The idea you wish to present should be clear in your mind; what you need to think about is your listeners and how they are getting your idea.

Forgetting the Audience a Common Fault

This attitude of attention to the listeners might seem to be a matter of course, something we achieve without effort. In reality, however, we constantly neglect it. The beginner at public speaking forgets his audience because he is not sure of himself, and his attention is fixed on what he wants to say, on his own posture, his voice, his hands. Later on, when the art of speaking to a group has become familiar so that he is no longer afraid of "getting stuck," his mind is apt to be fixed upon the ideas he wants to present. Without realizing the fact, he forgets his audience and just talks to himself.

In fact, we are all constantly subject to the temptation to lose ourselves in our own thoughts, to become so interested in working out our ideas and statements that we forget what we are uttering them for, or to whom we are speaking at the moment. Talking to ourselves in this way is common with all of us.

Some of the worst sinners are experienced speakers who ought to know better, people whose ideas are valuable and interesting, who can express themselves cleverly, perhaps strikingly. But they forget their listeners.

Mark Antony versus Brutus

The most famous example of all time is the speech assigned to Brutus in Shakespeare's play, *Julius Caesar,* the address to the crowd of citizens after the assassination of Caesar. Brutus, according to the play, is the leading senator in Rome, an experienced public man, a great statesman. On this occasion, he utters ideas that are lofty and earnest, in a form that is dignified, tasteful, gentlemanly. But his presentation as a whole is utterly unsuited to the crowd of emotional "men in the street." Then comes Mark Antony with a speech that is one of the best examples on record of a skillful "you"-appeal, and the crowd forgets Brutus and his sound ideas and swings over as one man to follow Antony.

Look up these two speeches and analyze them. You will recognize clearly the ineffectiveness of the speech of Brutus as compared to that of Antony, and the reason for it. Then, to follow up this analysis, read aloud Antony's speech, or better still, memorize it and practice delivering it. It will become for you a most valuable tool. It will be a yardstick not only with respect to the manifestation of enthusiasm, but also with respect to the art of watching an audience and adapting a message to their reactions.

While this speech of Antony's was of course "made up" by Shakespeare, it is based on what happened. Antony did actually win over the Roman crowd by an appeal of this character, the details of which of course are lost. Shakespeare's creative imagination has filled in the details and produced a speech which even today stirs a reader.

Study Other Speakers

An indispensable part of your self-training in effective speaking should consist of studying—as you have done in the case of the speeches of Brutus and Antony—the way speakers handle a situation. Form the habit of analyzing the speeches you hear at public meetings, or over the radio, to study the strategy of the speakers. You can very profitably apply the same sort of scrutiny to the way people talk in conversation. Such attention to the methods of other conversationalists will gradually develop in you the ability to watch yourself also, to keep aware of the methods you are employing when you address an audience or carry on a conversation. Then you will be on the straight road to becoming a really effective speaker, able to use at will all your resources of thought, language, and delivery. And even if you still have handicaps—a light voice, enunciation that is not quite clear-cut, a lack of fluency, and so forth—these handicaps will be minimized. They will count for less, with any audience, because you will be able to adapt yourself to the changing moods of your listeners and to feed into their minds, moment by moment, just the suggestions that they should be given.

Look at Your Audience

Now, paying attention to the audience involves looking at them. Direct your gaze right at their faces, not at the floor or ceiling, or out of the window. You are delivering a message to them. Look and see whether they are grasping it, and how they react to it. We have already spoken of the power of the eyes, for expression. But do not forget that the main function of your eyes is to enable you to see what is going on. So, look at your listeners. Some beginning speakers say, "Oh, I just can't look at the audience; I get rattled. So I look over their heads!" That is all wrong. If you do that you will talk over their heads. They will feel it; they can tell where you are looking and will lose interest.

But if you look at the individual faces of the audience and "lean" on them, if you study your listeners' responses as shown by their looks, postures, and movements while you talk, these things will go far toward insuring that your talk will not be a mere harangue, but, as it should be, a conversation.

Watching the Weather Signs

A conversation is a two-sided affair. But so also is a speech. While the audience may say nothing audibly, they are constantly revealing their reaction to the speaker's message and personality. The skillful speaker steadily watches these revelations of the reactions of his hearers; he watches the road signs. We might better say, the weather signs, because the things to notice have to do largely with the moods or feelings of the audience, which change from moment to moment, as does the weather. According to what he sees, he modifies the form and manner of presentation of his message.

Sizing Up the Room and the Audience

Here are some specific suggestions to keep in mind as you work through your speech:

Before you speak, examine the room. Note its size, shape, and probable acoustic properties—whether it is an easy room to speak in, whether there is an echo, and so forth. If it is a large room, you know you will have to exert your voice from the start. You will also have to exert your voice if the ceiling is low, or if the space is broken by pillars, as in many hotel dining rooms. If there seems to be an echo, you will need to speak more slowly.

Try to size up the audience beforehand. If there are other speakers, note how the audience reacts to them, and to the chairman's opening remarks. A beginner should avoid, if possible, speaking first on a program. If he can arrange to follow other speakers, he can get some idea of the character and mood of the audience.

You Are on Exhibition

If you are seated on the platform, remember that you are on exhibition even before you rise to speak. Don't slouch in your seat. Sit up. Listen to the other speakers. Don't whisper to the person next to you while someone else is speaking, and thereby set the audience the example of inattentiveness when it is your turn to speak.

Coming Forward to Speak—Some Do's and Don'ts

When introduced, stand up; bow very slightly to the chairman as you say, "Mr. Chairman" or "Mr. President"; then walk forward to the table or reading desk, if there is one, or to a point about six feet from the front of the platform. Do not stand right at the edge; the audience will be distracted, wondering whether you will step off. Stand facing the audience. Keep your feet together; do not straddle them apart, it looks awkward. Let your hands hang at your side. If there is a desk or table, do not use it as a place to lean on. Don't thrust your hands into your pockets at the beginning.

Do not address the audience until you have taken your position. To begin talking as you walk forward suggests uneasiness or embarrassment. Before beginning, glance over the audience a moment. This gives the people in the audience a chance to look you over. It will draw their eyes to you. That makes it easier for you to have their attention on your opening remark.

Ways of Beginning

As a rule, begin with a reference to the audience or the occasion. It always helps attention if you can tie your remarks to a matter which is in the mind of the audience. Sometimes it is effective to begin with a comment on something the chairman has said, or something said by a preceding speaker. In this case, the object should be not to take issue—that will not look well to the audience—but to support what has been said or give it a new application.

As a rule, do not begin with a reference to yourself. You are presumed to be there for the purpose of giving them a message; for you to be thinking of yourself at all is out of character. The only exception to this rule is when the situation gives opportunity for humor or a mild deprecating reference to yourself. For example, Newton D. Baker was a man rather small and slight of stature. When he began one speech, he stepped from behind a table with the remark, "Nature has ordained that I should never stand behind anything when I talk." Jimmy Walker, addressing a leading women's club just after taking office as mayor of New York, knew that all the women would note his diminutive size. He began his speech by saying, "Ladies, you see a little man in a large office."

Such a bit of mild self-banter prompts the audience to friendly sympathy for the speaker. With Newton D. Baker and James Walker it helped decidedly by stimulating the listeners to think of the importance and ability of the speaker in spite of this handicap of small size. Further, it helped to get all the listeners to think of the same thing.

Make Sure They Can Hear

Speak the first sentence distinctly and strongly, so that all can notice and get accustomed to the sound of your voice. In listening at a meeting, as in listening over the telephone, the ear is apt to find difficulty in catching the first words of a new speaker.

If you are not sure about the acoustics of the room—whether those in the rear can hear you—it may be well to begin with some remark on a minor point that is likely to call out an immediate response. If you begin with a short and humorous story, or ask a direct question, at least some of the listeners will be prompted to indicate by their faces that they have heard. Using an unimportant remark for this purpose enables you to save your important main thought until the audience is ready to listen. Moreover, you may also note by that time whether your voice is carrying to the back of the room.

See That All Are Paying Attention

Watch all the audience; do not direct your talk wholly to the front row or to the chairman. Look at one person, always, but not for long at the same person. Look about the room, remembering of course to avoid a mechanical swing of your gaze back and forth. If you see a particular group that is not listening, go after them. You may interrupt your argument or explanation with a story or joke or special remark addressed to that group or individual.

Notice whether they are all relaxed and still, as you talk. That shows they are absorbed. If they are stirring, coughing, or shifting in their seats, it shows they are not fully gripped by attention to what you are saying. In that case, interrupt your main speech and get their attention by some digression, and later resume the thread of your discourse.

Quieting a Noisy Audience

Here is one way of securing quiet from a noisy or restless crowd. Break off the thread of your discourse, and turn to a group in a front row and begin talking to them softly and in a confidential manner. Curiosity is one of the strong impulses in human nature. If the others think you are telling somebody a secret, they will quiet down, almost at once, to find out what it is. In a moment or two, when you have their attention, you can quietly go on with your speech.

With long speeches, of thirty minutes or more, there is a problem of letting the audience rest. If the rest or relief periods are properly managed, you can hold your audience as long as you have something to say. The author has found that if he is scheduled to speak in the middle or near the end of a long program, it is advisable to ask the audience to stand and stretch just before he begins his speech.

Interruptions

Sometimes there will be interruptions. In that case, wait until the racket is over. On one occasion a young speaker was addressing a large audience of men and women on a psychological subject. After some difficulty he had obtained their attention; at that point the janitor took a notion to go up into the gallery and open a window. The janitor had heavy shoes and a clumsy step. The gallery was nearly empty. The result was a measured succession of heavy footfalls followed by a deafening crash. The young speaker was obviously disconcerted by the noise and lost the attention of his hearers. An experienced speaker would merely have laughed with the audience, waited for quiet, and then resumed his speech with some such informal remark as, "Well, as I was saying before the crash . . ." The experienced speaker is able to make even interruptions strengthen his hold upon the audience.

The experienced speaker establishes a natural relation with the audience, that of magnified conversation. It is magnified, so that all can hear, slower than conversation with an individual, because the listeners' minds move at varying paces.

How Fast to Talk

This brings up the question of how fast to talk. The rapidity with which one speaks varies with the speaker. Some people naturally talk faster than others. Your speech must not be so fast it will not be readily understood by all. It must not be too slow—or it will seem labored, unnaturally solemn, or weighty. The rate of about 150 words a minute is likely to be right for an audience of moderate size, 100 to 200 persons. With a large audience—300 or over—speak somewhat more slowly, perhaps 120 words per minute. Then the rate of utterance allows you to shape all the syllables clearly and enunciate them properly.

Speaking Outdoors

Occasionally, you may have to speak to an audience outdoors. You will think this difficult, that your voice will not carry. That is not the fact. Speaking outdoors is not at all difficult if you use your breath properly, if you speak with resonance, and if you enunciate clearly. You need to speak more slowly than indoors, perhaps fewer than 100 words per minute. Let the words float out clearly.

In talking to large audiences or outdoors, take special care to sound the last word of every sentence clearly with a full tone. In this matter there is a special difference between the technique of public speaking and that of conversation. In conversation, many of your sentences do not need to be spoken fully. The listener catches your meaning before the sentence is completed. But in addressing an audience, every sentence pattern should be rounded out clearly. Dropping the voice at the end gives an unfinished careless effect.

Avoid Irrelevant Movements

Be careful about automatic irrelevant motions such as playing with a pencil, rolling a pencil or piece of chalk between your fingers, moving little articles on the table, and drawing lines on the table with your fingers. Such motions distract the attention of listeners from what you are saying. They look grotesque, comical. What is worse, they suggest that your interest is not concentrated upon your listeners. They give your talk an air of abstraction or preoccupation. A great many people are victims of such habits, very often without realizing it. The ideal is to keep your body quiet, to make no movements except those which definitely aid in expressing your thought and feeling. That is what a good actor does. Develop the same habit of control. Then every change of posture, every gesture, every turn of your head, will definitely count toward expressing your message.

Do Not Lean Over the Table

Do not lean over the table and use it as a place to rest, particularly if you are tall. A certain business executive, a man of great ability and also of commanding stature, was not accustomed to addressing audiences, and was very nervous when he had to speak. His nervousness took the form of leaning forward, almost sprawling on the table, on both hands. The position, almost on all fours, made him look grotesque. Once in a while in the middle of his talk, he would forget himself, warm to his subject, and begin to talk directly at the listeners. When he straightened up to his full height, threw back his head, and let his big voice boom out, he was a different man. He should have assumed the proper erect position at the beginning.

If you concentrate attention upon the audience from the start, you are likely to avoid such irrelevant movements and postures.

Utilize Pauses

The experienced speaker has learned the value of pauses. The beginner is apt to feel that he must keep going. Hence he rushes himself, failing to give his points time. And he goes from one point to another faster than the minds of his listeners can move with him.

Generally, point B is an outgrowth of point A, perhaps an answer to it. You must give your listeners' minds time for A to be grasped, and for the response to be prompted, or B is without meaning for them. The experienced speaker knows the value of pausing to let a point sink in. He remembers what Hamilton Mabie said of Emerson's use of pauses: "Emerson was a master of speech; he would pause, and into the pool of expectancy created by that pause drop just the right word."

How can you gain this effect? You can gain it by using your natural powers of expression as you use them in conversation. You make pauses when you are conversing; utilize them also in addressing an audience. Do not confuse this pause for emphasis with hesitation, or what has been called "the empty pause," the pause that is empty of thought. The pause which is made to impress the thought makes it vital. You and your audience both realize that it is made to give time for the idea to be fully grasped. It is that pool of expectancy of which Emerson was master.

Without pauses you cannot emphasize correctly, nor can you use inflection to its best advantage. Pause is part of the variety of our speech. Listen to the skilled political orator and note, when he makes a telling point, when he expresses some unusual thought, how naturally he pauses. That pause, far from giving his hearers the opinion that he has forgotten, adds to the interest with which they listen to him.

An Attitude of Friendliness

Much of your effectiveness will depend upon you, not upon your subject. Your attitude toward your hearers can make or spoil your talk. Assume a friendly attitude. Someone has said, "If you want friends, be a friend." Unless you are friendly toward others you cannot expect friendliness. Guard against an antagonistic attitude, a feeling of pique against some individuals who may be present. No matter how you try to hide your feelings, your audience will sense them. Sensing them, they will assume a corresponding attitude, and your talk will be marred. When you stand up to talk do not assume an artificial smile. That is unnecessary. Friendliness is shown by the way you stand, by your tone of voice, by the look in your eye, by your entire personality. Friendliness shines out from within. It is not a surface quality but an interior attitude.

No Airs of Superiority

Do not assume an air of superiority. "I always assume," said Lincoln, "that my audience is in many things wiser than I am, and I say the most sensible thing I can to them." Abraham Lincoln never felt superior to his audience. You are not superior to your audience. They are as intelligent as you. It is possible that they may not know your particular subject as well as you do, but each of them may know some subject better than you do. To quote Charles A. Beard:

> In the presence of an intricate question respecting the hydraulics of river improvement, the physics of hull design and water resistance or the strength of materials, the most intelligent and highly educated lawyer or editor in America is about as helpless as the most ignorant laborer.

And, we might add, the laborer may know some things that might inform the learned persons referred to by Charles Beard. Talk with your audience. You are making confidants of them. You should be showing them your thoughts. You reveal your thoughts to your intimates, not to strangers. You cannot treat your hearers as strangers and get results. Do not talk down to them, but talk with them as you do with equals.

The Matter of Time—Promptness

Watch your time. Do not be late for a speaking engagement. If you are prompt and ready when called on, all is well; there is no need for explanations; the audience is not vexed. And yet, in a very exceptional situation, if you wish to provoke special attention, it may be well to be late. A situation of this kind would be very, very unusual, however.

During a stormy political campaign in a small Eastern city, a public meeting was called to determine party policy. The main object of the meeting was to confront the party chairman—the storm center—with his assembled enemies and force his resignation. The hour of meeting arrived, and everyone was there on time except the one man they wanted to see. He kept them waiting an hour. When he nonchalantly walked in, his enemies were so angry that they lost their heads completely and said things they had not meant to say. Their intended victim got them fighting among themselves, turned their arguments against them, and walked out of the meeting with an endorsement. Perhaps we can say that a case of this kind is so exceptional that it proves the rule, which is· Always be on time.

Do Not Talk too Long

Do not talk too long. This is a great temptation. We are always impelled to tell everything. There are always some additional details which we feel are very important or very interesting, and we run over the time a little. We do worse. We say to the audience, "I must tell you that," or "I want to add just this." That reminds the audience that we are running over our time. It implies that we are not sufficiently master of our material to be able to tell the essentials quickly and briefly. Never talk over your time. Never let yourself appear too eager to talk.

The Close of Your Speech

Your closing sentence should be distinct, but not loud. Do not close with arm extended in a gesture. Pause, hold your position a moment, then bow slightly and walk back to your seat.

It is not necessary to say, "Thank you," after closing the speech, although many persons do this. You have been giving the audience a message, instruction, or earnest advice. The situation is one in which you are the dominant factor. You have been invited to speak or have been permitted to speak because of your conviction of the value of your message, or the belief of your audience that you have something worthwhile to say to them. For you to follow this with "Thank you" may suggest that you did not feel sure of your justification in speaking.

Watching the audience, as suggested in this chapter, is a matter of tact and shrewd management. From a practical standpoint, it is an exceedingly important factor in effective speaking. It enables you to set the stage for your speech and maintain the proper atmosphere. Thereby, you make sure that your message is not wasted, that your material is brought forward when the audience is in the right condition to make the response you desire.

Chapter 22

PARLIAMENTARY PROCEDURE—DISCUSSION—DEBATING

VERY often your speech does not stand alone but is a contribution to a discussion, in which several other speakers participate. In this situation there are problems of your relations with other speakers. The way you handle these relations may affect very greatly your main objective, which is the reaction of the audience to you and your message.

The Special Technique of Discussion

Many persons who can deliver a good individual speech do not fit well into the give-and-take conditions of discussion. They fail to make a good showing in the cooperative activities of a meeting. Sometimes they neglect the courtesies of such an occasion. More often they fail to make the most of the opportunities which it offers. Attention to these matters will greatly increase your all-round effectiveness as a speaker.

Your speech may be a part of the proceedings of an organized body, an association, lodge, club, chamber of commerce, or a governmental unit such as a city council. Or it may be delivered before an unorganized group, gathered more or less casually to consider a matter of mutual interest. In any event, there are certain special points of technique which you need to understand and observe.

There are first the rules of the road, providing for the orderly conduct of a meeting, variously called parliamentary procedure, parliamentary practice, or parliamentary law. In addition, there are various points of technique which relate to the courtesies of such occasions and the conditions of effectiveness, which you will find it profitable to consider.

Parliamentary Rules of Conduct

By parliamentary procedure is meant the body of rules for organizing and conducting the business of societies, clubs, conventions, and other groups so that those who participate are enabled to form a satisfactory consensus of opinion with fairness to all and with efficiency. In conducting meetings courtesy and fairness to all are essential. The majority should rule, but the rights of the minority must be respected.

The rules of parliamentary procedure are definitely standardized. They apply, in some degree or other, to large groups but not always to small informal discussion groups. Everyone who takes part in a meeting conducted under the rules of parliamentary procedure is presumed to observe them. Indeed, to be able to follow the course of business in a meeting and vote intelligently when decision is called for, you need to be familiar with parliamentary rules even though you never get up to make a speech.

Parliamentary procedure is the outgrowth of the custom of responsible governing bodies, such as our Congress and the British Parliament, as developed through years and even centuries of experience. For general use, the rules have been simplified and arranged in convenient form in various books, but particularly in *Robert's Rules of Order*. The following pages set forth briefly the essential principles and cover the aspects of procedure which come up most frequently. You may find it valuable, however, in connection with your study of effective speaking, to get a copy of *Robert's Rules of Order*, or some other similar comprehensive book, and familiarize yourself with the details of the subject.

The Meeting Guided by a Chairman

According to the underlying conception of parliamentary procedure, the conduct of a meeting is committed always to a presiding officer, a chairman, who is the representative and spokesman, or he may be merely some one selected for the occasion. It is his duty to see that the rights of both speakers and audience are preserved. For example, the chairman sees that every speaker has a fair chance to present his message without exceeding the time allotted him, and that certain courtesies of language and action are maintained.

The special duties of a chairman are explained in the next chapter, but certain points should be noted here which directly bear on the conduct of the speaker. According to parliamentary procedure, the discussion is presumed to be carried on by way of the chairman; that is, each speaker is required to apply to the chairman for permission to speak, and then to address his remarks "to the chair." In our national House of Representatives, for example, members address all their remarks to "Mr. Speaker," which is the title given to the chairman of the House. Of course, in many informal meetings, this presumption that remarks are addressed not to the listeners but to the chairman is largely or wholly disregarded. Always, however, the speaker is required to "address the chair" on beginning his speech, and to stop when the chairman bids him.

Definite Proposals–Motions

Another basic point in the theory of parliamentary procedure is that the discussion at a meeting must always grow out of a definite proposal for action or expression of opinion by the group, which has been presented to them in the form of a motion or resolution. Speakers are expected to confine their remarks to the motion which is "before the house." Here again there are many types of meetings in which no motions are made or referred to, in which the discussion consists merely of a series of speeches. In your study of effective speaking, you are primarily concerned with what to say and how to say it. However, you will find it desirable to have clearly in mind the nature of the motions recognized in parliamentary procedure, how they are made, and how they are followed up with group action.

According to parliamentary procedure, the motions or proposals for action which, by way of the chairman, may be presented to a meeting, are of four general types: main motions, subsidiary motions, incidental motions, and privileged motions—or questions of privilege.

Course of a Main Motion

A main motion is the formal statement of a resolution by which the meeting may take action or indicate its views. A main motion cannot be made when any other question is before the group as it does not take precedence over anything. All privileged, incidental, and subsidiary motions can be made while a main motion is under consideration. The steps in making and voting on a motion are as follows:

OBTAIN THE FLOOR

The member rises and addresses the presiding officer, as Mr. (or Madam) Chairman or President, as the case may be; if the audience is large, the member gives his name unless he is known by the presiding officer. If the member is entitled to the floor, the chairman repeats the name of the speaker; if the group is small and the members know each other, the chairman may merely nod to the member. This recognition gives the member the right to speak.

It is now out of order for a member to stand before the speaker has finished or to remain standing after another has been given the floor.

MAKE THE MOTION

The member then states his motion or offers his resolution. For example, he may say, "I move that we take action to secure a playground for this community." In order to state a motion properly the members of the organization should become accustomed to using the words "I move that" when introducing a motion.

SECOND THE MOTION

If anyone wishes the matter discussed and voted upon, a member of a small group says, "I second the motion," without rising or addressing the chair. In a large group the member generally rises, and without waiting until the chairman recognizes him, says, "Mr. Chairman, I second the motion." If no member seconds the motion immediately, the chairman repeats the motion and asks, "Is the motion seconded?" If the motion is not then seconded, the chairman may say, "There being no second, the motion is not before the assembly." There are various motions which do not require a second, such as questions of order, nominations, and leave to withdraw a motion. It is suggested that you consult a special book on parliamentary procedure if you are interested in the details of these various motions.

STATE THE MOTION

After the motion is seconded, the chairman then states the motion. For example, he may say, "It has been moved and seconded that we secure a speaker from Chicago for our meeting on May sixteenth." As this motion is debatable and amendable, the chair should then immediately ask. "Are you ready for the question?" or "Is there any discussion?" If the motion is not debatable or amendable (consult your parliamentary authority on a particular motion, if in doubt), the chair should immediately put the question to a vote.

DISCUSSION

After a motion has been stated by the chair, it is before the assembly for consideration and discussion. Speakers to the motion must (1) address their remarks to the chairman, (2) be courteous in their language and deportment, and (3) avoid all personalities. Speakers must observe the rules of the organization as to the number of times they may speak to a question and the length of the speeches. The maker of a motion may vote against, but not speak against, his motion. Discussion must relate to the immediately pending question.

PUT THE QUESTION

After sufficient opportunity has been given for debate, the chairman repeats the motion and says, "Are you ready for the question?" After waiting a moment, if no one claims the floor, the chairman then says, "All those in favor of the motion as stated, say aye, all opposed, say no."

ANNOUNCE THE VOTE

The chairman says, "The ayes have it, and the motion is adopted," or "The nos have it, and the motion is lost," as the case may be. In the event of a tie, the motion is lost unless the chairman votes in the affirmative in order to carry the motion. A tie loses because every question must be carried by at least a majority. If in doubt as to the result, the chairman calls for a rising vote, first for, and then against, the motion, asks the secretary to count the votes, and then announces the result.

Subsidiary Motions

After a main motion has been stated to the meeting by the chairman, members of the group may think it desirable to change it or to dispose of it in some way other than by the regular course of discussion and vote outlined above. Accordingly, various subsidiary motions may be presented.

MOTIONS TO AMEND

After the question has been stated to the assembly by the presiding officer, a member may rise, address the chair, and after being recognized say, "I move to amend the motion by adding the words, 'provided that the speaker's fee and expenses do not exceed fifty dollars.' " After the motion to amend has been seconded, the chairman states the amendment, and repeats the motion as it will read if amended, so that all may understand the effect the amendment will have on the main motion. The chairman then calls for remarks.

The discussion is now upon the proposed amendment and, after discussion is over, the chair puts the question and calls for a vote on the amendment. After announcing the result of the vote on the amendment, the chairman will then restate the motion that is before the house, in its original form if the amendment has been lost, or as amended if the amendment has been carried, and the vote is then taken upon it in its final form (if no further amendments are offered.)

When a motion or resolution is under consideration, only one amendment of the first degree is permitted at a time, but one amendment of that amendment—that is, an amendment of the second degree—is also in order. An amendment must relate to the subject to be amended.

The amendment of the second degree, if there is one before the assembly, receives first consideration. After disposal, unless another secondary amendment is offered, the amendment of the first degree is then pending. After all amendments have been disposed of, the main motion as amended, or in its original form if all of the amendments have been lost, is placed before the assembly for action.

MOTION TO REFER TO A COMMITTEE

At any time a matter under consideration may be referred either to a standing committee or to one especially designated to consider the matter in hand.

MOTION TO VOTE ON THE PREVIOUS QUESTION

The object is to stop debate. If the motion is seconded, a vote is taken and a two-thirds majority for the motion will end the debate and compel a vote on the main motion.

MOTION TO LAY ON THE TABLE

The object is to defer action until a more favorable time.

MOTION TO POSTPONE

If the postponement is to a definite time, the object is to bring about a vote under favorable conditions. If it is to postpone indefinitely, the object is to dispose of the motion without voting on its merits. Indefinite postponements are out of order if amendments are pending.

MOTION TO RECONSIDER

The object is to bring up for fresh consideration a matter already voted. The motion must be made by some one who has voted on the prevailing side of the motion as previously carried.

Incidental Motions

Incidental motions arise from another question which is pending. They take precedence over and must be decided before the question which gave rise to them. They may also be incidental to a question that has just been pending, and they should be decided before other business is considered. Questions of order and appeal, suspension of the rules, and methods of voting are illustrations of incidental motions.

Privileged Motions

Privileged motions are not directly connected with the main motion under consideration. They have to do with the conduct of the meeting.

MOTION TO ADJOURN

This motion may be made at any time except when someone is speaking or when voting is in progress. It is not debatable and may not be amended. If the motion to adjourn specifies a certain time and place, and if no other business is pending, it may be treated as a main motion and amendments offered.

MOTION TO RISE TO A QUESTION OF PRIVILEGE

At any moment, except when motions to adjourn or recess are being considered, a matter affecting the efficiency of the organization or the rights and privileges of its members may be brought up. The form to be used is, "Mr. Chairman, I rise to a question of privilege." The chairman's answer is, "State your question." If the chairman decides that the question of privilege should be granted, he will say, "The question is well taken and the privilege will be granted." If the decision is adverse, he will say, "The privilege is not granted."

MOTION TO RISE TO A POINT OF ORDER

At any time when no other privileged motion is pending, a member who observes a violation of a rule of the organization or of the parliamentary procedure which it follows may rise and say, "Mr. Chairman, I rise to a point of order." The chairman asks the point and gives his ruling. If he is in doubt, he will ask the meeting to decide the question for him.

Value of Mastery of Parliamentary Procedure

Knowledge of parliamentary procedure is very helpful. It frequently enables an organization to accomplish smoothly and regularly some purpose which otherwise could not easily be attained. Furthermore, it sometimes happens that members of a group will try to take advantage of a situation by a technicality; and in that event, it is useful to know the resources of parliamentary procedure in order to prevent such attempts. To make a display of familiarity with parliamentary procedure is of course foolish. On most occasions, in informal meetings, minor infractions of the rules are harmless and may well be passed over. But when it is evident that careless action is leading an organization into trouble, it is desirable to have a knowledge of parliamentary procedure by which you can help to straighten out the situation.

Discussion Etiquette and Strategy

In addition to these formal rules of the road, in connection with a discussion, there are also points of etiquette and points of strategy which you will do well to observe.

Avoid Needless Repetition

Do not waste time repeating what others have said. In a discussion in which different aspects of a subject are given to a series of speakers for presentation, it is far too common for each of the speakers to inflict upon the audience a lengthy introduction to the main subject, in which he covers essentially what all the others cover. Nothing does more to kill the interest of an audience in a speaker. If you find when it comes to your turn, that some preliminary aspects of the topic have been inadequately treated, it is always in order to go back and fill in the topics which were not covered fully. But do not feel it your duty to fill in everything that has been omitted or to correct every minor error.

Do Not Hesitate to Speak

On the other hand, do not hang back or shrink from giving your view when your ideas are really different from those that have been expressed. Even though your general conclusions are the same, if the process by which you have reached them is radically different that fact may be interesting and useful. Your individual reaction is always of interest and you may express it briefly but adequately.

Build on What Has Been Said

The right way is to build upon what others have contributed. Make your talk grow out of something that has been planted in the mind of the audience by another speaker. If you follow this method you will find that the discussion offers a special opportunity to put over an idea in which you are interested. When you are the only speaker, you have to do all the work yourself; you must introduce the subject, get the audience ready to listen, cover all the points needed, and state the conclusion. But when there are other speakers you can count upon their doing their share. As indicated above, you can utilize items presented by them which support your views, and thus reinforce your own ideas by whatever prestige the other speakers possess. You can in this way focus your effort upon the points which you desire especially to stress.

Friendly Attitude toward Other Speakers

Remember also to maintain always a friendly attitude toward the other speakers. If your views differ sharply from those of previous speakers, so you have to take issue with them, be tactful and friendly. If you assume an antagonistic attitude toward another speaker, you cannot hope to win his support. Do not argue; explain. You have facts. You have, presumably, considered already the ideas which he has presented and discarded them because of some inadequacy. You should be able to show him, or at least be able to show the other members of the group, why your views are better. Be especially tactful in your introduction. First, talk about the points on which you agree, and try to win the other speaker over to you. Take the attitude that he is sincere in his views just as you are sincere in yours. He has not seen the question from the same viewpoint that you have. If we could all look at a problem from the same angle, we would all agree. Place him in a position where he can look at the matter from your viewpoint.

Simple Language

Take pains to put your ideas in language that the other speakers, and of course the audience, will understand readily and will like.

That is how Lincoln gained his power over audiences. Lincoln said:

You see, when I was a boy over in Indiana all the local politicians used to come to our cabin to discuss politics with my father. I used to sit by and listen to them, but father would not let me ask many questions, and there were a good many things I did not understand. Well, I'd go up to my room in the attic and sit down or pace back and forth until I made out just what they meant. And then I'd be awake for hours just a-putting their ideas into words that the boys around our way could understand.

Lincoln made the preparation for a particular group, for "the boys around our way." You should do the same. In a discussion, even more so when you are the only speaker, it is imperative that you "watch your audience"—and watch the other speakers.

Debating

There is one special form of discussion that deserves a brief mention—debating. Sometimes your view is squarely challenged by another speaker, or you may find it necessary to challenge another person's view. The issue is joined between the two of you. Your object is to establish your point and to overthrow that of the other speaker.

Debating exists in two forms. There is first the real clash of opinion that develops between persons who consider a matter from opposing points of view. Such a clash of opinion is found constantly in a highly specialized form, in the law courts. A lawyer is debating all the time. Similarly, there is a constant clash of opinion in political life, in national, state, and municipal campaigns. In connection with the policy of a business organization, or of an association, lodge, or club, such occasions for differences of opinion occur, but of course less frequently.

Debating as a Sport

There is also what might be called the "artificial" form of debating, considered as educational activity in colleges and high schools, and in special debating clubs outside. Debating, as carried on in this way, is artificial in that questions are formally set up and weighed, the contestants are grouped in teams, and certain conventions and rules of procedure are followed.

Participating in debating activities is very useful as a means of training in the logical, forceful, concise presentation of material. Many men who have achieved distinction as lawyers or in public life undoubtedly had rigorous practice in debating classes or clubs in youth. If you have an opportunity to become a member of a debating club, you may wish to take advantage of it. It will strongly reinforce the training you derive from studying this book.

Obviously, also, anyone who is a member of such a club, or whose activity in law or in politics calls for frequent debating, should find the broader training given in this book practical and beneficial.

Rules of Effective Debating

Any lengthy consideration of the special technique of debating should not be necessary here. A few points may be noted, however, which will be helpful on any occasion when you are required to engage in controversy with another speaker, or when you wish to argue a point. A discussion of debating technique involves a restatement, with somewhat different emphasis, of the directions for formulating material which we have previously presented.

A Clear Statement

Take care, always, before entering a debate, to work out definitely the question to be debated. This issue should be clearly drawn.

Definite Points

Break down your arguments into a few definite points. Take pains to express each of these points sharply and explicitly. In a speech on a subject that is controversial, it is always important to keep the audience reminded as to just where you are in your argument, how far you have come on the road, what is the relation of the item under consideration at the moment to preceding items and to those which are to follow.

Take care to arrange these points so that taken together they give a complete, constructive case, and so that they build up to a climax. The listeners will then be led, step by step, to the conclusion you desire. In a debate, remember, you are seeking a definite decision. There should be no waste material in a debate; everything you say should contribute to proving the point you seek to make.

Definite Evidence

Support each point by definite evidence. Present facts, not mere opinions or assertions. Take care to cite the source of your evidence, so that the listeners, if they desire, may verify it. Do not give too many facts, as that will only confuse your hearers, but choose a few which are strong and significant. Dramatize these facts. Put them in concrete, human terms.

Remember to point out explicitly the bearing of each item upon your case, just what it shows; do not leave this to be inferred.

Rebuttal

After you have presented your own case, or perhaps in the course of it, remember to take up and overthrow the points presented by the other side. Do not ignore them, or dodge them. But do not waste time upon trifles. Pick out the few vital points and drive hard against these.

Aggressiveness

In framing your points, in your language, in your delivery, drive hard. Your purpose is to win the decision, not merely to display knowledge of the subject. Do not be unfair. Any suspicion of unfairness will discredit you with the listeners; but do not be "easy." Debating is a friendly fight, and in a fight you are expected to hit hard enough to win.

Brevity

Be brief. A quick, well arranged, clean-cut presentation is far more powerful than a lengthy disquisition.

Discussion Is Invaluable Training

This chapter has dealt with situations when you are, in one way or another, brought into competition with other speakers, and with the requirements and the possibilities which grow out of that relationship. The further you go in your self-education in effective speaking, the more clearly you will see the bearing of what is said in this chapter upon all your speaking. For you are always competing against other speakers, whether or not they are actually present. The people who listen to you today, are comparing you, more or less consciously, with the men and women to whom they listened yesterday or last week. They are certain to appraise your knowledge of parliamentary procedure, your observance of the courtesies of discussion, your ability to make full use of the possibilities of controversy in terms of these other speakers. The more you know about the technique of discussion and debating and apply it to your own performance, even when you are the only speaker, the better your speeches will stand up in this final appraisal.

Chapter 23

THE DUTIES OF A CHAIRMAN

THERE is one type of public speaking with very special requirements and a special technique. That is the speaking which is required of the chairman of a meeting. You should not neglect it. As you become more active as a speaker in your organization, your lodge, your town, you will undoubtedly be called upon to preside at meetings, and you will find more need than ever for a command of effective speaking.

Importance of Chairman's Work

A good chairman does not talk much, but he needs to talk well. Indeed, he needs to have at his ready command all the varied resources discussed in this book. A great many of the persons who undertake to preside over meetings do it very badly. They never learn the special requirements of the situation. The result, often, is waste of time, confusion, and friction. Yet the technique of the chairman's office is not difficult to learn, and you will certainly find it convenient and useful to know.

Two Functions

The chairman of a meeting is generally the representative and spokesman of the group. He is thus at once the voice of authority and the host.

In embodying authority, the chairman has the responsibility of carrying through the program. He is expected to keep order, and to see that the requirements of parliamentary procedure are observed as far as they apply to the situation. With regard to the speakers, he is expected to see that they have an opportunity to deliver their messages without interference, but without overstepping their rights.

In addition, the chairman occupies the position of a host. He is expected to look out for the physical comfort of speakers and audience, with respect to quiet, ventilation, comfort, convenient lighting, and warmth. More than this, he is expected to make everyone feel at home, to establish and maintain an atmosphere of interest and good humor. It is no exaggeration to say that the success or failure of a meeting may depend very largely upon how well the chairman measures up to his responsibilities.

Keeping Order

With respect to keeping order the chairman should have a good knowledge of the principles of parliamentary procedure. If the meeting consists merely of a series of speeches, this knowledge may never be needed. But whenever there is discussion, there is always the risk that some persons will overstep the proper limits of courtesy or reasonableness, and cause delay, embarrassment, and friction. If the chairman knows his parliamentary law, he can handle the situation firmly and tactfully. If you are chosen to act as chairman of a meeting, procure one of the little manuals of parliamentary law beforehand, and prepare yourself for your responsibilities.

Alertness, Decisiveness, Fairness

This aspect of your duty as chairman calls for alertness of ear, eye, and brain. It calls for decisiveness; not, of course, noisy bluster, but quick, firm rulings. Your audience will expect you to "run the show"; they do not like a dilatory or indecisive chairman. You must be fair. Your decisions and your entire attitude must be impartial. Whatever may be your personal feeling with regard to a speaker or what he says, or with regard to members of the group, when you take charge of the meeting you put your personal feelings aside. For the time being, you represent not your own party but the entire assembly. In meetings of regularly organized groups, this is almost always the case. In too many meetings of less formal character, however, it is not the case. Whatever you can do by precept and example to raise the standard of presiding at a meeting is desirable.

Ready Command of Speech

Your work as chairman, keeping order, gives you excellent training in expressing yourself with readiness, clearness, decisiveness, and tact. When you are making a speech of your own, even a short speech, you have several minutes to present a point. But when you speak as chairman of the meeting, you are expected to say what is necessary in not more than a few sentences. Accordingly, you learn to choose words that will be accurate, expressive, and free from untactful suggestions. You learn to have a voice, enunciation, and posture under ready command, so that your brief statement and look may be fully effective. Such intensive training in tact and self-command is of the utmost aid, indirectly, to the effectiveness of your speaking at other times.

Bringing the Audience Forward

One little duty which often presents itself, particularly in meetings of unorganized groups, is that of inducing the audience to come forward. If the room is large, and the audience is not numerous, many of those present are almost certain to take rear seats, leaving an expanse of empty chairs between them and the speakers. That is not conducive to a good meeting. An experienced chair man makes it one of his first duties to get these diffident or lukewarm listeners to move forward to the front part of the room. It is sometimes a real test of his powers of good-humored persuasion.

Introducing Speakers

The chairman is an intermediary between the speaker and the audience. A good chairman can do a great deal to help a speaker present his message adequately.

In the first place, there is the matter of introducing the speakers. If you are appointed to preside at a meeting or dinner, remember that there is an art in introducing individuals to an audience. We say of one man that he is a magnificent toastmaster. He seems to know how to handle any situation that comes up. His introduction of the speakers is smooth and varies according to the topic.

As a rule, introductions should be short. But they may be so short as to be meaningless. William Jennings Bryan tells of one short introduction that he received. The chairman of the meeting said merely:

> Ladies and Gentlemen: I have been requested to introduce to you William Jennings Bryan who will talk to you. I have now done so. He will now do so.

The mere announcement: "Mr. Smith will now address you," is never sufficient to put the speaker at ease and cause a friendly attitude on the part of the audience.

On some occasions the message to be delivered, or the individual who is to be introduced, justifies a longer introduction. The term, longer, is merely relative; most introductions should not last more than from four to five minutes. You can say a great deal in five minutes. A speech of five minutes, transcribed on the typewriter, will cover two double-spaced typewritten pages, 8½ inches by 11 inches in size.

Planning in Advance

In order to carry out smoothly the introductions necessary at any function, the chairman must be prepared. He must plan. If there are a number of speakers to be called upon, he has the responsibility of choosing the speaker who is to begin the program. He must endeavor to pick the most effective speaker for the climax, the end of the program. Figures, statistical data, are sometimes dry and uninteresting. Accordingly, if you have a speaker on your program whose subject demands the use of a great deal of such material, introduce him at the beginning of the program, although not as the very first speaker.

If the speakers who are to appear are not known to you personally, endeavor to secure information in regard to them and their subjects. Do not wait to secure this information until immediately before the gathering takes place. It is embarrassing to the speaker and will be embarrassing to you if just before introducing a person you have to ask him to note on a card, or tell you, something about himself. Get the facts beforehand. And make sure that you have met the speakers before the meeting. The committee which arranged the program should introduce the speakers to you and to others who will take part in the function. It is even better if you have taken part in the selection of the speakers so that you will be certain to be chairman of what you believe is a worthwhile program.

Paving the Way for a Speaker

Do not make your introduction of the speaker too elaborate. Tell of your acquaintance with him. Say something of his reputation. Always bear in mind, however, that your function as presiding officer is merely to introduce the speaker, to pave the way for his talk. Do not make his speech for him. Be careful not to steal his thunder. That is a grave breach of tact.

Do not tell a large number of anecdotes or funny stories at the beginning. A good story, appropriately used, is always in good taste if it easily fits into your remarks, but never try to be facetious at the expense of the speaker unless you are very well acquainted with him and he is known to the audience. Your task is to put the speaker at ease and to make the audience want to listen to him. You are to introduce the speaker as a friend, to prepare the way for him. With your help he will get results, and his effectiveness will redound to your own credit.

Sometimes it is necessary to call upon someone who has not been notified before the meeting that he is to talk. In that case be sure that he receives some warning before you actually introduce him. Also, in justice to him, let the audience know in your introduction that he had not been given the usual invitation prior to the meeting.

Watching the Time

The chairman should keep careful watch of the time. It is easy to allow time to be wasted needlessly. The fault may be failure to make sure that all persons who are to take part in a program are in their places; or it may be overlong introductory remarks by the chairman himself. It may also result from permitting the speakers to overrun their allotted time.

You should have a definite understanding with those on the program with regard to the time each one is to consume in his talk. This is very often neglected. It is embarrassing to be told, "Talk as long as you like," and then find when the time comes to make your address that you have but ten or fifteen minutes in which to cover your subject. Whatever time limit has been set for a speaker, let him know it definitely beforehand. On the other hand, if a speaker runs over his time, do not hesitate to call his attention to the fact, tactfully and unobtrusively, and bring his talk to a close. You are the representative of the audience, with a responsibility for carrying the meeting through on time. It is better that a careless speaker should be embarrassed if he will not stop, than that the time of the other speakers should be taken and the whole audience inconvenienced.

Tact in Meeting Emergencies

The presiding officer frequently has on his shoulders the burden of handling embarrassing moments. There is need of tact in dealing with speakers, no less than in the handling of the audience itself. The tactful person says the right thing at the right time in the right way. He uses his imagination. He has breadth of sympathy. He not only avoids giving offense but enters readily into the experiences of others.

It is related that Mr. Robinson, the speaker of the Virginia House of Burgesses when George Washington was a member of that body, expressed the thanks of the House to him for his distinguished military service. The eloquence of the tribute so embarrassed Washington that when he arose to respond, he was overcome with confusion. Mr. Robinson relieved him by saying: "Sit down, Mr. Washington, your modesty is equal to your valor; and that surpasses the power of any language that I possess." It was an example of alertness, tact, and courtesy. A good presiding officer will emulate Mr. Robinson.

Conducting a Discussion

When there is a discussion, you as chairman have an added responsibility. Your duty to audience and speakers alike is to keep the discussion moving forward. You must not try to influence the speakers' thoughts. But you can do much, by means of a tactful remark or question here and there, to aid the group in keeping on the track, in avoiding digressions, or disputes over points that do not matter. You can also do much to get the group as a whole into the discussion and to make sure that all pertinent points of view are expressed. From the way individuals listen, an experienced chairman can usually discover those who really have something worth saying, but need a little urging to speak up. By drawing out these diffident or reticent people, through well-timed comments and questions, and occasionally a direct appeal, you can often turn a discussion that began unpromisingly into one that is spirited and constructive.

The Chairman's Talk

Besides introducing the speakers, and keeping your fingers on the discussion, you are expected in the capacity of chairman to open the meeting, to make announcements, and to close the meeting. In each of these situations, while your remarks should be brief, they need to be appropriate and skillful. You have the responsibility of guiding the proceedings.

Opening the Meeting

At the beginning, and particularly in the case of a special meeting, you have the task of opening the program. You are expected to state the reason for the gathering and welcome the guests. The purpose may be the celebration of a memorable event. It may be to honor a distinguished citizen. The voicing of public opinion may be the purpose. Perhaps a campaign for funds for a hospital is being started. Whatever the reason for the gathering, the presiding officer must state it concisely and gracefully.

Making Announcements

Frequently, the chairman will have to make an announcement. Generally this has to do with some feature of the organization's activity which presumably is of interest to the group as a whole. Do not speak in a perfunctory manner. Take pains to frame the announcement in simple and attractive language. Utter it distinctly, as if you cared about it.

Closing the Meeting

After the speakers have finished, you have the task of bringing the meeting to a close. You will not permit yourself to make a speech of course. Lengthy good-bys of any sort are out of place. On the other hand, merely to rap on the table with a blunt: "That is all. The meeting is adjourned," is equally unsatisfactory; it suggests that the chairman, at least, has had little interest in the proceedings; it comes like a dash of cold water. Instead, speaking as the representative of the audience, you should express in two or three short sentences their appreciation of what they have heard, and of the courtesy of the speakers in addressing them. If you can give your remarks a good-humored turn, sending the audience away with a smile, that is perhaps the best sort of conclusion.

Acting as Chairman Is Valuable Training

The good chairman does not show off or attract attention to himself. He keeps his personal views and feelings in the background and seeks to help others to speak. This, it should be repeated, requires constant alertness and tact. It requires also ready command of the art of language, to be able to say much in a few words, to say just enough to give the cue to someone else, or to ease an embarrassing situation. Nothing will do more to develop the power of expressing yourself in brief, colorful, tactful, effective remarks.

Serving as chairman of meetings offers a real opportunity to distinguish yourself. A good chairman is always in demand. The fact that you can be trusted to take charge of a meeting and run it skillfully and successfully may put you ahead on the road to recognition and influence. Incidentally, such work offers a distinct opportunity for the person who has good judgment and intelligence, but may lack fluency. Such a person is generally ready enough with single remarks which often have pungency and pleasant humor. There have been instances of persons quite lacking in fluency who have made names for themselves for skill in handling meetings.

What This Book Should Have Done for You

You should find that this book on effective speaking helps you in ways you had not considered before you read it. It should make you alert to determine just what you want to say on any occasion when your opinion is sought. It should bring readiness in framing your ideas in a form that is not only understandable but pleasing to the persons you address. It should already have given you surer command of the mechanism of delivery, made your voice better, your utterance more distinct, your manner more expressive.

A Wider Range of Interest

But more than this, your study of expression should widen your range of interests. Your mind should work more accurately. That of itself should make you more interesting. And this development and enrichment of your personality should aid you in your business or profession. The fact that you can talk effectively, whether to an individual or to a large audience, decisively and tactfully, may easily lead to acquaintanceship with people of standing and influence and bring you opportunities for leadership.

PART V

Valuable Reference Material in the Preparation of Your Speeches

Chapter 24

INTERESTING SELECTIONS FROM SPEECHES AND SERMONS

IN the pages which follow you will find selections from a great many speeches and sermons. Some of these selections consist of stories, illustrations, and humorous comments that you may find useful in your own speeches; others consist of interesting observations or summaries of facts that will help you with your speeches. You may also find occasions when you wish to quote from some of these speakers, giving credit to them for their remarks. These selections can be invaluable to you for reference and study.

Not Easy to Understand

I sat down with my income tax recently. They want me to guess what I am going to make this year! I expect to write down any old number and send it in without signing it. If I have got to guess what I am going to make, let them guess who sent it in.

I don't understand what emanates from Washington. For some reason I do not understand, the Department of Interior banded a lot of crows and set them loose. They wanted to put Washington Department of Biological Service and everything on the band, but there wasn't room so they shortened it to "Wash. Biol. Ser." Later, I understand a letter came in which said "I caught one of your tame crows. I followed your directions. I washed it. I boiled it, and served it, and it tasted awful. Why don't you quit trying to fool people?"—*From an address by Tom Collins.*

Freedom

It must be obvious that liberty necessarily means freedom to choose foolishly as well as wisely; freedom to choose evil as well as good; freedom to enjoy the rewards of good judgment and freedom to suffer the penalties of bad judgment. If this is not true, the word "freedom" has no meaning. Yet there are persons in America who wish to pass laws to force people to do only "good," or at least their concept of what is good. These would-be dictators are not content with a preventive law which punishes a person who deliberately chooses to injure his neighbor; a law that prevents any person from forcing his viewpoint upon any other person; a law which penalizes the person who interferes with the liberty.—*From an address by Admiral Ben Moreell, President, Jones & Laughlin Steel Corporation.*

Successful Retailing

Perhaps some of you believe I am romantizing when I say that in an intelligently run business, the immediate and vital objective is to satisfy a public need. Here the skeptics say: "Aren't you in business to make money?"

Let's answer that question, too, with an analogy from baseball. The batter standing at the plate is in business to hit a home run if he can, or a base hit. But his chances of making a hit, or even a sacrifice bunt, are pretty slim if he keeps his eye on where he wants the ball to go, instead of on the ball.

Obviously, a business has to make money or cease to exist—just as a batter has to score a reasonable average of hits, or be dropped from the team. But what we are concerned about is how the objective can be achieved. In baseball, and in business, the man who tries to brush aside the elementary principles of the game isn't likely to get very far.

There are some people who, when the principles of business success are explained to them, do not find the answer sufficiently intellectual to be satisfying. In retailing, the formula happens to be a basic liking for human beings, plus integrity, plus industry, plus a creative imagination that manifests itself in the ability to see the other fellow's point of view. Now, these individuals, when a chemistry teacher tells them that the formula for water is two parts hydrogen and one part oxygen, don't complain that the formula is unsophisticated. When a physics teacher explains the laws of leverage, no one protests about their lack of originality. But in the field of merchandising they turn up their noses at the basic truths, because these are too commonplace.

In any field, whether the arts, the sciences, or business, it takes people with uncommon imagination to see the challenge of the commonplace. Frederick W. Taylor was such a person. He was fascinated by the problem of developing an improved type of steel for cutting tools. After forty thousand separate experiments, he produced the high-speed steel on which present-day mass production is based.

Today, the world needs a system of distribution that will keep pace with our wonderful productive ability. Just as a body requires a steady circulation of blood to maintain normal health, the economic arteries of the country need a brisk flow of materials. We must keep striving for more and more merchandise, at lower and lower prices, so that the fruits of modern industry reach everywhere and benefit everyone. Helping in that process should be an inspiring objective.—*From an address to the students of Stephens College, Columbia, Missouri, by J. C. Penney, founder of J. C. Penney Company, Inc.*

Answering a Difficult Question

Years ago my father gave me some advice that stands me in good stead this morning. Said he, "Flattery is like perfume, it should be sniffed but not swallowed." I'm flattered by your invitation to speak, but I'm not taken in. . . . You see, I too happen to know that Plato said, "When you have a really difficult question to ask, ask it of a young man, for he will be audacious enough to offer an answer—and because of his youth his elders will be charitable enough to forgive his errors." —*From an address by Newton L. Margulies, attorney, Des Moines, Iowa.*

Different Ideas

We don't always have the same ideas. A hen and a pig were going down the road and they came to a sign, "Ham and Eggs."

The hen said, "See, we are partners!"

The pig said, "Yes, it is a day's work for you, but it is a real sacrifice to me."—*From an address by Tom Collins.*

Character of a Nation's Citizens

It is as true today as in Plato's time, that "types of government correspond to the types of human nature. States are made, not from rocks or trees, but from the character of their citizens which turn the scale and draw everything after them."

The character of the individual citizen, then, is the key to our future. And as the astronomer scans the distances of the universe to discover the forces which control the earth's movements and keep it in place, so man must plumb the depths of his own nature to learn the basis of his own behavior—the fears, the jealousies, the ambitions and desires that motivate men in all their relationships—in international affairs, in business, in labor, in learning, and in the ordinary contacts of daily life; and to understand that these emotions may be in opposition to his avowed principles. A citizenship conscious of its purpose is a barrier to dictatorship by group or individual, economic or political, a solvent of confusion, and repellent to domestic weeds and to poisonous pollen from afar.

Science makes giant strides forward because the scientists have had the intelligence to base their experiments on the proven grounds of the past. They weigh the accumulated theories, both true and false, and discard those lines of attack known to be unrewarding. So will human relationships most surely be aided in their advance if guided by man's experiments in living, which in the course of time become history. Over and over again, in these experiments in living, man finds recurring the same lines of false reasoning, the same selfish insistence upon ends profitable only for the moment, the same persistent misrepresentation of truth, which have always led to war, to disaster, to destruction of civilizations. And yet with bland indifference he has ignored these lessons of history; he has always said to himself—"But that was long ago and in another country. . . ."

Historians and philosophers, however, and all thinking men, know that there is a common factor in the crises of all countries and all times. The insistence of so many educators on the value of the classics is not because antiquity makes them sacrosanct; it is because they show so plainly that problems in human relations have not changed, however much external conditions may have done so, and that the ethics of ancient Greece and Egypt, the sturdy virtues of the early Roman citizens, the precepts of all holy religions, are still the only means of survival for the human race today.

Are these things trite? Then so is the law of gravity, which a child begins to understand and respect with his first blocks; an understanding which develops as he matures and which he uses throughout his entire life. The architect of a great cathedral, the engineer who translates the dream into the reality, the steel worker, the carpenter, the mason responsible for the smallest stone—even the man who quarries that stone—all accept the principle of the law of gravity and find it necessary to their performance.

In our present need to build for the world that structure of the spirit which might be called a cathedral of freedom, we must make use of those principles, those spiritual laws, which govern men's creative emotional life as surely as the law of gravity is involved in their material life. And as men first encounter the law of gravity at nursery age, so ought they at the same age become conscious of simple principles of disciplined freedom in the family circle. This consciousness and acceptance of moral law, growing and maturing as it is fostered by the teaching of church and school, will become in the adult an integral part of his thinking.

So nurtured, the individual citizen will not spinelessly abdicate his franchise in the face of threat, but each within his province—architect, engineer, mason, whatever he be—will act, build, construct, in the firm faith that the structure of freedom he establishes will send its triumphant spires towering into the heavens, "the cynosure of neighboring eyes," to be recognized from every point of the compass.

Enough, if something from our hands have power
To live, and act, and serve the future hour.

—From an address by Frank Diehl Fackenthal, formerly Acting President, Columbia University, delivered at the 194th Commencement of Columbia University, New York City.

The Destiny of Our America

The invitation to address this patriotic meeting of my fellow Americans of the Negro race brings to me an honor and a privilege. I stand before you not to teach, but rather to discuss, on common ground, our common interest in the destiny of our America.

We, of all races, who now together constitute the whole of our America, match surely, and in all extremes, from high nobility in leadership to every form of human weakness, the best and worst of all mankind.

In all your living may be seen, by those who look through friendly eyes, reflections of the victories and defeats by which the God of all has seasoned the souls of men of earth as they have struggled toward the light.

Your preference for self-discipline and orderly participation in the life of your community, your history in America attests.

Your ancient love of arts and crafts you have preserved.

Your skills have helped you mightily to stand abreast of other men in modern industry.

Your valor in battle for your country has enshrined you in the hearts of men of freedom everywhere.

Men of your race have written, in the lasting literature of America, their honest thought.

In fields of science and invention your great and modest brother, Carver, rose from slavery to place within the reach of all of us rich fruits of his communion with the mysteries of lowly things found growing at his feet.

From sand lots to Olympic Games, your skills and courtesies in sports have won for you your share of laurels, and of high respect, often in contests with all the champions your nation and the world could put beside you.

The melodic rhythm of your soulful songs stirs in all hearts a cordial sense of brotherhood.

The resilience of spirit in which you once submitted to servitude in America—and your emergence with your will to happiness all unimpaired—hold promise that your courage will endure.

Only your faith in our common destiny can fortify your dignity and your integrity for tests to come.

Who lacks faith in your destiny lacks faith in your America. Who lacks faith in your America can have little hope for the future of your race.

We stand or fall together, as we help or hurt each other.—*From an address by John W. Anderson, President, The Anderson Company, Gary, Indiana.*

Let Freedom Ring

My subject this morning is "Let Freedom Ring." Paul writing to the Galatians says in the fifth chapter and the thirteenth verse, the first half of that verse, "For, brethren, ye have been called unto liberty." The call to liberty is one of man's greatest aspirations. From the dawn of history down to this moment men have been in search of freedom. They have heard the call to liberty. One hundred seventy-two years ago this day our independence was declared. Our forefathers had heard "sweet freedom's song" and they did something about it and the result is that today across this land and in many lands what they did there is being called to remembrance.

Professor Brested, perhaps the greatest Egyptologist the world has ever known and one of its greatest archeologists, has pointed out that man has been fashioning destructive weapons for a million years whereas conscience emerged less than five thousand years ago. So the odds against us are about two hundred to one. A million years against five thousand years. Conscience, you see, in comparison to the length of time men have been fashioning lethal weapons, is a newcomer on the scene of activity. Conscience is new; bludgeoning weapons are very old. But because that conscience as a social force dawned five thousand years ago men have been seeking increasingly their liberty, but they have recognized that without severe disciplines and without the acceptance of responsibility liberty is quite impossible. They have noted, too, that once they have gained liberty they can't be sure of retaining it. There's a possibility of losing liberty. The fact that you've won it once doesn't guarantee that you'll have it forever. It can be taken from you. Enemies may descend in the night and wrest it from you by force and there are many who keep watch on the fortress of democracy lest these subversive forces from the outside or from within penetrate and destroy.

But there are other ways of losing our much-vaunted freedom. Indifference, taking for granted this priceless gift of ours, is an easier way of losing it. It is well that we set aside the Fourth of July and remind ourselves of what our forebears did and trace for a moment the long laborious process by which this liberty of ours was won. Not only do we gain from the vantage point of the years the perspective of what has happened, but in discovering the contribution that men of other days have made find that which inspires us and sends us forth in noble endeavor and high courage to carry on in the noble tradition of yester-year.

In about the year 1850 a man from Sicily, homesick for his Mediterranean land, brought to Australia in a small pot a plant of prickly pears. Today Australia spends hundreds of thousands of dollars each year in an endeavor to curtail the spread of the prickly pear. It has all but taken over Australia. In that short period of time that little plant in the pot reverted to the jungle and has invaded an entire continent. Each year it reclaims for the jungle about a square kilometer of ground —that's five-eighths of a statute mile. You know here in Southern California that it doesn't take long for the jungle to win back your garden unless you stay everlastingly at it. Indifference to things spiritual results in like catastrophe, and human nature has a way, unless it is sustained by effort and by discipline and by a recognition of responsibility, of reverting to the jungle. The fact that we have won this hard-earned victory of liberty and freedom does not guarantee that we shall always possess it. Indifference can lose us our liberty as it has lost others theirs—*From a Fourth of July address by Dr. Donald H. Tippett, Senior Minister, First Methodist Church, Los Angeles, California.*

The Vernacular

My wife says that when I start talking without notes, as I did here today, I usually return to the vernacular of the prairie, which I presume is correct.

One time when I was going to school at Phillips, Indian territory, night school, we had a Scotchman teaching school, and after a long time the professor introduced us to a new writer—that is, he was new to me; I had never heard of him before. His name was William Shakespeare.

We got the idea that he expressed himself rather well, and you know how you are when you find out something new. You want to pass it along to the congregation, so we decided we'd put on a Shakespearian play.

We chose one of Shakespeare's more simple little plays, *Julius Caesar.* You recall in that play where Shakespeare used the supernatural, when the ghost walks the night before Philippi, saying, "Beware the Ides of March." You remember Brutus was supposed to be lying on a Roman couch in his tent.

We didn't have a Roman couch, so we put an army cot in the tent. We had an old boy lying on the cot, and when it came his turn, he was supposed to hop off the cot, throw back the flap of his tent, and say, in a deep voice, "Cassius, where art thou?" Well, this old boy hopped off the cot, threw back the flap of his tent, forgot his lines, and said, "Cassius, where you at?"—*Excerpt from extemporaneous remarks in a question-and-answer period following an address by General Patrick J. Hurley.*

Knowledge Accumulates

When Dr. Charles W. Eliot was president of Harvard, a friend of his asked him: "Is there really anything to be learned at a place like this?" Dr. Eliot answered: "Well, sir, the freshmen always bring some knowledge with them, and the seniors don't take any of it away, and knowledge accumulates."—*From an address to the students of Stephens College, Columbia, Missouri, by J. C. Penney, founder of J. C. Penney Company, Inc.*

Education

When Washington was President, and Alexander Hamilton was Secretary of the Treasury, the latter had difficulty in raising three hundred thousand dollars for the new republic in the world mart of Amsterdam. But Jefferson and Franklin were both ambassadors to Paris; Hamilton, Madison, and John Jay had produced in *The Federalist,* what an *Englishman* described as "the greatest state papers in political philosophy since Aristotle's *Politics.*" And though pigs ran through the streets of Manhattan, the whole world sensed that on the eastern seaboard of a roaring wilderness, something great was moving and stirring.

Ladies and gentlemen, the eighty-six papers of *The Federalist,* written by Hamilton, Madison, and Jay, were published as newspaper articles to be read by the public. A large part of the public of those days—and most of the women—could not read them, because many were illiterate. But the public that was exercising the leadership of the nation could, and did, and interpreted them to the people in the cracker-box assemblages of those days.

Today we are "statistically" the most "educated" country in the world. One fifth of the entire population are going to school. Education is the largest American industry. We have approximately a million and a quarter teachers. We have over thirty-two million students. A larger percentage of our youth get college degrees than in any other country. And yet, I say it advisedly, the average American today *could* not read the *Federalist Papers* with any understanding. He has not the vocabulary to do so.

About four years ago an analysis was made of the knowledge of freshmen entering one of our better state universities. Remember that these young people had already had *twelve years of schooling.* Yet forty per cent of them had had no mathematics beyond arithmetic—and many of these could not do a problem in long division; one third had had no training at all in grammar; less than half could spell words in common English usage; and four out of ten could not read quickly or accurately, to say nothing of being able to write a single paragraph of correct, coherent prose.

What in the world *had* they been exposed to?—*From an address by Dorothy Thompson, author and commentator, before the Women's Luncheon, 38th Annual Meeting of the Chamber of Commerce of the United States, Washington, D. C.*

Opportunity Plus

I remember interviewing the late Charles Schwab. He had a million-dollar-a-year job. I didn't. I thought it might be done. I asked him how he got it, if luck had anything to do with it.

He said, "Not at all, young man. I never worked for anybody but Andrew Carnegie. My job was shoving cars of ore along the track. I sang while I worked. One day the foreman came along and said, 'What is your name, boy? Mr. Carnegie likes your singing at your job and he wants you moved up where he can hear you sing.' " They did it.

Then they saw that Mr. Schwab not only sang well, but he worked well too. Finally he was boosted up until he ran the place. He didn't believe in luck. What if he sang like I sing? What if Mr. Carnegie had been deaf? What if he had said, "You tell that young fellow to save his breath and put it into his job. If we wanted a singer, we would have hired a singer." The point is he got under the boss' nose and he worked well. It is a pretty good place to be when you know your oats.

He had opportunity. Did he make it? Probably not, but he used it. —*From an address by Tom Collins.*

An Educated Person

We live in a democracy, which means that the final decisions in all things rest with a majority of the people. We have a tendency to believe that this mere fact, in itself, will save us. It will do nothing of the kind. It will not save us, and it can even wreck us, unless the majority of the people are adequately educated. What *is* an educated person—at any level? It is a person who is able to perform satisfactorily all of the duties of life. To be a competent and responsible father or mother, maintain a home, do a job of work as well as it can be done, and view public affairs at least with common sense. An educated person is one who does not depend on others for his primary satisfactions; who is not afraid to be a nonconformist; and who can amuse himself. On the higher levels an educated person is one who has control over those instruments through which alone a person can *think*—the symbols, which are words, and numbers. He has a purpose in his existence which is beyond money. He has a philosophy to guide him through the hazards and griefs of life. He has sound values—which are the same values, applied in however changing a society, which have always guided men through personal and social hazards. He is *not* a mass man. . . .

Who is this mass man? Do not believe, for a moment, that he is necessarily a poor man. The Vermont farmer is poor, but he is not a mass man. Quite the contrary.

The mass man does not know how to *do anything* really well—and that includes the mass woman—whether to make a bed or cook a meal or keep a house clean. He does not understand the fundamental processes of life—how milk, for instance, gets on the shelves of the A and P. He feels forlorn and insecure unless he is in the midst of a crowd. That is one reason he drifts to great cities, until now, in this vast continental country, twelve per cent of our entire population live in five cities—and the trend is increasing.

The modern technological processes of industry can use him, to perform some simple repetitive act. Or, he possesses some single minor skill which he can sell. But he possesses no capacity whatsoever to turn his hand to more than that single skill, and he depends—to sell his labor—on a great and complex organization, in which he is a small unit. If, therefore, he loses his job, he loses, in effect, his life, unless the state will support him, as it has to do.

The mass man is not a moron. He is the creation of modern technological society and its complex system of division of labor which has produced such miraculous amounts of goods. But it has also produced its own Frankenstein in this *type* of man. In earlier and more primitive civilization, he would simply have starved to death, or been aided by his neighbors. But he would not have starved. He would have developed numerous skills out of necessity—sufficient carpentering to build a shelter for himself; knowledge of animals; and of seasons; how to plow and tend a field. How to live at home with himself and his family. And all that would have been education—real education, even if he could not read or write. And he would have had the inner satisfaction of genuinely creative and personal activity, without which nobody can ever be happy.

But the modern mass man, lacking roots or contacts with more than a small segment of life, is both truculent—because he is unconsciously frustrated—and conformist, because he is unconsciously afraid. He is easily influenced—by the advertisements which urge him to buy what he can't afford but promise him happiness; by slogans of all kinds; by the dreams he sees in movies, which with radio, television, and spectator sports fill his leisure time, and by whatever has power at the moment. Because being conformist, he is fickle. He runs with the crowd.

And unless, by education, the mass man is demassed, he will destroy human culture and human freedom, here, as he has done in so many places, and in various ways, for he is a man being trained for slavery.—*From an address by Dorothy Thompson, author and commentator, before the Women's Luncheon, 38th Annual Meeting of the Chamber of Commerce of the United States, Washington, D. C.*

Two Views of Life

There are people who believe that . . . God is the very beginning of all things. He pervades everything, He is eternal, unchanging, shall endure for always, His laws are immutable, and that it is the part of wisdom to learn what those laws are and adjust ourselves to them; that one's understanding of them may change, that their application in our lives may vary from time to time, but that the laws themselves are immutable.

There is another point of view—with many others in between, to be sure—which goes to another extreme. This says in effect that what we call God isn't anything absolute; that the thing you call religion is just one of a number of things that man has to develop and build to satisfy his needs. He has need for religion and builds his religion according to his needs. He worships that which he does not understand, as once he worshiped the sun. And you can go through history again and discover that as man's understanding of physical things improves or increases, as he knows more and more, his ideas of God have also changed; therefore, this point of view tells us, religion itself is not an absolute or fixed thing. It is simply one of a number of things which man evolves himself to serve his own needs, and the God of Abraham and Jacob and Moses and Jesus is not necessarily the God of all the world. And this point of view finally brings us to the position, as Karl Marx so thoroughly anticipated, that there really isn't any God at all; that what you call God is only the feeling of a vacuum occasioned by man's inadequate knowledge of the world in which he lives, and inadequate knowledge of himself. You see, it is a very different point of view.

Now, depending upon which one you accept, or which one you lean to, you are going to build your personal philosophy and even your economic system. If you take the first, then you will recognize in the writings of the Bible, you will recognize in the speaking and writing of the so-called saints, men who have honestly sought out God and in some measure, at least, have found Him. You will take what you find in the nature of things as they are, and recognize your God, that Eternal Power, as the Being to whom you are ultimately responsible; not to states, not to organizations, not to devices of one kind or another, but to God Almighty Himself. Then it becomes your quest as an intelligent human being to understand God, come closer and closer to Him, and build the rest of your life accordingly.

Again, if you take this point of view you have in effect also chosen a point of view with regard to reform. You are going to find the improvement of the world not in the setting up of governmental controls or devices. You will use them to facilitate justice, to be sure, but you won't rely on them as means of curing our ills. You will go back to the same point of view that the Master took. You will find your answer not in machinery but in men; in building the kind of men who, when they exercise their freedom of choice, will choose rightly. Because, you see, as we implement this point of view we are forced, if you please, to recognize controls by a Power greater than any group of men, any state or social device, and therefore remedy our ills by conducting ourselves in accord with that Power.

The easy way to remedy our ills may seem to be to set up human controls preventing men from choosing unsound courses of action. When one grows impatient with the slowness of human improvement, he is tempted to accept that alternative. To say to himself, "We can't wait" —as a very prominent clergyman said three years ago in Pittsburgh. He said, "The improvement of mankind through religion is nice to think about; but, after all, we are dealing with sin. Religion has its place, to be sure, but we must be practical about these things." In that little talk he set forth the idea which many other men have followed, that if God won't do His job Himself, we will have to get Caesar to do the job for Him.

Now, you can see what lies back of that. What in many cases appears to be a splendidly motivated approach, an approach motivated by love for one's fellow men, motivated by a genuine desire for the good of men, is coupled with impatience with the speed with which God is working things out. We cannot wait for the visibleness, the availableness of God, if you please. So we set out to implement our aims in social and governmental devices. It means, in the last analysis, that those who follow this course have lost faith in God!

A strange thing for a business man to be talking about, isn't it? And yet, after all, it's the most basic thing in your life and mine.

I have come to the point in my thinking where I am convinced that these opposing points of view separate us into two broad groups. In one group a few—and God knows, only too few—believe so thoroughly in this God, in His justice, in His laws revealed in the nature of things as they are, that they are willing to risk their lives on the soundness of those laws. In the other group are many who say, "After all, I haven't ever seen God—" They don't admit it in so many words, but in effect they say, "I have never seen God come down on earth and do these things. I have prayed to Him, but He has never answered my prayers or come into my bedroom and stood alongside of me and told me just what to do. I am afraid God is either deaf or dead." So we must take these Christian principles as ethical principles, if you please, and do as Karl Marx might have suggested—set up the necessary state controls that will make men do the things you and I think they ought to do. Thereby God would find that He is justified finally by the things that Caesar does for Him. This grows out of a lack of faith in God, in my judgment.—*From an address by Dr. Alfred P. Haake, Chicago, Illinois, Trustee, National Small Business Men's Association, delivered before the Economic Club of Detroit.*

To Listen and to Inquire

Lesson: Luke II, 25-34; 40-52. (Luke II, 46:) "And it came to pass that after three days they found Him in the temple, sitting in the midst of the doctors, both hearing them and asking questions." The passage from the Bible read this morning from which I have taken this text recounts the only incident of the youth of Jesus which has been preserved for us in the Gospels; the sole incident which throws any light on his education previous to his active ministry. It is rich in its suggestion of preparation for that ministry. It touches the heart of every parent of a growing youth and the sensibilities of every member of the teaching profession.

Mary and Joseph came every year to Jerusalem for the feast of the Passover. On this occasion as Jesus had reached the age which made him "a son of the law" and bound by its rules he accompanied them. But when they came to leave for home the twelve-year-old slipped away from them, as boys will; and they taking for granted that he was somewhere safe with friends in the returning caravan, themselves started back for Nazareth. Only after they had journeyed a day did they discover that he was not with the group of travelers. One imagines the anxiety with which they hurried back to the city, fighting down the fears of disaster which their imagination conjured up, anxiety which must have become fevered during the three days that passed before they found him. And then their astonishment in what must have been the last place they thought of looking. Here in the court was their son of twelve arguing with the learned doctors of the Temple. Relief mingled with bewilderment doubtless exceeded their pride, and one feels the poignancy of the mother's exclamation: "Son, why hast thou thus dealt with us? Behold thy father and I have sought thee sorrowing"; and her wonder at his reply: "How is it that ye sought me? wist ye not that I must be about my Father's business?"

But for the teaching profession the incident sets forth a glowing example of the right sort of education. The ideal preparation for a career of service that demanded brains as well as heart. A boy intellectually mature beyond his years, certainly. There was nothing miraculous about this. In the early days of Yale, college students would matriculate at eleven or twelve; Nathan Hale was only fourteen when he came here as a freshman. The teacher, however, is deeply struck by the picture of Jesus "sitting in the midst of the doctors, both hearing them and asking questions." This is the true educational process for which colleges exist in their duty to prepare youth for future leadership: to listen and to inquire. Later in his life Jesus spoke with authority; but in his preparation for his Father's business he heard the doctors and he asked questions.

A college education offers precisely this privilege, the privilege of forming the habit of inquiry. It is the obligation of the college to see to it not merely that the faculty ask questions on examination papers, but that the students themselves learn how to ask questions, to listen to the answers, and to form their own opinions. Free and untrammeled inquiry is not merely a privilege, it is an obligation that lies upon all educated men in a democracy; upon its safeguarding and its active prosecution the strength of a democracy will depend. Our citizens must always be alive to the necessity of asking questions, otherwise civilization dies of dry rot.

The spirit of curiosity which impels us to ask questions does not make for placidity. Anyone with children knows that. Pandora discovered it when her curiosity got the better of her caution and she opened the mysterious box letting loose all the stinging and buzzing troubles of the world. Questioners are troublemakers and not generally popular. Socrates was put to death because in his search for truth he asked questions which the authorities regarded as disturbing to the spirit of Athenian youth.—*From an address by Charles Seymour, former President, Yale University, at the baccalaureate services opening Yale's 247th commencement, New Haven, Connecticut.*

Charge to the Graduating Classes of Northwestern University

The concept of freedom which we Americans cherish is a many-sided one. It implies freedom to fail as well as to succeed. We learned long ago that the rewards of victory are tawdry indeed unless they are won under the hazard of defeat. Who would watch a football game with only one team on the field? Yet that is precisely the condition that some of our social planners would like to see established. They would remove all elements of conflict, of struggle, of hazard, from life; or, as they put it, they would extend security "from the cradle to the grave." The men and women who listen to the blandishments of these theorists forget that as Mr. Justice Holmes put it, "Security is generally an illusion," and that the slavery imposed by a planned economy can be much worse than that of poverty or disease. The pioneers who settled this state of ours were not seeking a life of either ease or security. They were eager to work, and gloried in the opportunity, not the security, which they found here west of Lake Michigan.

As an indication of our belief in freedom we have been careful to protect a man's right to stop work, when he thinks that by doing so he can better himself economically. The right to strike is part of our many-sided American freedom. I hope you young Americans are also interested in the right of a man to remain on the job if he wishes to—a right which is too often denied him. We are careful, here in America, to make sure that a man receives a fair day's pay for a fair day's work. This is eminently proper; concern for the welfare of labor lies at the foundation of our whole economic structure. But I hope you also believe that the man who furnishes the capital should receive a fair return on his investment. Remember that without Mr. Ford's millions plowed back into the business there would be no sixty thousand jobs at River Rouge. If the unjustified demands of labor or the unchecked greed of the tax assessor or the theorizing of the planner stops men from saving money and investing it in agriculture or in industry, the United States fifty years from now will be a sorry place in which to hold a class reunion!

Some people tell me that our worries concerning the future would disappear if all college students could be required seriously to study American history. Well, I yield to no one in my interest in the history of this country of ours. Only against the background of the past can one understand the present, or venture tentatively to anticipate the future. But sometimes I wonder whether it would not do us more good to ponder the history of ancient Rome. For Rome can be seen in perspective; it does not press so close upon us as to distort our vision and our judgments.

What a magnificent story it was! Five hundred years of the Republic, and then another five hundred of the Empire. During many of those ten centuries Rome was quite literally the mistress of the world, and maintained peace wherever her eagles gleamed in the sun. The Roman citizen, like you and me, enjoyed freedom within a law of his own making, and accorded justice to everyone, even to the captive of war and the slave. Courts, hospitals, banks, markets, roads, systems of transportation—all these "modern developments" were features of Roman culture. Literature reached higher levels than it was to attain till the spacious days of Queen Elizabeth. A magnificent army threw a protecting barrier around the empire; the Roman navy held the Mediterranean in fee, and pushed boldly beyond the straits of Gibraltar to the white cliffs of England. Behind these human ramparts the great city-state lived proudly on her seven hills, and received tribute from all corners of the globe.

And then, not swiftly, but steadily, inexorably, as darkness wraps itself around the earth after sunset, the Empire crumbled. The Goth and the Vandal pillaged the city; Alaric and Attila led their barbarian hordes in triumph up the Capitoline. Why? Not because of superior physical force. Rome fell because the nation collapsed spiritually; because a hardy race succumbed to the insidious poison of the idea that "the government will do it"; because rulers bought power at home and favor abroad by gifts of treasure and food; because integrity and thrift and industry gave place to corruption and waste and indolence; because the nation bartered its ancient heritage of hard-won freedom for the specious ease and false security which a corrupt government promised it. Then and only then the Centurions' swords were blunted in their hands; their spears rattled harmlessly to the ground. Then and only then the invaders from the north and east took over the empty shell of the Empire.

Sometimes I wonder about this land of yours and mine. What destiny waits for it behind the thin veil of the future? I have no fear that any power in the world can forcibly break through the steel wall of our young manhood. Twice within a single quarter-century we turned back the barbarian from our gates; a third assault would be crushed in the same way. But too many of us are asking the federal government to do for us what our grandparents would have done for themselves; too many office holders are keeping themselves in power by promising spectacular gifts to the electorate; the old concepts of thrift and economy are laughed out of court by theorists who delight in squandering money that other people have earned; what seems to be a wasteful and inefficient federal government is reaching out like an octopus to wrap itself around more and ever more phases of your lives and of mine. If these trends continue unchecked, we may well destroy ourselves from within as did Rome.

I hope that no such fate awaits this country of ours. I hope that the intuitive common sense of one hundred forty million people is still strong enough to assert itself, and to re-establish the antique virtues of courage and honesty and industry and thrift in the minds and hearts of our citizens. I hope that the young people who this month are graduating from American colleges and universities still have the hardihood of their pioneer ancestors, and do not wish to be nursed and coddled by the government as if they were weaklings. I hope the college men and women of this country will make their voices heard in every legislative hall when they say: "Our universities encouraged us to think and to live like free men, and we do not propose to surrender the freedom which above all else makes life worth living. We shall plan our lives as we think best, with due regard for the happiness of other people, and any bureaucrat who tries to plan them for us we shall toss out of office. We shall not be enslaved by foreign conqueror or domestic theorist or even by our own government. We want no state socialism in this land of ours; we want no special favors for ourselves; all we ask is the freedom which is our birthright as Americans; and that freedom we shall certainly maintain!"

If you will say something like that to your representatives at Springfield and at Washington, ladies and gentlemen, and keep saying it, they will listen to you, and you need have no worries about your fiftieth reunion. It will be a pleasant occasion!

And now I claim from you the pledge traditionally taken by all Northwestern men and women before they receive their diplomas. Please rise and repeat after me the words printed on the inner cover page of your programs:

> With a solemn sense of my responsibility
> I pledge myself
> To hold my degree as a sacred trust,
> With untarnished honor to myself,
> In generous loyalty to Alma Mater,
> And with fidelity to my country,
> My fellow men, and my God.

And may the Lord direct you in all your doings, and further you with His continued help; that in all your works, begun, continued, and ended in Him, you may glorify His Holy Name, and finally by His mercy, obtain Everlasting Life.—*From the charge to the graduating classes of Northwestern University by Franklyn B. Snyder, former President of the University, Evanston, Illinois.*

The Heritage of America

As citizens of the United States, you and I—and all Americans in every corner of our land—must be forever mindful that the heritage of America and the strength of America are expressed in three fundamental principles: first, that individual freedom is our most precious possession; second, that all our freedoms are a single bundle, all must be secure if any is to be preserved; third, that freedom to compete and readiness to cooperate make our system the most productive on earth. Only within the framework of these principles can we hope to continue the growth that has marked our history. Only thus can our millions reach the fullness of intellectual, moral, and physical welfare that is justly ours—and avoid any risk of submission to the all-powerful State. Moreover, only thus can the world have any hope of reaching the millennium of world peace—for without the example of strength, prosperity, and progress in a free America, there is nothing to inspire men to victory in today's struggle between freedom and totalitarianism.

As friends of free people everywhere in the world, we can by our own example—our conduct in every crisis, real or counterfeit; our resistance to propaganda and passion; our readiness to seek adjustment and compromise of difference—we can by our own example ceaselessly expand understanding among the nations. We must never forget that international friendship is achieved through rumors ignored, propaganda challenged and exposed; through patient loyalty to those who have proved themselves worthy of it; through help freely given, where help is needed and merited. In this sense there is no great, no humble among us. In rights and in opportunity, in loyalty and in responsibility to ideals, we are and must remain equal. Peace is more the product of our day-to-day living than of a spectacular program, intermittently executed.

The best foreign policy is to live our daily lives in honesty, decency and integrity; at home, making our own land a more fitting habitation for free men; and, abroad, joining with those of like mind and heart, to make all the world a place where all men can dwell in peace.

Neither palsied by fear nor duped by dreams, but strong in the rightness of our purpose, we can then place our case and cause before the bar of world opinion—history's final arbiter between nations.—*From an address by General Dwight D. Eisenhower, President of Columbia University, in a series of lectures dedicated to the cause of international peace, Columbia University, New York City.*

The Corporation's Responsibility to the Future

The first responsibility of the corporation is:

To be a productive and creative force in society.

American companies, both large and small, have marked up amazing records of producing vast quantities of goods. They just continue this productivity and seek to enhance it by vigorous cultivation of that ingenuity which characterizes industry in this nation.

The kind of output needed in today's world calls for organization on a big scale—for big companies. Today we hear much said about bigness in industry. Many people seem to be afraid of it. Actually, bigness in industry is what has made possible mass production and mass distribution. In a free country, bigness is simply a technique for achieving results—big results.

Far from being antisocial, it is a significant social achievement, an example of practical, productive cooperation by large numbers of people. This cooperation of large groups is one of the outstanding accomplishments of the modern corporation. It includes the pooling of resources by thousands, often hundreds of thousands, of investors. It includes the cooperation of employees, many thousands of them, and management. It includes cooperation with customers and the public at large, not to mention the government.

Furthermore, the existence of big companies certainly does not hinder the founding of new enterprises. Many hundreds of thousands of new businesses have been established just since the war. In the twelve months ending July, 1949, the number of firms entering business exceeded those going out of business by one hundred thirty thousand.

Large-scale operations are a legitimate and healthy child of our times. Bigness in organization is no more strange or dangerous than bigness in equipment and machines. Big machines, big operations, and big organizations are related; they are prime producers of our high standards of living.

I am confident that great opportunities lie ahead for industry in the field of production; invention; the physical and chemical sciences; and the whole vast area where modern American enterprise has such spectacular achievements to its credit.

Plainly, then, the basic responsibility of the corporation is to meet the continuous needs of consumers in a world where the number of consumers is steadily growing.

However, important as physical productivity is, it cannot, by any means, be considered the sum total of responsibility. Corporations are not merely aggregations of materials and machines. More importantly, they are people. In Jersey Standard we regard our employees as the company's most valuable asset. A particular oil field may become exhausted, a plant may be destroyed or lost by accident or war, but as long as the company has people—loyal, experienced, and working together as an effective team—new oil fields can be found, new plants built.

This brings me to what I believe is the second great responsibility of corporations. It relates to people, and it is this:

To continue seeking better ways to make industrial work satisfying and rewarding. The modern corporation is not only a producer of goods and services, it is a major factor in the mode of daily life for millions of people. As our country has become more highly industrialized, a larger proportion of the employed people work for corporations. And these people spend half their waking hours in store or plant or factory.

Although the labor of the employee has a value that can be expressed in terms of money, a financial return is not the only thing he wants from his job. Some operations in modern mass production tend to be monotonous. Some of them represent such a small part of the over-all process as to seem pointless, perhaps, to the person performing them. Under such circumstances, the individual does not find in his job a satisfaction for the creative impulse which is in all human beings. He feels, instead, like a cog in a machine.

Ways must be found to give the individual worker, at every rank, a sense of accomplishment, a feeling of personal worth, a realization of the true importance of his effort to the broad scheme. The individual employee wants not only fair pay and reasonable security but just dealing, respect, and a feeling of accomplishment. He wants, too, the opportunity to advance in his chosen career, and to build a fuller life for his family.

What I am now talking about, of course, is the wide field of human relations. Considerable progress has already been made in this field by corporations. Companies have become increasingly aware of the human factor in their operations and have, accordingly, taken actions in this respect. In my own company, for example, we have long had safety and health programs, paid vacations for all employees, thrift and retirement plans for all ranks, cash rewards for suggested improvements, job training and educational assistance plans.

We have seen, in this country, that the individual—when not hedged in and hampered, but given opportunity to learn and to grow—represents a tremendous creative force. It has been demonstrated that freedom and opportunity for the individual not only are morally right but pay magnificently, and not only in material terms but in spiritual values as well.

It is the growing realization of this truth, I think, that accounts for the movement, in American corporations, toward decentralization through delegation of authority. This is not something that has happened in the past few months or past few years; it has been going on for a long time.

This movement represents, in my opinion, a significant development of the democratic idea. In fact, I think that corporations may be leading the way along the path of democracy. Certainly in government and in many labor organizations the trend at present appears to be toward centralization of authority rather than toward decentralization.

Large companies, especially, are moving toward decentralization as a matter of common sense. Even if the head of a large business wanted to run the organization in a dictatorial way, he would find it impossible to do so. He might give all the appearance of success for a time, but the mere scope of the enterprise, the amount of knowledge required for proper administration, would mean that the effort was doomed to failure.

The company with which I work, if you will permit another personal reference, does business in almost every language, in almost every currency, and under almost every system of laws in the world. To attempt to operate such a business in dictator fashion would be plainly absurd.

We operate, therefore, as a kind of family of autonomous affiliates, each of which is responsible for its own activities and has very wide latitude for the exercise of judgment and initiative. We have *no* faith in the infallibility of any small group of individuals at the peak of a pyramid. We *do* have great confidence in talent, training, and experience. We do *not* believe those qualities are to be found in any special class of society. We *do* go to great trouble to insure the continuous "bubbling up" of vigorous, ambitious young men.

It is our conviction that such a method is good not only for the individuals all the way down the line but for the company and the stockholders who own it.

The heads of today's large corporations are professional managers. They know that their success is measured not alone by this year's or next year's profits, but far more by whether they turn the enterprise over to those who follow them in as good or better shape than they received it. They want the enterprises they head to outlast their own tenure of office. They know that the only way to do this is to delegate authority and to assign responsibility broadly, thus providing opportunities to many individuals for training and growth.

It is because the extent of decentralization in business is not widely realized, I believe, that one hears misgivings about the large size of some companies. It is because many people have a notion that corporations are run in a dictatorial fashion that they readily accept criticisms of what is called "Big Business." The truth is that there are many influences in the big units of a free, competitive economy which act against autocratic methods.

But many questions of human relations remain unanswered. I have an impression that human relations is a field that has not been approached with the same painstaking care shown in many other areas of inquiry. It seems to me that modern corporations can make significant contributions in this field because they are accustomed to approaching problems from the research standpoint. In addition, I feel that this is a field in which cooperation between companies and universities should be employed as a means of enlarging our knowledge.

There is another branch of the social sciences which, I believe, merits particular mention—one that brings me to a third responsibility of the corporation:

To undertake on its own account, and to aid others, to develop sound economic thought.

I have pointed out that there has been a great increase in world population. Technical advances and people's needs have brought about mass production requiring huge and intricate machines. The large-scale corporation has arisen to meet these conditions and is a relatively new development.

Yet it seems to me that much discussion in the economic field today does not give sufficient weight to these developments, but is based on beliefs that do not conform to reality. For example, it is often assumed that a large-scale economic organization—that is, a corporation—reacts to the same impulses and in the same way as an individual enterpriser.

In many important respects this is not entirely so. The policy-making executives of a large company are not its owners. They are answerable not just to themselves and the law, as an individual enterpriser is, but to hundreds or thousands of stockholders. Because of the relative prominence of their positions, corporation executives find that the forces of public opinion focus more strongly on them than on the sole proprietor. Further, the sole proprietor has a definite limit on his life, whereas, as I mentioned earlier, the managers of a corporation expect the company to continue long after they have left the business scene. As a consequence, the objective of continuity and the long-range view generally weigh more heavily in a corporation's conduct than in that of the individual business man.

When Galileo discovered new facts about the universe—new, at least, so far as man's knowledge of them was concerned—the science of astronomy had to be revised and expanded. The discoveries of Newton and Einstein made revisions and widening necessary in the science of physics. A similar expansion of economic thought seems to me necessary today.

Economic study is a natural subject for corporations. They have an obvious interest in it, and they have a great deal of statistical information useful to the scholar. This is another place, it seems to me, where cooperation between colleges and universities on the one hand and corporations on the other would represent a fruitful approach to the problem. For the subject is too complex for any one mind. It is probably too vast to be mastered even by a group of minds having similar background and outlook. Neither the business man nor the professor has all the answers. The job calls for what General Eisenhower has described as "the merger of the academic and the practical."

In Jersey Standard we have tried to contribute to such an interchange of information by holding conferences with people from college faculties and by having professors visit the company for discussion and observation. Many of them have told us that the experience has helped them to understand better the operation of a large company.

We have seen the surprise of academic economists as they got their initial first-hand view of how a corporation really works. They saw that the actuality often had little in common with theory. On the other hand, we too have learned much from these contacts. A fresh mind can often see new points of view which we miss.

Another method that might have merit would be to make the experienced background of corporation executives available to colleges, through lectures or through part-time service on faculties. These men could bring their knowledge and experience directly to the campus for discussion and examination. Still another method might be to have more graduate economics students live with the practical problems of a corporation.

The conditions of every new period, especially one which has seen so much change as the last century and a quarter, are strange and unfamiliar. But changes in old theories, developed to explain the new conditions, must be based not on assumptions but on solid facts, if they are to have any value and not mislead us into harmful actions. In the development of modern, sound, economic thought, industry and business might well take more initiative.

These are by no means all the responsibilities of a corporation, but they represent some of the important problems we face in the coming years.

I would summarize very briefly what I have tried to say in this way:

First, the corporation has a responsibility to continue as a creative force in society. American companies on the whole have an admirable record of turning out more and better goods for growing numbers of people. They must continue this productivity. In addition, they owe it to their millions of customers and millions of owners to resist the idea that "bigness" is unavoidably "badness" because that would hamstring the production which is the basis of our high standard of living.

Second, the corporation has a responsibility to study and to promote better human relations with employees, stockholders, and the public. This includes the responsibility to find ways to delegate authority and decentralize operation, with top management acting to set sound policies and to see that they are carried out. In this way it meets its further responsibility of becoming a better example of democratic procedure.

Third, the corporation has a responsibility to study the present-day economic situations of which it is both an effect and a cause, to cooperate with others in this task, and to make economic truth as widely known as possible.

Let me say again that I deeply appreciate this opportunity to address so notable an audience on such an historic occasion. Speaking for myself and for the company I represent, I would like to congratulate Rensselaer Polytechnic Institute on her great achievements of the past one hundred twenty-five years, as an institution and as a mother of distinguished men.

We here honor ourselves in honoring R.P.I.—*From an address by Eugene Holman, President, Standard Oil Company of New Jersey, at Rensselaer Polytechnic Institute, Troy, New York.*

Spoilers

The spoilers are legion. We meet them everywhere. They are inevitable and unavoidable. Nobody travels far without meeting one of the breed. Having spoiled their own lives, they can't rest until they spoil other lives too. There is a spoiler in every fraternity who will pull everyone to his own level if he can. Everytime you read in the newspaper of some delinquent boy or girl you can be very sure there was a spoiler in the background. Every man who is elected to responsible public office is fair game for the spoilers who will corrupt him if they are able. Every home is exposed to the gossiping spoilers who tell half-truths with subtle purpose.

We cannot escape the spoilers, and they leave their marks upon us. There are motion pictures that are spoilers, simply because they glorify a kind of living that is cheap and utterly devoid of permanent values. There are novels that are spoilers because they leave us with the feeling that right and wrong are mere expedients in a universe indifferent to ethical values. There are philosophies that are spoilers because they reduce everything to the level of economics and sex. No matter where you turn you meet influences that challenge the integrity of your soul.

You can give up, then, saying as the potter might have said: "What's the use of trying to make something beautiful when somebody always spoils it before it is finished?" "What's the use trying to live a beautiful life when somebody always mars it?" There are those who say just that and then let themselves go. They simply give up trying to be Christian. —*From a sermon by Dr. Harold Blake Walker, Minister, the First Presbyterian Church, Evanston, Illinois.*

Moral Values

The towering enemy of man is not his science but his moral inadequacy. Around the world today, laboratories supported by almost limitless resources are feverishly pushing their research in the development of physical and bacteriological weapons which overnight could turn this planet into a gigantic slaughterhouse. On what moral basis will the decision be made to use these weapons? What ethical restraints will have developed to curb the hysteria, fright and passion of men against such a blind paroxysm of destruction? For if this final Nemesis overtakes the pretensions of modern man, it will not be his science that has betrayed him, but rather the complete prostration of his moral values. It will not be this telescope and all that it symbolizes that have led him to the doorstep of doom; it will be the impotence and immaturity of his ethical codes.

There is a sense, of course, in which the problem we face is not new. Over scores of centuries, man's progressive accessions of power have always outstripped his capacity for control, and the gap between his morality and the physical force at his disposal has always been uncomfortably wide. But never before have his curiosity and ingenuity led him within the space of a few years to weapons by which he could completely obliterate his own institutions and decimate the planet on which he lives.

This may seem too somber a note to be sounded at the dedication of a mighty instrument whose purpose is in line with man's noblest instincts; but in the twenty years that this telescope has been under construction, the human race has lived through its greatest tragedy. We know now that knowledge is not a gift; it is a challenge. It is not merely an augmentation of facts; it is a test of human character. And our generation is presented with what may well be the final choice between the use of knowledge to build a rational world or its use to arm, for one last, desperate affray, the savage and uncivilized passions of mankind.—*From an address by Raymond B. Fosdick, President, the Rockefeller Foundation, at the dedication of the 200-inch telescope on Mount Palomar, California.*

Levity

A well-known public speaker once remarked ruefully after disastrous consequences had followed misplaced humor, as they often do, "I rose by my gravity and fell by my levity."—*From an address by Dr. Robert A. Millikan, Professor Emeritus of Physics, California Institute of Technology, at the 53rd Annual Congress of American Industry, New York, New York.*

Pure Science and Industry

Mankind's fundamental beliefs about the nature of the world and his place in it are in the last analysis the great moving forces behind all his activities. Hence the enormous practical importance of correct understanding as a guide to all actions. It is man's beliefs about the nature of his world that determine whether in Africa he spends his time and his energies in beating tomtoms to drive away the evil spirits, or in Phoenicia in building a great "burning fiery furnace" to Moloch into which to throw his children as a sacrifice to his god, or in Attica in making war on his fellow Greeks because the Delphic Oracle, or the flight of birds, or the appearance of an animal's entrails bids him to do so, or in medieval Europe in preparing for the millennium to the neglect of all his normal activities and duties as he did to the extent of bringing on a world disaster in the year 1000 A.D., or whether he spent his energies in burning heretics in Flanders or drowning witches in Salem, or in making perpetual-motion machines in Philadelphia or magnetic belts in Los Angeles, or soothing syrups in New England.

The invention of the airplane and the radio are looked upon by every one as wonderful and pre-eminently useful achievements, and so they are—perhaps one-tenth as useful as some of the discoveries in pure science. . . .

Look, then, for a moment at the historic background out of which these modern marvels, the airplane and the radio, have sprung. Neither of them would have been at all possible without two hundred years of work in fundamental science before any bread-and-butter applications were dreamed of—work beginning in the sixteenth century with Copernicus and Kepler and then Galileo, whose discoveries for the first time began to cause mankind to glimpse a nature and a nature's God, not of caprice and whim as had been all the gods of the ancient world, but instead a God who rules through law, a nature which can be counted upon and hence is worth knowing and worth carefully studying. This discovery, which began to be made about 1600 A.D., I call the supremely useful discovery of all the ages, for before any so-called practical application was ever dreamed of, it began to change the whole philosophical and religious outlook of the race, it began to effect a spiritual, and an intellectual, not at first a material revolution—the material revolution came later. . . . It was this new knowledge that began to change man's conception of his duty, which is the essence of religion—to inspire man to know his universe so as to be able to live in it more rationally.

As a result of that inspiration there followed two hundred years (1600–1800) of pure science involved in the development of the mathematics and of the celestial mechanics necessary merely to understand the movements of the heavenly bodies,—useless knowledge to the unthinking, but all constituting an indispensable foundation for the development of the terrestrial mechanics—the power machines—and the industrial civilization which actually followed in the nineteenth century; for the very laws of force and motion essential to the design of all power machines of every sort were not only completely unknown to the ancient world, but completely unknown up to the time of Galileo and Newton.—*From an address by Dr. Robert A. Millikan, Professor Emeritus of Physics, California Institute of Technology, at the 53rd Annual Congress of American Industry, New York.*

THE DOCTOR

It was, I believe, H. G. Wells, the late English writer and historian, who made the pertinent remark that education is a race against catastrophe. It seems to me especially significant that we are gathered here at this time to evaluate our experience in the field of health and medicine while at the same time it would seem that the world is tottering on the brink of a terrible abyss opened up by the advent of the atomic age.

It would perhaps be more accurate to state that the threat of disaster comes not from the enormous strides taken by science, for these steps could lead to a peaceful world—a world in which man could realize his potentialities more than ever before. No, the fault is in the failure of the human mind to evolve proper methods of dealing with the new tools which scientific research has made available.

In a sense, we who devote ourselves to the health and welfare of mankind, individually as well as collectively, stand as a thin line of shock troops against the destructive forces which are threatening to nullify all the advances of science which have enabled man to rise above the savagery of his primordial days to the comparatively advanced civilization in which we live today. But we are a *thin* line. The strength of the opposing forces, now still but a threat, is so enormous that, should it materialize, the accumulated work of centuries of progress will be obliterated in a moment. Within the experience of most of us, two violent wars have occurred and each of these has had its retrogressive effect upon our general well-being. It must be plain to anyone who thinks about the situation that the general level of health cannot but suffer a decline, when the very flower of our race is periodically sacrificed to the gods of war.

Thus, it appears to me that we are in a position now where not only must we work to our utmost, to rectify the blunders of the past, but we must strive in every way to keep the frail plant of human existence from becoming uprooted by the gathering storm.—*From an address by Leo F. Simpson, M.D., President of the Medical Society of the State of New York, before the Annual Conference of Health Officers and Nurses, Saratoga Springs, New York.*

A Valid Ideal

The history of man attests the eternal restlessness of his spirit. Animals migrate by a sort of blind instinct but it is man that explores and pioneers. The body of the beast becomes adjusted to its climatic environment but man adjusts his environment to his body and then is not satisfied. He is not content to use his ears to hear the sounds of nature; he creates melodies and harmonies of his own. He is not satisfied to use his eyes merely for food and safety; he possesses a subtle taste for beauty which craves Sistine Madonnas and Taj Mahals.

Not all man's restlessness, however, is wholesome. There is a devilish discontent as well as a divine discontent. There are desires which drive man feverishly only to leave him frustrated. There are ambitions which keep him climbing toward the summits of supposed success only to leave him buried under an avalanche of freezing regrets. It is therefore imperative that we discriminate between our incentives.

The search for the Holy Grail might well stand as the symbol of the pilgrim spirit at its purest. The legend is entwined in the literature of almost all Western lands. The Arthurian cycle of Tennyson has preserved it for the English. French poets have elaborately embroidered the myth. Wagner immortalized it in his *Parsifal*. And our own James Russell Lowell has etched it on our American minds in "The Vision of Sir Launfal." Lowell makes his knight say:

> "My golden spurs now bring to me,
> And bring to me my richest mail,
> For tomorrow I go over land and sea,
> In search of the Holy Grail."

When a man thus sets out to give his utmost for the highest, he must examine his incentives. He must look to his spurs, and only the best will do. Let us, then, here at the commencement season, when careers are at their threshold, call for our "golden spurs."

Consider first the golden spur of a *valid ideal*. Commencement is the time for taking pictures. But more important than the photographs taken of you are the pictures you are taking of the person you plan to be twenty, thirty, forty years hence. Your lives will be shaped by them. When the imagination and the will are in conflict, the imagination wins. David Starr Jordan was wont to ask his students at Leland Stanford to catch a vision of their "after self." And then he would ask them what they were going to leave to that self which was waiting his turn in those decades ahead. Would they leave him a fair chance when his time came or would they rob him of his rightful opportunity by present ignorance or indulgence?

There is a certain poignant sadness about the fact that men never fully attain their ideals. When the Epistle of the Hebrews lists the noble characters in Israel's Hall of Fame, it says of them, "These all died in faith, not having received the promise." While this seems sad, there is a disappointment far more tragic, and that is to pursue an ideal only to find that the struggle and sacrifice have been spent on an unworthy objective.—*From a baccalaureate address by Dr. Ralph W. Sockman, Minister, Christ Church, New York City, at New York University, New York City.*

Keep America Close to God

My friends, I am a priest of God, but I speak also as a citizen. You, as you graduate tonight, go forth as citizens into the civil community but without exception you are the children of God and you are responsive to the things of the spirit. I need not ask you to remember the classroom lessons you have learned at Marquette, but I do ask you to retain always the sense acquired here of the true place of religion in education, of piety in patriotism, of spiritual values in social stability. I beg you be vigilant against those who are attempting to drive the spirit of religion out of community affairs, the values of religion out of education. A nation is cradled in its homes, but it is made in its schools. Unless God be present in both the home and the school, college and university, I know not how He can enter the national life. This only thing I know: Reason, revelation, and history all agree that a nation without God is a nation doomed. Blessed is the nation whose Lord is God. Keep close to God yourselves—keep America close to God. Then you shall have faith and freedom—life, liberty, and happiness—all these, and heaven, too.—*From a commencement address by the Most Reverend Richard J. Cushing, D.D., Archbishop of Boston, at Marquette University, Milwaukee, Wisconsin.*

Creative Endeavor

In his book, *Possession,* written some twenty years ago, Louis Bromfield makes one of his characters, a young man of twenty-one out in the Middle West say: "My grandfathers set out into this wilderness to conquer and subdue it. It was a land filled with savages and adventure. I too must have my chance. I am of a race of pioneers but I no longer have any frontier." In that statement was voiced the yeasty restlessness of youth following World War I. It was in those days we talked much about "flaming youth" and the "revolt of youth."

Some ten years passed, and in 1936 *Fortune* took a survey of student opinion. We quote from its findings: "The present-day college generation is fatalistic . . . the investigator is struck by the dominant and pervasive color of a generation that will not stick its neck out. It keeps its shirt on, . . . its chin up and its mouth shut. If we take the mean average to be the truth, it is a cautious, subdued, unadventurous generation, unwilling to storm heaven, afraid to make a fool of itself, unable to dramatize its predicament. It may be likened to a very intelligent turtle. . . . The turtle has security and . . . security is the *summum bonum* of the present college generation. . . . Yearners for security do not set foot on Everest or discover the Mountains of the Moon."

Whether such a generalization was accurate, I do not venture to say. But the suspicion lurks in my mind that the depression of the 1930's did help to transform the frontier-seeking adventuresomeness of the 1920's into a security-consciousness.

And what has been the effect on youth of World War II? Perhaps it is too early to tell, but certainly ours is a security-conscious generation. Nations and individuals are living on the defensive. And a defensive mood never develops very creative or progressive living. We need to break through our present cautious patterns of personal and public policies and do some dynamic adventuring. There is no zest or virtue in goodness unless it exceed the righteousness of the merely respectable. There is no thrill or satisfaction in work until it has a pilgrim pioneering spirit.

To be sure, the "brave new world" dreamed by the youth of the 1920's is now a broken old world. But there is more real achievement in recreating the old than in creating the new. To take an old farm as Mr. Bromfield has done, and make it into a new adventure of living; to take an old community and make it a frontier of new social experience; to take an old broken embittered world and transform it into a place of hope and promise—such are some of the goals which still beckon the pilgrim spirits. The golden spur of creative endeavor is still available.—*From a baccalaureate address by Dr. Ralph W. Sockman, Minister, Christ Church, New York City, at New York University, New York City.*

Good Enough

It is a curious fact that good enough is good enough for most people, but sooner or later somebody comes along who makes a better mouse trap or a better television and then good enough is not good enough. Good enough goes out of business, like as not complaining of unfair competition. Good enough is good enough until hard times, and then good enough is unemployed and down on its luck. Good enough to get by is good enough in good weather, but it involves sleepless nights and troubled days when the weather turns bad. Somewhere there is a story of a farmer who needed a hired hand. He met a man in the village who wanted work and asked him for references. The man had no references, but he remarked "I'm a man who can sleep through a storm at night." The farmer was puzzled by the remark, but he liked the young fellow and hired him.

Time went on, and after a few weeks the farmer awoke one night, startled by a storm raging outside. He donned his clothes and rushed outside to the barn. He climbed into the loft where the hired man was sleeping. He called, he shook the bed, but the hired man would not stir. So the farmer hurried down into the barn. There he found every horse securely tied in his stall, the cows carefully bedded down, the doors and windows all securely locked. He went to the chicken coop. The windows were closed and fastened and everything was in order.

He knew then what the hired man meant when he said he was a man who could sleep through a storm.

Shoddy work and casual character may get us by with the crowd, but they will not let us sleep through storms that test our courage and try our faith. Sooner or later we are caught by the consequences of mediocre living and cheap ideals. In due time we learn that good enough to get by is not good enough for God. We can't sleep and the days become a burden we cannot bear. We know then we need God to refashion our lives, to stir our passion for the best, to make us restless until we reject what is good enough in favor of what is abidingly excellent.—*From a sermon by Dr. Harold Blake Walker, Minister, the First Presbyterian Church, Evanston, Illinois.*

GRUB-STAKING

The history of America is the history of stout and serviceable men—everything accomplished goes back to some individual having the freedom—who initiated something new, spurred on by incentive of reward, of gain, or profit.

Queen Isabella didn't back Columbus just for the trip. She wanted new treasures from a new land and he brought them back. It was her capital that made possible the discovery of America. The California forty-niners, prospecting for gold, were grub-staked by Easterners. Americans have been the greatest grub-stakers in the world; they will back anyone or anything in which they have faith. Sometimes they lose, or it may take a short or long time to make something, but there is the incentive grub-staking. Call it the profit system, or better yet the profit and loss system.—*From a speech by Harold C. Stassen in Detroit, Michigan.*

NATURAL WEALTH

Many seek to defend our democracy on the ground that it produces great material wealth. They cite the large number of automobiles and radios that our economy produces and think that that ought to persuade others to follow in our way. In fact, that argument falls on deaf ears and that is as it should be. Those who seek first the Kingdom of God and His righteousness may have material things added to them. But these material things are by-products and never looked to as the sole or primary justification of any system, that in itself is evidence of moral bankruptcy. So, while material productivity is good, because it can free men from worldly cares and give increased opportunity for spiritual and intellectual growth, material wealth is never in itself an end or justification.—*From an address by John Foster Dulles at Union College commencement, Schenectady, New York.*

Calamity or Opportunity

Our Father, when we long for life without trials and work, without difficulties, remind us that oaks grow strong in contrary winds and diamonds are made under pressure. With stout hearts may we see in every calamity an opportunity and not give way to the pessimism that sees in every opportunity a calamity.—*A prayer once offered in the United States Senate by the late Dr. Peter Marshall.*

Challenging Custom

In all probability no living creature has such a strong guarantee of security as the clam. All he has to do to get nourishment is to open his doors and food comes in. He hides comfortably in his shell, safe from danger, secure from attack. He has no neck to stick out or risk. He simply lives. On the other hand, the eagle lives a hazardous life. He builds his nest on rocky crags and takes his life in his hands every time he swoops down to the earth for food. He has to be challenging the elements around him from dawn until dark, beating the winds with his wings, defying storms, overcoming the cold. Having seen an eagle, who wants to be a clam? Maybe that is why we have made the eagle the symbol of our nation.

Curiously enough, we Christians have become more like clams than eagles. We do not wish to soar above the customs that ought to be changed in the name of Christ. We feel a little as Charles felt about Joan of Arc in Bernard Shaw's play, when Charles, nearly distracted, said: "Why doesn't she shut up or go home?" No doubt the Pharisees felt that way about Jesus. Mentally and spiritually he soared above the confining customs of his time. He would not shut up. He would not stay put like a clam. He was forever saying: "Ye have heard it said of olden time . . . but I say unto you," challenging custom and changing conventions.

But we, who are his followers, have turned into clams, and nothing will be changed if we are silent. Who wants to change the habit of government inefficiency and graft? Certainly not those who profit by it. Who wants to change the custom of race discrimination? Certainly not those who are satisfied with it. Who wants to change the custom of settling disputes by violence? Certainly not those who are untroubled by the disintegration of the American home. Who wants to change the custom of scorning spiritual values in the name of realism. Certainly not those who feel no desperate spiritual need.

It takes courage to challenge custom, to say what we think and then march off in new directions, but courage is the hinge on the door to the future. Stephen, the man who challenged custom for the sake of his Lord, lost his life in the bargain, but he left a mark the ages cannot erase. Nobody ever remembered a clam with a monument, or elected a clam to be a saint. Nobody ever erected a church in honor of St. Clam.—*From a sermon by Dr. Harold Blake Walker, Minister, the First Presbyterian Church, Evanston, Illinois.*

Beating the Game

Nothing is more certain in this world than the fact that you can't beat the game. You may be able to beat it for a while, but it will beat you after a while.

One fellow said: "I am sick in my side." His friend said, "Go to a doctor. See Doctor Jones. He will charge $25 for the first visit and $5 for the rest."

The little fellow said, "I do not like that first visit." All night long he tried to work out a scheme so he could start on the second visit.

The next morning he had it. He rushed to the doctor's office and said, "Hello, doctor, here I am again."

He gave the doctor $5. The doctor took it, put it in his pocket; he looked him over and said, "Well, just go on with the same medicine I gave you last week."—*From a speech by William Rainey Bennett.*

Not All Sweet

The little boy thought he would always like to eat brown sugar and his father said: "All right. There is the sugar barrel. Eat all you want." And after the boy had been eating and eating his father came along but the boy was not eating brown sugar. He was leaning over on the barrel sort of seasick, and his father asked: "Don't you like brown sugar?" And the boy said: "Yes, I like brown sugar, but I've come to a place in this here barrel where the sugar ain't no good." There is not a single sugar barrel on earth that tastes sweet all the way through. Not one.—*From a speech by Major Thornton Anthony Mills.*

Knew What He Wanted

A Frenchman went into a restaurant. He knew what he wanted, but he could not remember the name of it. He called the waitress and said, "Mademoiselle, what is the name of the national bird, the cock-a-doodle-doo?"

"The rooster?"

"Oui, ze rooster. And how it is that you call the madam of the rooster?"

"The hen."

"Oui, ze hen. And who is the child of the madam of the rooster?"

"The chick."

"Oui, ze chick. And what is the chick before he is a chick?"

"The egg."

"Oui, two of him."

You see, he knew what he wanted all the time, but it took him a little while to get it.—*From a speech by Charles Milton Newcomb.*

Optimist

One of my first lessons in inspiration and optimism came to me one day at the city hall, when a little chap had fallen downstairs. I rushed over to him, lifted him up, brushed his clothes and asked him, "Are you hurt?" He said, "No, I was coming down anyway."—*From a speech by Edward James Cattell.*

Loyalty to Father

Three boys in a little town got into an argument. One boy was the son of a lawyer, one was the son of a doctor, and one was the son of a minister.

The son of the lawyer said: "My father talks to the jury and whispers in the judge's ear; and the fellow who has done something wrong does not have to go to jail, and he gets so glad of it that he gives my father money."

The son of the doctor said: "My father cuts a fellow open and then takes something out of him and sews him up; and then he goes out feeling so good that he gives my daddy a thousand dollars."

The minister's son looked up and said: "Hey, you fellows, every Sunday morning my daddy talks for a half an hour, and then it takes six men with baskets to bring him all the money."—*From a speech by T. Dinsmore Upton.*

Leadership

Now, let us not fool ourselves. There is no magic in democracy that does away with the need of great leadership. Democracy must both create and control its own leadership. And it cannot afford to neglect either half of this responsibility. If a democracy thinks only of the creation of leadership, forgetting its control, it may end the vassal of a dictator, or a secret oligarchy, but if a democracy thinks only of the control of leadership, forgetting its creation, it will end the victim of mediocre leaders who are more interested in holding a job than in doing a job. Democracy is still young and we may yet go on the rocks if we blunder in this business of creating and controlling our leaders. When humanity smashed the twin traditions of the divinity of kings and the docility of subjects, the whole problem of finding and following leaders had to be worked out on a new basis. So far we have not—if we are willing to be honest—made a brilliant success of our venture.

We spend half our time crying for great leadership, and the other half crucifying great leaders when we are lucky enough to find them. The danger of our democracy, as I see it, lies in our tendency to select leaders who are similar to the rank and file of us, whereas the hope of democracy seems to me to lie in our selecting leaders who are superior to the rank and file of us. This cuts to the heart of the whole problem of leadership in a democracy. Just what should we look for in our leaders? Should we hunt for leaders who will lead us or for leaders who will follow us?

I think it was during the French Revolution, you may remember, that a very famous political leader was seen by an old comrade running about two blocks behind a mob that was going toward a certain building in Paris. This old comrade came up and said: "You must not get entangled in this mob, you will get hurt." The old man turned around and said: "My God, I must follow them. I am their leader." Now, shall we hunt for leaders who will lead us, or for leaders who will follow us? Should we look for leaders who will always think like us or for leaders who might be able to think for us in a pinch and respecting problems of which we did not have basic information? Should we elect men to office because they promise to vote for certain measures or because we can trust their mind and their morals to guide them aright on measures in general, once all the facts are before them? Can we run American democracy on the theory that the patient should always dictate the physician's prescription?

Our republic began as a government by trusted representatives. Experience proved that very often representatives do not represent. For self-protection we began to throw all sorts of restrictions around our representatives. And I pass no criticism upon the fact that we did throw these restrictions like the initiative, the referendum, the recall, the popular petition, and now the widespread practice of the post-card referendum, around our political representatives. Let me be clear about this matter. These devices were called into being by the obvious failures of trusted representatives.

I think we were perfectly justified in the restrictions we threw around representatives, because if a representative does not represent we have to lasso him, that is all, but I suggest that it just may be barely possible that all of the systems that we have devised for checking and controlling, and hampering and hobbling our leadership, while it was justified in the sense that some measures of control had to be set up, it may be just possible that the practical results are not the practical results expected. Now, what do I mean by that? I mean that any impartial student of the American social order today must be aware of the fact that we are rapidly drifting into government by instructed delegates rather than government by real representatives. The riddle we have not yet solved is this: How can a republic hobble its faithless representatives without hamstringing its faithful representatives?

The theory of leadership upon which our republic is based is that representatives shall be human substitutes for their constituencies; our current practice respecting leadership is to make our representatives phonograph records of the fluctuating moods of their constituencies. And a democracy is always in danger when its most popular leaders are those who most quickly carry out the orders of a post-card bombardment from the folks back home. Democracy will be doomed if it finally makes subserviency of spirit a bigger political asset than superiority of mind.

We began with the theory of a responsible government. We are acting on the theory of a responsive government. Somewhere between the two we shall find great leadership and good government. Unfortunately, strong men often become poisoned by their own power and so forfeit the confidence of their fellows. This may be why democracies have always been suspicious of their powerful men. But we dare not ignore the fact that no form of government can endure that trusts only its mediocre men in positions of leadership. The most difficult lesson American democracy has to learn is this—to learn to tolerate leaders who are great enough to differ from their constituencies when necessary.

Until democracy learns this lesson it cannot hope for really great leadership in public affairs. For no man of authentic greatness of mind and character will purchase political position at the price of adjourning his own intelligence and becoming the errand boy either of Main Street or of Wall Street. The great leader will be the creative servant of the real interests of both Main Street and Wall Street, but the cringing slave of neither.—*From an address by the late Dr. Glenn Frank, President of the University of Wisconsin.*

INDEX